THE ACTIVE LEARNER

SUCCESSFUL STUDY STRATEGIES

Third Edition

Sallie A. Brown, M.A., English
Emerita, El Camino College

Douglas E. Miller, M.A., History
Educational Consultant

Foreword by Gene Kerstiens, Ed.D

Roxbury Publishing Company
Los Angeles, California

NOTE TO INSTRUCTORS: A comprehensive *Instructor's Manual/Testing Program* is available from the publisher.

The Active Learner: Sucessful Study Strategies, 3rd Edition / Sallie A. Brown,
  Douglas E. Miller
  p. cm.
  Includes bibliographical references and index.
  ISBN 1-891487-18-3
1. Study skills—Handbooks, manuals, etc. 2. Active learning—Handbooks,
  manuals, etc. I. Miller, Douglas E. II. Title.
LB1049.B69 2001
371.3'028'1—dc21   98-46241
                                                    CIP

THE ACTIVE LEARNER: SUCCESSFUL STUDY STRATEGIES

Publisher: Claude Teweles
Managing Editor: Dawn VanDercreek
Production Editor: Joshua H. R. Levine
Copy Editor: Jackie Estrada
Production Assistant: Teresa Gonzalez
Typography: Synergistic Data Systems
Cover Design: Marnie Kenney

Printed on acid-free paper in the United States of America. This book meets the standards for recycling of the Environmental Protection Agency.

ISBN 1-891487-18-3

Roxbury Publishing Company
P.O. Box 491044
Los Angeles, California 90049-9044
Tel.: (310) 473-3312 • Fax: (310) 473-4490
E-mail: roxbury@roxbury.net
Website: www.roxbury.net

Dedication

To the late Ingrid Herman Reese, our trustworthy editor of the first two editions of *The Active Learner.* Her compassion and sense of humor greatly calmed the rough waves during the editing process.

Contents

Part One: Study Strategies and Techniques

Part Two: College Texts

Foreword

Gene Kerstiens, Ed.D.
Andragogy Associates
(Member, Board of Editors, Journal of Developmental Education)

The Third Edition of *The Active Learner* focuses on helping students to learn more in less time—and with greater ease and confidence—while engaging in college-level assignments. Together with an array of study-reading techniques, the authors introduce proven strategies for vocabulary building, memory improvement, test-taking skills, and library research tactics. To achieve greater ease and efficiency in carrying out academic assignments, the book incorporates the latest research in learning theory and presents a complete set of optional strategies based upon competent research and practice—resulting in significantly greater flexibility of presentation and application.

In keeping with current research and practice concerning learning theory, the layout of the *The Active Learner* is generous, encouraging noting tactics that increase comprehension and retention. The authors rightly consider student goals, life styles, and learning styles as factors that affect students' understanding of difficult passages as well as time-management considerations involved in completing long-term assignments. In a student-friendly progression, students take brief diagnostic surveys followed by guided practice in strategies to improve performance on certain tasks.

The book also incorporates metacognitive aids to promote reading comprehension, takes advantage of innovative hypertext delivery strategies that support vocabulary and mnemonic development, encourages concentration, and directs attention to detail. Perhaps the most outstanding and innovative feature for both students and instructors is the book's modular format, which can be adopted to individual needs. Content is not necessarily sequential and accommodates the emerging needs of the learning environment.

Finally, authors recognize that studying *is* work. Like all productive endeavors, it requires time and energy. However, when approached with more efficient strategies and attitudes, studying can prove rewarding and even exciting as it produces better learning.

Acknowledgments

To our loving, supportive families.

To all the students who taught us with such patience and wisdom.

To the many colleagues and educators who not only influenced us but whose ideas are reflected in these pages. Special thanks to math instructor Dick Sewill, foreign language instructor Bob Davis, and science instructor Laurie Turner.

To our artistic friends who contributed their talents: Morgan Mazzoni, photographer, and Shelley Higuera, graphic artist.

To our supportive publisher Claude Teweles and patient editors Joshua Levine and Dawn VanDercreek.

To the candid reviewers whose ideas helped shape and polish this book. They will recognize the changes made due to their suggestions:

Debra C. Catts, *Delaware State University*

Sally Goss, *Cerro Coso Community College*

Diana Guereña, *Southwestern College*

Regina Jack, *Clarion University*

Patricia Kelly, *Southwestern College*

Kay Lesh, *Pima Community College*

Betty Lingren-Young, *Skyline Community College*

Carlos Maldonado, *University of Southern Colorado*

Carolyn Allen Roper, *San Bernardino Community College*

Linda Skaug, *Portland Community College*

Sandra Sowers, *Delaware State University*

Christy White, *East Arkansas Community College*

Copyright Acknowledgments

Preface for Instructors

The Third Edition of *The Active Learner: Successful Study Strategies* is designed to assist both the instructor and student in their search for a more meaningful way to ensure student academic success. Based on the success of the previous editions, this new edition is an innovative, interactive learning text that combines:

- chapters that can be used in any order, according to need.

- a metacognitive approach to develop students' awareness of their thought processes and to guide them through changes in their study strategies.

- a holistic approach to help students integrate study strategies through exercises keyed to both across-the-curriculum text excerpts and two complete textbook narratives. Skills are then immediately applied to students' texts from other classes.

Students analyze and record their reactions in Personal Response Checks and problem-solving Journal Entries. Doing so provides metacognitive feedback as they monitor self-contracts and develop their own personal study strategies.

The text:

- offers students ten simple steps in a flexible format that allows selective teaching. Lessons are designed to self-activate and guide students.

- encourages students to read actively and critically, using multicultural and across-the-curriculum readings.

- features built-in cooperative learning strategies as suggested activities.

The following features are new in the Third Edition:

- A new step: "Write a Research Paper."

- A revised "Use Your Library" section.

- An additional college textbook excerpt: "Stress and Health Psychology."

- A new history text excerpt: "The Roaring Twenties."

- Rearrangement of some of the steps.

- Journal entries moved to the end of each step.

- Changes to multicultural reading selections.

- Spatial step summaries.

- New and additional exercises.

Also available is a revised, comprehensive ***Instructor's Manual/Testing Program*** offering suggested lesson plans and camera-ready handout masters, along with reference material on the latest research in learning theory to support the study strategies in this book. The Instructor's Manual offers suggested curriculum outlines for six- and nine-week courses.

Preface for Students

So you want to be a more successful student?

Think back:

- When you were a small child, you did not simply stand up and begin to walk. You actively experimented with different strategies for moving forward without falling down. With practice, you eventually learned to walk with confidence.

- When you first began to communicate with others, you learned, through active trial and error, what techniques were most successful.

- When you learned to play a sport, again you first had to learn the basics, then actively experiment to find the approach that let you enjoy the game and win. Then came practice, practice, and more practice.

You did not make progress by passively sitting back, hoping that any of these skills would somehow miraculously seep into your brain. You learned by *active participation*.

Improving your study skills is no different.

In this book you will follow ten steps to help you become an *active learner*. As you will see, the active learner assimilates new information by becoming actively involved in—you might say "interacting" with—the subject matter. This is a process of questioning and thinking through an assignment—of taking responsibility for your own learning curve. It involves posing questions about content, organizing your thoughts, and making your own critical thinking connections between ideas. The techniques you will learn in this book are far more effective than the passive, inactive approaches you are already familiar with, such as rereading and rote memorization.

As a student you are bombarded with so much new information that it can be difficult to know how or where to begin studying. You are drowning in a sea of words, sentences, paragraphs, ideas, details, charts, formulas, and illustrations. You need ways of handling and processing all this incoming data. Because people differ fundamentally in how they learn, there is no set formula for achieving this. However, certain study techniques will prove more efficient. As you move through the ten steps in *The Active Learner*, you will not only master many new study techniques, you will learn *how* and *when* to use them and how to decide which strategies work best for *you*.

As with any textbook, it is important to understand the "game plan" of this book. *The Active Learner* is divided into two parts:

- Part I will teach you study techniques.

- Part II provides an American history narrative and an excerpt from a psychology text on which to practice these techniques.

You will also apply these techniques to textbooks and lecture notes in your other classes.

Old habits do not die easily. You will need to practice these new study techniques constantly until they become almost second nature. At first you may be uncomfortable or feel clumsy with a new method of studying, but give each technique a fair chance. If you become restless because of the time it takes to master a new technique, be patient with yourself. Little in life is achieved without effort.

Your Emergency Needs

If you find yourself in a situation that requires immediate help from a later section of this book, check the Table of Contents or the Index for help.

For example, if your most serious problem is concentration, study the 'Beat the Clock' strategy in Step 4. If you will be facing a major test soon and lack test-taking skills, turn to Step 8. If your notes are so hopeless that you are failing a course, begin with Step 6. In other words, do not hesitate to pick and choose the steps you need immediately.

Part One

*Study Strategies
and Techniques*

Stage One
Take Inventory: Learning How You Learn

The unexamined life is not worth living.
                                        —Socrates

Objectives

❑ To identify your strengths and weaknesses as a student

❑ To examine where you have been, where you are now, and where you want to be as a student

Contents

❑ Inventory One: Personal Profile

❑ Personal Response Checks

❑ Inventory Two: Lifestyle Goals

❑ Inventory Three: Learning and Teaching Styles
   Learning Styles, Part A
   Learning Styles, Part B
   Learning Styles, Part C
   Learning Styles, Part D

❑ Inventory Four: Present Study Inventory

❑ Inventory Five: Preferred Teaching Styles

❑ Summary of Inventories

❑ Summary Map of Stage One

❑ Journal Entries: Introduction

Key Terms

inventory
metacognition
short- and long-term goals
generalist
detailer
auditory memory system
visual memory system
kinesthetic memory system
personal response checks
journal entries
self-contract

3

Introduction to Stage One

As a student, it can be helpful to take an **inventory** of both the internal and external factors that influence how well you do in school.

Internal factors include your learning style, attitude and motivation, degree of commitment, goals, and priorities. You control these aspects of your life. For example, you can motivate yourself to study when you are not in the mood, make a firm commitment to raise your grades, or set your priorities for studying on a daily basis.

External factors include the teaching styles of your instructors, financial constraints, family and job responsibilities, and the attitude of the people close to you about your education. Obviously, these elements are not completely within your control. When an instructor's teaching style doesn't match your learning style, you are the one who will have to adapt. Family and work commitments may affect how many classes you take, the hours when you can be at school, and when and where you study. Family members or friends who feel that you are outgrowing them or resent the loss of your attention may unconsciously sabotage your study priorities.

Fortunately, you have more power over many external factors than you may realize. You can get more cooperation from family members by communicating that your education is a top priority, by including them in your progress as much as possible, and by letting them know how much you need their support. Discussing your educational goals with your employer can result in fewer conflicts between work and school. The friends you spend time with should care enough about you to want you to succeed.

The more you adapt the various aspects of your life to your educational needs, the more you will develop your academic potential. Stages 1 and 2 offer inventories to help you examine the internal and external areas of control in your life.

Inventory One: Personal Profile

Be completely honest in answering these questions.

1. My main goals in school are (rank each goal as 1, 2, or 3, with 1 as most important)

    to spend time with my friends.   _____
    to obtain a degree (certificate, diploma).   _____
    to become qualified for a well-paying career.   _____
    to find a satisfying job.   _____
    to enjoy the process of learning.   _____
    to advance in my present career.   _____
    other_____

2. The person(s) who influenced me most to attend college was/were (select one or two)

    friends   _____
    parents   _____
    other family members   _____
    employer(s)   _____
    former teacher(s)   _____
    other_____

3. An event/situation that influenced me to attend college was

    _____

    _____

Suggested Activity: Form groups with two or three classmates to discuss your educational goals and who/what influenced you.

---

4. Based on my previous educational experience, I would describe my profile as a student as follows (Check the most appropriate response in each of the six groups.)

_____highly motivated	_____good grades
_____average in motivation	_____average grades
_____poorly motivated	_____poor grades
_____managed time well	_____very little social life
_____allotted enough time	_____average social life
_____managed time poorly	_____controlled by social life
_____variety of study skills	_____good test-taking skills
_____sufficient study skills	_____sufficient test-taking skills
_____very few study skills	_____poor test-taking skills

5. My top three priorities are (rank 1, 2, and 3, with 1 as most important and 3 as least important)

_____my social life	_____my home life
_____my work life	_____my future life
_____my school life	_____my_____

6. In the table on the following page, I will list my positive and negative attributes that have an effect on my educational goals.

POSITIVES		NEGATIVES	
Examples:	*Supportive family* *Strongly motivated*	Examples:	*Can't concentrate* *Lack math basics*

Personal Response Checks

Throughout this book, you will be asked to keep a brief record of your positive and negative reactions to the process of taking stock of yourself and trying out new study strategies. Writing is a form of self-discovery. As you note your positive and negative reactions, you will learn much about yourself as a learner. This knowledge will assist you in developing your own Personal Study Profile in Stage 4.

Personal Response Check: Based on my responses to Inventory One,

I realize that   (1)_____

(2)_____

Inventory Two: Lifestyle Goals

Unless you have specific goals you want to achieve, you may not be fully committed to your education, and without commitment you will not be motivated. You must know exactly what you are striving for to be sufficiently motivated to spend long hours attending classes and studying. Do you ever daydream about how you want your life to be when you finish school? These dreams will keep you motivated if you put them on paper and make them specific. To say that your dream is "to be happy" is too vague, but to say that you want to travel four weeks a year is something that you can visualize. This inventory will help you make a detailed list of your dreams.

Long-Term Goals

List what you want ten years from now. Be as specific as possible: list a spouse and three children rather than simply a family. List working with teenagers rather than being active in the community. Consider every aspect of your future life: family, career, friends, leisure time, material possessions, bank account, income, home, educational degree, and other desires.

1. _____

2. _____

3. _____

4. _____

5. _____

6. _____

7. _____

8. _____

9. _____

10. _____

Suggested Activity: Discuss your goals with a group of classmates. What sacrifices are you willing to make to achieve these goals?

Short-Term Goals

Goals for one year from now: To achieve your ten-year, long-term goals, what must you do during the next year? For example, if your long-term goal is to become a doctor, then you'll want to concentrate on receiving A's and B's in your classes so that you will be able to get into medical school.

1. _____

2. _____

3. _____

4. _____

5. _____

Goals for this semester: To achieve your goals for the next year, what must you accomplish this semester? Examples: earn a B in biology, discuss interest in a nursing career with a career counselor, plan your courses for next term.

1. _____

2. _____

3. _____

4. _____

5. _____

Personal Response Check: As a result of examining my long- and short-term goals, I realize that   (1)_____

(2)_____

Inventory Three: Learning and Teaching Styles

All education is really self-education.

—Anonymous

If you keep in mind the axiom that all education is really self-education, you will come to depend on yourself to learn rather than counting on an instructor. Of course, instructors can help by providing information and resources, but in reality you are teaching yourself when you read textbooks, take notes, and review.

To understand how to learn more efficiently, you first need to understand how you learn best. This process of understanding how you learn is called **metacognition.** The prefix *meta* means "beyond," and the word *cognition* means "to know." Metacognition means to go beyond just knowing: you need to know how you know and learn how you learn. Using the metacognitive process, you observe your own learning process, evaluate which study strategies fit the way you learn best, and "fine-tune" or adjust them as needed.[1] Psychologist Carl Rogers aptly described the metacognitive process when he said, "The only person who is educated is the person who has learned to learn; the person who has learned how to adapt and change; the person who has realized that no knowledge is secure, that only the process of seeking knowledge gives a basis for security."[2]

To learn more about how the metacognitive process relates to you, take the following four inventories to examine four types of learning styles and situations.

Part A: Learning Styles

We each have a unique learning system, but do we know which study techniques work best for us? The following questionnaire is designed to help you analyze how you go about studying. After reading the statements A and B on the following pages, choose the one which best describes your method in most situations. (Note: There are no right or wrong answers.)

---

[1]A. L. Brown. (1980). "Metacognitive Development and Reading," in R. J. Spiro, B. C. Bruce, and W. F. Brewer (eds.), *Theoretical Issues in Reading Comprehension,* Pp. 453–481. Hillsdale, NJ: Earlbaum.

[2]Quoted in Michael J. Rabalais' editorial. (May 1991). "I'm Already Good, and I Want to Get Better: Improving Instruction Through Effective Teaching," *Teaching English in the Two-Year College.* 18:2, Pp. 81–92.

_____ 1. When beginning a new chapter in a textbook, I tend to
A. skim over titles, subtitles, and graphics before I begin to read.
B. begin by reading the chapter and progress from page to page.

_____ 2. When I study, I
A. combine lecture and text notes into a simple master outline.
B. concentrate on all the lecture/text notes without an outline.

_____ 3. When I take notes in class, I concentrate mainly on
A. general ideas.
B. details and facts.

_____ 4. When I review, I test myself by writing or reciting
A. general summaries.
B. specific details.

_____ 5. When listening in class, I mainly listen for
A. important principles, theories, and ideas.
B. important facts such as who, when, and where.

_____ 6. When reading an assignment for the first time, I concentrate on
A. only three or four major ideas in a chapter.
B. details and then decide what the major ideas are.

_____ 7. When studying a topic, I read
A. other books and materials on the topic.
B. only the assigned material.

_____ 8. When reading a book for the first time, I
A. read over the table of contents first.
B. begin to read the first chapter assigned.

_____ 9. When reading a chapter, I
A. read the introduction, the summary, and questions first.
B. read it in sequential order.

_____10. When I read an assignment, I formulate questions
A. that I want to answer before I begin to read.
B. as I read.

_____11. Before writing an essay, I
A. create an outline on paper or in my head.
B. write as ideas occur to me.

_____12. When I think about questions that might appear on a test, I stress
A. main ideas.
B. specific facts.

_____13. When asking my instructor for information, I tend to ask
   A. broad questions that require lengthy answers.
   B. specific questions that require only a word, phrase, or sentence to answer.

_____14. When I listen to my instructor, I prefer to concentrate on information that
   A. goes beyond what I will be tested on.
   B. pertains only to the subject I will be tested on.

_____15. Study the two pictures below. The illustration on the right is a detail from the stained glass window on the left. Examine one illustration for a few moments, then the other.

If you began by examining the entire stained glass window and then the smaller section, mark A in the space provided for 15 above. If you began with the detailed section, mark B.

Now calculate your total number of A's and B's in Part A:

   Total number of A's = _____   Total number of B's = _____

Results of Part A

Did you sense any difference between A- and B-type responses while you were taking inventory? The A statements indicate a preference for working with general ideas as opposed to a preference for specific details that lead to general ideas, which is represented by the B statements.

If you chose more A statements, you tend to be a **generalist,** or *deductive thinker.* You prefer to

- seek an overall view before moving into detailed work.
- organize major ideas and concepts quickly.
- make a "panoramic sweep" before you zoom in on the details.

If you have more B statements, you tend to be a **detailer** or *inductive thinker.* You usually prefer to

- move from specifics to form a general picture.
- work with details and examples to draw conclusions.
- examine minor points to seek main patterns.

The generalist prefers to appreciate a stained-glass window by standing far enough away to see the design of the whole window before moving closer to examine the specific details. The detailer prefers to appreciate the details of the window before moving back for a broader view to see how the parts create the whole.

Neither style of learning is inherently better than the other, but you should become adept at using both styles. Whenever possible, begin as a generalist, looking for the overall picture before shifting into the detailer mode and examining the specifics. However, some study situations do not clearly reveal the big picture and require working with details before the overall design emerges.

Personal Response Check: As a result of learning about generalists and detailers,

I realize that   (1) _____

(2) _____

Part B: Learning Styles

For each section, check the statements that are usually true for you. (For now, ignore the long blank lines after the numbers of the sections.)

Section I: _____

1. I prefer to think for myself rather than work with others. _____

2. I prefer self-paced lessons from a text to lectures. _____

3. I like to be given a general essay topic and then be allowed to narrow it to a specific topic. _____

4. I do not like step-by-step deadline checks for portions of my papers to be completed. I prefer to be given a final deadline for the entire project. _____

Section II: _____

1. I prefer lectures followed by discussions. _____

2. I prefer to take notes while I am studying. _____

3. I like to do extra reading and research about topics I am studying. _____

4. I often think of examples from my own experiences that relate to the topics I am studying. _____

Section III: _____

1. I like to answer questions in class. _____

2. I like to be a group leader in class. _____

3. I like an instructor to acknowledge my participation in class. _____

4. I like to get the highest grade in a class. _____

Section IV: _____

1. I like to take classes on a no-credit basis rather than for a grade. _____

2. I like it when the instructor provides a lecture outline. _____

3. I prefer to listen and let the other students respond to questions. _____

4. In group work, I prefer to let other students offer ideas. _____

Section V: _____

1. I like to study with classmates outside of class.   _____
2. I prefer a class that includes group work.   _____
3. I like doing group projects rather than individual projects.   _____
4. I like to share my ideas with other students.   _____

   Total number of checks in each section: I ___ II ____ III ____ IV ____ V ____

Results of Part B

Consider the sections in which you had the most check marks. These responses should give you a clue as to the type of learning style you prefer.

Beside Section I, write *Independent Learner* in the blank. This type of learner functions well without much direction from the instructor or interaction with other students. This student is usually self-confident, prefers to guide his or her own education as much as possible, and likes general guidelines rather than specific directions. This student's reward is being able to control the learning process.

Beside Section II, write *Discovery Learner.* This type of learner has a sense of curiosity and enjoys most subjects. This student goes beyond what the class requirements dictate and explores topics in more depth. This learner's reward is experiencing the discovery of new information.

Beside Section III, write *Competitive Learner.* This type of learner finds a reward in being the best and in receiving admiration from the instructor and classmates. This student will work long hours to succeed.

Beside Section IV, write *Dependent Learner.* This type of learner prefers that the instructor provide structure and lets classmates lead the way. This student will tend to learn only what is required, may lean on others for learning, and is probably a passive learner.

Beside Section V, write *Cooperative Learner.* This type of learner prefers to interact with others by sharing ideas and leadership. This student likes people and finds reward in social and intellectual interaction with others.

You will probably find that you are a combination of several types of learners. For example, you may be an independent/competitive learner, a discovery/cooperative learner, or any other combination of the five models. You may be an independent learner in one class but a dependent learner in another. These labels are less important than your own self-awareness about how you prefer to learn and your willingness to adopt new learning styles.

> ***Personal Response Check:*** As a result of exploring learning styles in Part B,
>
> I realize that   (1)_____
>
> (2) _____

Part C: Learning Styles

Write in the letter for the phrase that best describes your preferred learning style.

_____ 1. When I am listening to a lecture, I tend to
    A. remember most of the content without needing to take notes.
    B. take notes as much as possible.
    C. make flow charts and organizational maps of the information rather than take regular notes.

_____ 2. When reviewing my notes, I tend to
    A. read them aloud.
    B. add information and formulate questions.
    C. mark them with symbols and draw maps to help me assimilate the information.

_____ 3. When I sign up for a class, I always hope that
    A. most of the learning will come from what I hear.
    B. most of the learning will come from what I read.
    C. most of the learning will come from lab experiments or field study.

_____ 4. If I have a choice of the method of testing, I would choose to
    A. verbally explain my knowledge.
    B. write my knowledge.
    C. demonstrate my knowledge.

_____ 5. When I study, I prefer to
    A. review the material aloud or discuss it with classmates.
    B. reread my text and notes.
    C. make review sheets with graphic outlines: charts, graphs, or pictures.

_____ 6. When memorizing, I tend to
    A. read the information out loud.
    B. keep rereading the material.
    C. create visual memory devices.

_____ 7. If assigned a project on emotions in a psychology class, I would prefer to
    A. give an oral explanation.
    B. write a paper.
    C. present a dramatization.

Record your answers:

Number of A's:_____   Number of B's:_____   Number of C's:_____

After reading the next section, return to this page and fill in the terms for these three types of learners.

Type A Learner:_____   Type B Learner:_____

Type C Learner:_____

Results of Part C

The A's represent a preference for an **auditory memory system** that relies on hearing information from others and listening to oneself. Auditory learners can listen to a lecture and remember it with a minimum of notes. They also benefit by listening to lectures they have taped, discussing topics with others, and simply listening to themselves review aloud.

The B learners prefer a **visual memory system,** depending heavily on their eyes to receive information. These students absorb what they see in writing, pictures, film, or other visual representations. They must take notes so that they can see what they are hearing. Since they do not retain what they hear for very long, they like to refer to textbooks or notes.

The C's represent those who depend on their **kinesthetic memory system.** Their preference is for learning through action, and they like to use their motor skills to learn. These learners would rather demonstrate a chemistry experiment than write about it or explain it verbally.

Personal Response Check: As a result of examining these three memory systems,
I realize that   (1)_____

(2) _____

Part D: Learning Styles

Respond to the situations below by indicating your preference. Select either A or B, not both.

1. In thinking about your future college career, have you

   _____A. picked out the courses you will need to take and arranged them in a logical sequence?

   _____B. taken courses that sound interesting, leaving the required courses for a later time?

2. When reading a text that also presents the same information in a graphic display, do you concentrate on

   _____A. the written information?

   _____B. the graphic display?

3. When a friend shares a problem, do you

   _____A. explore the positive and negative effects of each potential solution?

   _____B. share your concern and assure your friend that everything will be fine?

4. When a friend is irritable, do you

   _____A. explain how that person's mood is affecting you and what he or she might do to feel better?

   _____B. get the person to laugh and forget his or her problems?

5. If something is troubling you, do you

   _____A. try to figure out what has caused this feeling by examining possible reasons?

   _____B. shake the feeling by doing something that you enjoy?

6. When taking a test, do you prefer

   _____A. multiple-choice questions?

   _____B. open-ended questions?

7. When meeting a new person, does your attention center on

   _____A. what the person is saying?

   _____B. the person's body language?

8. Do you tend to remember people you have recently met by their

   _____A. names?

   _____B. faces?

9. Do you like your week to be

    _____A. carefully planned?

    _____B. unplanned and spontaneous?

10. Do you prefer classes in which you

    _____A. break problems down, examine them in some kind of order, and then draw a conclusion?

    _____B. look at each problem as a whole and approach it by using hunches?

Total number of A's = _____   Total number of B's = _____

Wait to fill this in until you have read the results below.

A signifies_____-brain dominance. B signifies_____-brain dominance.

Results of Part D

Research on how the brain functions indicates that the left and right sides of the brain tend to handle different thinking processes, although the two sides are always in communication with each other.[3] For example, a friend breaks down and cries, telling you that she and her boyfriend are breaking up. You have an emotional reaction (right side of the brain), but then you think of logical ways to explain to your friend how she can win her boyfriend back (left side of the brain). Your friend does not understand, so you explain by describing images of her boyfriend sitting sadly by the phone waiting for her call (right side of the brain).

The American public school system favors left-dominant students who function well in a structured, authoritarian environment, who use a systematic, logical approach to their studies, and who prefer to read books and listen to lectures (all A answers in Part C).[4] Right-dominant students function better in a freer, less structured environment, preferring to discuss, experiment, follow their hunches, and play around with ideas (all B answers in Part C). Neither learning style is wrong. They are simply different.

---

[3] R. E. Ornstein. (1972). *The Psychology of Consciousness.* San Francisco: Freeman.

[4] J. D. Fenton. (1977). "Cognitive Learning Style and the Brain," *Proceedings of the Tenth Annual Conference of the Western College Reading Association* 10:179–183.

To be a successful student, you need to know what your learning style is and how to adjust it when circumstances warrant a different approach. For instance, if you are a science student, you probably function well with left-dominant strategies. However, many aspects of science require right-dominant activities. What if you decide to take a creative writing course in which you are expected to be creative rather than analytical? What if you are an art major and have to take a chemistry class?

What is important here is not whether you are left or right dominant but how you handle study situations.

Personal Response Check: As a result of thinking about brain dominance,

I realize that   (1)_____

(2)_____

Inventory Four:
Present Study Inventory

List strategies that you currently use in the left column. As you adopt new strategies, describe them in the right column. A record of your test scores will indicate whether the new or old strategies are more effective. *You may want to photocopy this page to use for different courses.*

Study Strategies

Present study techniques for this course	New study strategies for this course
(Example: Begin by reading first page of chapter.)	(Date) Scan chapter headings and subheadings before reading chapter.
Reading strategies	
Note-taking strategies	
Reviewing strategies	
Test-taking strategies	
Other strategies	

In addition to internal and external factors, where you study, how you study, and how you utilize your time have a significant impact on your academic success. The following inventories will add to your understanding of how you learn.

Grade Status Inventory

Too often students prefer not to know what their grade average is and what a particular course requires because they fear they might receive bad news. However, you need to be constantly aware of your status in every course you take. Do you know whether you are passing? If you are alert to how you are doing in each course, you can determine where your attention is most needed. For instance, you may be focusing most of your attention on a course in which you are successful and unconsciously ignoring your poor achievement in another.

Course Title:_____

Instructor:_____

Office Hours: Mon.____Tues.____Wed.____Thurs.____Fri.____

Office Location:_____ Telephone:_____

Record your grades below:

	Date: _____		Date:
Test 1_____(____)	Research Paper Grade:	_____	_____
Test 2_____(____)	Lab Grade:	_____	_____
Test 3_____(____)	Extra Credit Grades:	_____	_____
Test 4_____(____)		_____	_____
Test 5_____(____)		_____	_____

Date: _____

Mid-term Exam: _____(____)

Final Exam: _____(____) Final Grade: _____

Number of absences allowed: _____ Number of late arrivals allowed: _____

Dates of absences:_____

Dates of late arrivals:_____

Other class information:_____

Many instructors factor attendance and tardiness into your final grade but don't necessarily say so. Find out each instructor's policies and keep a careful record.

Study Atmosphere Inventory

Have you ever given any thought to where you do most of your studying? Your study area can affect your concentration and your grades. In the following exercise, list three places where you work on your assignments. Many students who receive high grades spend much of their study time in the library, so you may want to include it as one work area.

Example Study Areas: A ___my bedroom___   B__at work_____   C___library_____

My Study Areas: A_____ B_____ C_____

Relate your answers to the following descriptive statements about the areas in which you normally study. Rate each statement below as 3 for true, 2 for sometimes true, and 1 for not true.

A   B   C

2   1   3   (Example) There is no telephone nearby to interrupt or tempt me.

___ ___ ___   1. There is little or no distracting conversation around me.

___ ___ ___   2. There is no refrigerator to attract me.

___ ___ ___   3. There is no television to distract me.

___ ___ ___   4. There is very little noise from outdoors.

___ ___ ___   5. My family members do not interrupt me.

___ ___ ___   6. There is not a couch or a bed where I might lie down and grow drowsy.

___ ___ ___   7. A desk or sufficient table space is cleared for studying.

___ ___ ___   8. Study equipment is available: paper, pens, computer, etc.

___ ___ ___   9. Encyclopedias and a dictionary are nearby or available online.

___ ___ ___   10. Lighting is sufficient for long-term studying.

___ ___ ___   11. Room temperature is comfortable, but a little on the cool side.

___ ___ ___   Total Scores

The highest score indicates that (choose A, B, or C)_____is the best study area for me.

Study Materials

When you study, you need your study tools readily available. Take inventory of your study tools by putting a check mark where you can locate the following items. (Later, add needed items to your home study area and book bag.)

Item	Home	Book Bag	School
Computer	_____	_____	_____
Dictionary (large, hardbound)	_____	_____	_____
Dictionary (paperback)	_____	_____	_____
Grammar/composition handbook	_____	_____	_____
Encyclopedia (1–2 volume set)	_____	_____	_____
Encyclopedia (full set)*	_____	_____	_____
World atlas	_____	_____	_____
Thesaurus (synonyms/antonyms)	_____	_____	_____
Packages of 3 x 5 cards (or larger)	_____	_____	_____
Stapler	_____	_____	_____
Supply of staples	_____	_____	_____
Scotch tape	_____	_____	_____
Paper clips	_____	_____	_____
Hole puncher	_____	_____	_____
Ruler	_____	_____	_____
Eraser	_____	_____	_____
Notebook paper, lined	_____	_____	_____
Paper, white, unlined	_____	_____	_____
Work station	_____	_____	_____
Colored pens	_____	_____	_____
Colored highlighters	_____	_____	_____
Pencils	_____	_____	_____
Portable desk or plastic pouch**	_____	_____	_____
Precise-point pen	_____	_____	_____
Calculator	_____	_____	_____
_____	_____	_____	_____
_____	_____	_____	_____

---

*A note about encyclopedias: They often supplement or explain textbook information. Your local thrift stores may have a used set that is affordable. Although it will probably not be current, the volumes can serve as a temporary source of information until you can get to the library or you can visit an online encyclopedia.

**Office supply stores sell small carrying cases that include many of the smaller items listed here. They also sell three-hole plastic pouches to insert in your notebook.

Inventory Five: Preferred Teaching Styles

Just as you prefer certain ways of learning, your instructors have specific ways they like to teach. Often an instructor's teaching style will not match your learning style. With some "shopping around," however, you can prepare a list of instructors who teach the way you like to learn.

Mark the teaching style you prefer:

_____ 1. Lecture only: the instructor lectures with little or no interaction with students.

_____ 2. Lecture with discussion: the instructor stops often to invite questions and comments.

_____ 3. Group discussion: the instructor regularly allows time for students to learn together.

_____ 4. Lecture/lab: class time is divided between lectures and student experimentation on lecture topics in a lab environment.

_____ 5. Other_____

Results of Inventory Five

From time to time during the course of your education you are sure to have some instructors whose teaching styles do not match your learning style. When that happens, you need a variety of study strategies and a flexible approach.

For example, if you are an independent learner in a class where you must participate in group discussion, you might take notes to study later when you are alone. If you are a cooperative learner in a class with no group participation or class interaction, you can form an out-of-class study group. If you are a student who needs specific instructions for a project but have an instructor who provides only general guidelines, arrange a meeting to ask for more detailed directions.

Don't sit by idly and hope for the best if you find yourself in an uncomfortable teaching environment. To earn good grades you must actively seek out study strategies and approaches that will be most helpful to you in adapting to the instructor's teaching style.

Personal Response Check: As a result of thinking about teaching styles,

I realize that   (1)_____

                 (2)_____

Summary of Inventories

1. I approach studying mainly as a ____ generalist ____ detailer

2. My main styles of learning can be ranked as (rank from 1 to 4, using 1 to indicate your main style and 4 as the style you use least):

    ____independent   ____discovery   ____competitive

    ____dependent   ____cooperative

3. My memory system preferences are ranked as: 1 (*most used*) 2 (*often used*) 3 (*least used*)

    ____auditory   ____visual   ____kinesthetic

4. I tend to be

    ____A. left-brain dominant

    ____B. right-brain dominant

    ____C. balanced

5. My preferred teaching style is

    ____lecture only   _____lecture with discussion

    ____regular group discussion _____lecture/lab

    other_____

    Explain the expression "All education is really self-education."_____
    _____
    _____
    _____

This summary begins your profile as a student. You will add to the profile in each of the subsequent steps in this text when you record your reactions in Self-Awareness Checks, Personal Response Checks, and Journal Entries. These reactions will guide you in examining your current study methods, testing new study strategies, and analyzing which strategies work best for you. Students who adopt new study methods based on their preferred learning style gain confidence, earn higher grades, and often spend less time studying.

Throughout this book you will read comments from former study-skills students as they share their academic problems, solutions, and victories. For example, Gilbert Rodenberry was a typical freshman student who had never been taught how to study, nor had he ever seriously examined his study habits and attitudes before taking a course in study techniques. Here are some of his comments:

> *This class has made me aware of my bad habits and how to change them into positive habits. I've had to take a look at my future goals, how I manage my time, and, most of all, my willingness to make sacrifices for my education. With all of this information, I think I have a better chance at making it through the first year.*
> —**Gilbert Rodenberry**

Summary Map of Stage One

Personal goals
- Short-term
- Long-term

Metacognition
- Journal entries
- Personal response checks
- Self-contracts

Learning styles
- Study method
  - Generalist
  - Detailer

- Type of learner
  - Independent
  - Discovery
  - Competitive
  - Cooperative
  - Dependent

- Memory system
  - Visual
  - Auditory
  - Kinesthetic

- Brain dominance
  - Left
  - Right

Journal Entries: Introduction

You began this book working with inventories and the first of several personal response checks. Journal entries will now help you probe deeper into your attitudes, habits, and strategies as a student. Done conscientiously and systematically, writing your deepest thoughts will give you an awareness of the changes you want to make and possibly serve as a guide to your future. Furthermore, these journal writings will prepare you to develop a Personal Study Profile in Stage 4.

Journal writing is *freewriting*—writing free of any restrictions or concerns for "proper English," without stopping. Write whatever is on your mind. When you freewrite, unconscious thoughts may emerge. Here is an example from a student who recorded thoughts about her motivation for attending college, unaware of what would show up:

I used to go to school because I was expected to go. In fact, the more my parents insisted that I go, the more I didn't want to go. Stubborn. Lazy. No plans for the future—I was going no place fast. Now. What now? Where am I going? I don't really know. The future is so hazy I get scared. Now I have more reason to work. I want a good job. Not the one I've got now. No more "yes, sir!" "no, sir!" to someone I can't stand. I know I want to be independent. Maybe I want to be a boss? Or own my own business?

Stage One Journal Entry

Date:_____

Henri Bergson talks about "creating oneself endlessly." In order to continue changing, you need to take inventory periodically to know who and what you are, to learn what works and doesn't work for you, and to consider alternative options.

For ten minutes, freewrite, *without stopping,* about the most interesting aspects that you discovered about yourself as a result of taking the inventories in Stage One. What are some of the positives you learned about yourself? What are some of the changes you want to make? Don't worry if you ramble. Don't stop writing to condemn or censure yourself.

_____

_____

_____

_____

_____

_____

_____

_____

_____

_____

_____

_____

_____

_____

_____

_____

_____

_____

_____

_____

_____

_____

_____

_____

_____

_____

_____

_____

_____

_____

_____

_____

_____

_____

_____

Now that you have finished, go back and underline anything that you want to think about more. Examples: "I am here because my parents expect me to go to college"; "I dread going to chemistry class because I don't understand what chemistry has to do with the rest of my life;" "I find Professor X extremely dull."

Stage Two

Evaluate Present Study Strategies and Time Management

If you don't control time, time will control you.
                                                        —Alan Lakein

Key Terms

Time Management Log
time-wasters
2:1 formula
20:10:20 formula
prime-time energy
prioritize
procrastination

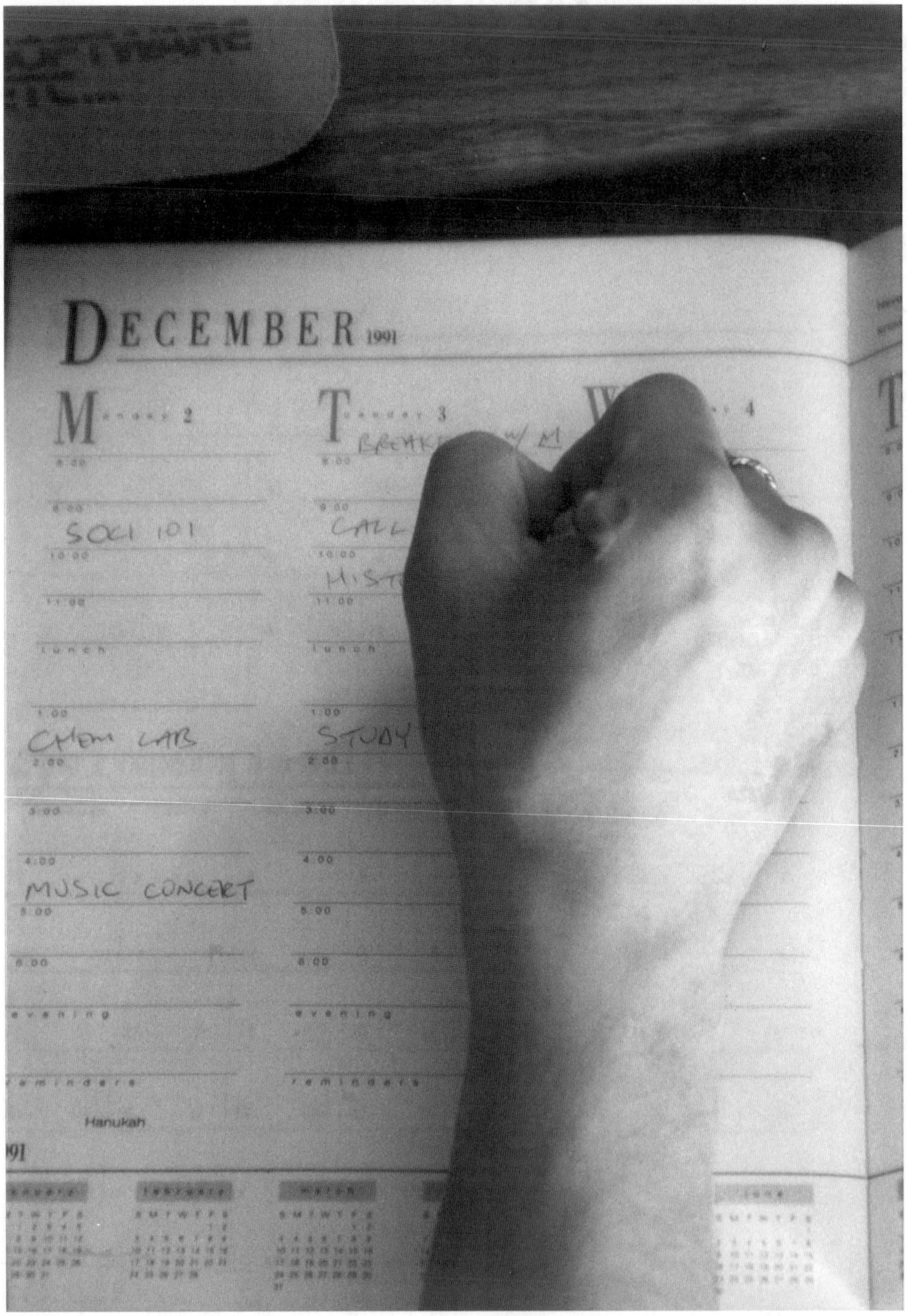
DECEMBER 1991
SOCI 101
CHEM LAB
STUDY
MUSIC CONCERT
lunch
evening
reminders
Hanukah

Self-Awareness Check:

Check the following items on the appropriate blank:	Often	Sometimes	Rarely
1. I spend too much time socializing.	___	___	___
2. I am aware of how I waste time.	___	___	___
3. I work too many hours to make good grades.	___	___	___
4. I don't study at regularly scheduled times.	___	___	___
5. I use an appointment book every day.	___	___	___

Introduction to Stage Two

In addition to the internal and external factors examined in Stage One, how you utilize your time has a significant impact on your academic success. The following inventories will add to your understanding of how you learn.

Basic Principles of Time Management

Most of us complain about always being too busy—never having enough hours in the day to accomplish what we need to do at school, home, or work. You may have experienced this problem yourself. Somehow the hours slip by too quickly, and by the end of the day you feel like a juggler who keeps dropping the balls.

Since you have only 24 hours in a day and 168 hours in a week, you need to treat time as you would money. If you were broke all the time, you would begin analyzing where your money was going and plan a realistic financial budget. Because time is money, this section will help you begin analyzing time the same way.

Estimating How You Think You Spend Your Time

Before you begin to record how you actually spend your time, take a few moments to estimate how you think you use it. Note what percentage of time you estimate you spend per week on the following activities.

Sleeping_____%

With friends_____%

In class_____%

Watching TV_____%

Studying_____%

Working_____%

Recording How You Actually Spend Your Time

Keep track of how you spend your time for one week. Record your activities throughout the day so that you do not forget what you actually did. Note them in units of 30–60 minutes, using general categories such as those listed to the right of the box.

	Monday	Tuesday	Wednesday
12-6 a.m.	Sleep ↓	Sleep ↓	Sleep ↓
6-7	Dress / Eat		Dress / Eat
7-8	Commute / Socialize	Dress / Eat	Commute / Study
8-9	History	Commute / Math	History
9-10	Chemistry	Math	Chemistry
10-11	Study	Commute / Work	Study
11-12	P.E.		P.E.
12-1 p.m.	Eat / Socialize	↓	Eat / Study

Dress/eat
Commute
Socialize
Attend class
Study
Work
Television
Telephone
Sleep
Errands/chores
Child care
Home care

Fill out the **Time Management Log** on the next page for a seven-day period, recording as often as possible. If you wait until the end of the day or put off recording for several days, you may forget about significant ways in which you spent your time. At the end of each day, total your class and study hours. At the end of the week, total those hours in the boxes on the far right.

In Stage One, you read Gilbert's thoughts about being a student. Here, other students share their time-management problems.

I took on a full-time job and full-time school schedule without thinking it would be too much, but it was. I now know that to survive in college, you need to be dedicated and willing to make a lot of sacrifices.

—Dawn Hernandez

As a single mother with two children, my time is very limited. I have to schedule my time carefully to find enough time to study.

—Sabrina Merritt

TIME MANAGEMENT LOG

	Monday	Tuesday	Wednesday	Thursday	Friday	Saturday	Sunday
12–6 a.m.							
6–7							
7–8							
8–9							
10–11							
12–1p.m.							
1–2							
2–3							
4–5							
6–7							
8–9							
10–11							
11–12							

Weekly Totals:

Daily Class Hours								Class Hours:
Daily Study Hours								Study Hours:

Analyzing How You Spend Your Time

Use your completed Time Management Log to calculate how much time you spend on each activity listed in the Activities Breakdown below. The blank lines are for any additional situations that take up your time. After you have totaled all the items you can think of, figure out how much free time you have.

ACTIVITIES BREAKDOWN

Activities	Hours per Week
1. Class time	_____
2. Study time, reviewing, projects, papers	_____
3. Commuting	_____
4. Dressing and eating	_____
5. Hours of outside employment	_____
6. Responsibilities at home	_____
7. Telephone	_____
8. Television, internet	_____
9. Dating, outings, sports, movies, clubs, etc.	_____
10. Sleeping	_____
11. _____	_____
12. _____	_____

Total: _____

Total number of hours per week =   168

Subtract your total   _____

Total free hours per week   _____

Personal Response Check: As a result of analyzing my time log,
I realize that   (1)_____

(2)_____

Becoming Aware of Time-Wasters

Before you can decide how to use your 24 hours more productively, you must first determine ways in which you are wasting your time.

Using the Time Management Log you have just completed, list in Column A all the activities that do not contribute to achieving your ultimate goal of being successful in college. (Ignore Column B for now.) Recording these **time-wasters** does not necessarily mean that you are giving them up. You will make that decision later.

MY LIST OF TIME-WASTERS

Column A	**Column B**
Example: *Watch 2-3 hours of television daily*	
1.	
2.	
3.	
4.	
5.	
6.	
7.	
8.	
9.	
10.	

Suggested Activity: In a small group, discuss the time-wasters each person has identified. If you recognize any that belong on your list, add them.

Now go back to Column B and indicate which time-wasting activities you can delegate to others, which ones you can decrease, and which ones you can eliminate.

Examples:

Column A	**Column B**
Talked one hour in cafeteria	*Decrease to ten min. after I eat*
Mother calls daily for ½ hour	*Decrease to five min.*
I work overtime	*Eliminate overtime work*
I drive my kids to school	*Delegate to others to share & carpool*

Personal Response Check: As a result of thinking about how I waste time, I realize that   (1)_____

(2)_____

Using the 2:1 Formula

For many years the **2:1 Formula** has helped students determine how much time to allot for studying. This reliable rule-of-thumb calls for approximately two hours of study for every hour of class. While you may not need two hours for every hour you attend a physical education class, you may need far more than two hours for physics or English. The formula takes into consideration that you will probably have a mixture of easy and difficult courses.

Return to the Time Management Log and record your weekly totals from the right–hand column.

Total Class Hours:_____ Total Study Hours:_____

Are your study hours approximately double your class hours? If not, are you getting the grades that you want? If they are not satisfactory and you are not using the 2:1 formula, you may want to consider changing the way you prioritize your time. For example, you might save money and time by finding a job closer to your home or on campus. Only you can decide whether you need to follow the 2:l formula and how to create enough hours to study.

Another formula to consider is **20:10:20.** If you work 20 hours or more a week, you probably should not spend more than 10 hours in class, because you will need 20 hours for study. This total of 50 hours a week equals more than a full-time job.

Being in Business for Yourself

Consider yourself self-employed while you are a student. The hours you spend attending classes and studying are an investment in yourself. No one else can make this investment for you.

How much are you worth per hour? Select a dollar amount that is comparable to what you think you will earn per hour after you're established in your career.

Record the amount that you are worth: $_____ per hour

When you waste an hour, you are in effect wasting the amount of money that your time is worth. If you spent two hours watching television last night when you needed to study and you value your time at $25 an hour, those programs actually cost you $50. Were they worth it?

Personal Response Check: As a result of thinking about how much I am worth per hour and the 2:1 Formula,

I realize that   (1)_____

  (2)_____

Using Prime-Time Energy

There are times in the day when you feel at your best, times when your energy level peaks, and times when you begin to lag. For instance, a "morning person" often feels most mentally alert and energetic in the hours before lunch. "Night owls," on the other hand, notice that their energy levels rise later in the day.

Do you schedule your study periods to take advantage of your peak hours—your **prime-time energy?** Students often mistakenly think they should be in class during their peak hours. But the energy of your instructors and classmates will keep you alert even during low-energy hours. If not, you can at least keep your eyes open and take notes. At work, interaction with other people will keep you functioning. But when you are alone during a low-energy period, you will probably want to nap, eat, watch television—do anything but study. Try to plan your classes and work schedule around your lower energy times and save your peak time for studying.

In the chart below, write the word *Study* in the time slots that best correspond with your prime-time periods. Then fill in the slots when you think it would be best for you to attend classes and work.

	High Energy	Middle Energy	Low Energy
Morning			
Afternoon			
Night			

When I was working in the aerospace industry, I used to be exhausted by the time I hit campus at four p.m. One day I sat down and added up my expenses. I realized that I could survive on less money if I lived within walking distance of the college. All I'd need would be a part-time job on campus. I could save money on driving and clothes. In addition, by cutting back on work, I could also graduate in half the time. I was willing to make the sacrifice. So I sold my old car, and now I walk or take a bus—with the promise that when I get my degree I'll pick out the car of my dreams and buy a closet full of new clothes. The best thing is that I have more energy now, so my classes don't seem nearly as difficult.

—**Chris Lisecki**

Planning an Ideal Time-Management Log

Now that you know how you actually spend your time and have considered what your prime-energy time is, consider how to rearrange your life this semester to spend your time more wisely.

You may not be able to make as many changes as you would like, but you can design a time plan that is both realistic and more effective than your current schedule.

As you work on your ideal (but realistic) time plan on the next page, remember the old adage: We always find time to do what we really want to do. Write in when you plan to study for each course as well as when you plan to sleep, attend class, work, socialize, and meet other commitments.

IDEAL TIME-MANAGEMENT LOG

	Monday	Tuesday	Wednesday	Thursday	Friday	Saturday	Sunday	
12–6 a.m.								
6–7								
7–8								
8–9								
10–11								
12–1p.m.								
1–2								
2–3								
4–5								
6–7								
8–9								
10–11								
11–12								**Weekly Totals:**
Daily Class Hours								**Class Hours:**
Daily Study Hours								**Study Hours:**

Managing Your Time

A chief reason some students miss achieving their goals is that they tend to wander from day to day with no clear road map of where they are going or when they will reach their destination. They need a do-it-now plan of action to manage their time, and they need to stick to it (except for emergencies).

Your first Time-Management Log revealed how you tend to spend your time. The following three simple tools will help you organize your time to achieve your ideal Time-Management Log:

- ■ a monthly calendar

- ■ an appointment book

- ■ a daily Things To Do list

These organizers will give you the peace of mind that comes from being in charge of your life. Don't let other people—even friends and family—create "emergencies" and then try to impose them on you. Stick to your set plan of action as best you can.

1. *Monthly Calendar.* A calendar will give you an overview of dates for taking tests, turning in papers, attending mandatory special events, and other academic responsibilities. If you glance over the month, you can block off chunks of time to prepare for a school project. You won't be tempted to plan social events if you are already committed.

SAMPLE MONTH

Sunday	Monday	Tuesday	Wednesday	Thursday	Friday	Saturday
	1	2	*Due:* 3 *Art project proposal*	4	*Chem* 5 *exam*	6
7	8	9	10	11	12	13
14	15	16	17	18	*Chem* 19 *exam*	20
21	22	23	24	25	26	27
28	*Due:* 29 *Art project*	*math* 30 *exam*	31			

2. *Weekly Appointment Book.* Maintaining an appointment book will give you a sense of control because you know what to plan for and expect in the week ahead. Record everything you need to do for the week, including your schoolwork. While your calendar alerts you to major deadlines in what may seem like the faraway future, your appointment book will tip you off to everything you need to do during the week at hand.

Most important, be sure to *make appointments with yourself to study.* This may sound unnecessary, but unless you have an appointment to study, it is too easy to keep telling yourself that you'll "get around to it tomorrow." But when tomorrow comes, will you be ready for a test?

Whenever an instructor gives you an assignment, make a point of writing it down in your appointment book. Consider this a sort of "study appointment," remembering to schedule it during your prime energy hours. Keep track of any appointments that you break and note the reasons why. Also, periodically examine the reasons for your broken appointments. Does a pattern emerge? Is it a pattern you want to break?

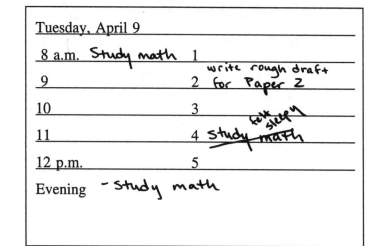

Note broken appointment and reason

Note rescheduled appointment

3. *Things To Do Today List.* Jot down the day's activities on a notepad and keep it where it is easily accessible. During the day you may wish to add to it or cross off tasks as you complete them. Most weekly or monthly appointment books do not have the space for a long list of daily tasks, and that is why a separate daily notepad is advisable. Include an estimated time for completing each task, a step that will convince you that simple tasks add up quickly, leaving no spare moments for time-wasters. The sample form on the next page is for you to photocopy and use for the next four days so that you can test this method. Time management specialists suggest that you **prioritize** each item so that you are sure to take care of the most important tasks first.[1]

> A = top priority (must be done today)
> B = second priority (should be done today)
> C = lowest priority (should be done soon)
> D = delegate this to someone

Things To Do Today: Tuesday

A – call math study group	(15 min)
C – pick up laundry	(10)
B – check library sources, Paper 2	(30)
B – talk to art instructor	(15)
D – get ½ gal milk	(10)
C – call Aunt Celia	(15)
A – call tel. co.	(5)
B – talk to chem. tutor	(10)
D – wash car	

---

[1] Alan Lakein. (1989). *How to Get Control of Your Time and Your Life,* 28–29. New York: Signet.

For the tasks that you need to accomplish within the next 24 hours, fill out your own list and prioritize each item with an A, B, C, or D.

Things To Do Today:

_____

_____

_____

_____

_____

_____

_____

_____

_____

_____

Suggested Activity: Exchange time management ideas with a small group of your fellow students. What are the methods each of you use to plan your time? Which ones sound the most useful? Make up a list for a group report to the class.

Personal Response Check: As a result of reading about organizing my time with a calendar, an appointment book, and a Things To Do List,

I realize that   (1)_____

                         (2)_____

When you get right down to the meaning of the word "succeed," you find that it simply means to follow through.

—F. W. Nichol

Avoiding Procrastination

If you are like most people, you are subject to occasional **procrastination.** Most of us procrastinate when faced with unwelcome tasks, but eventually we get them done. However, serious procrastinators need to examine why they make excuses, such as:

I'm too tired.

My friend needs me to talk.

I don't know how to do this.

The grass needs to be mowed.

I have to buy groceries.

Add some of your favorite excuses to this list:

_____

_____

_____

People who delay action until all factors are favorable are the kind who do nothing.

—William Feather

I have a terrible habit of procrastinating to the point of sometimes having to drop classes because I can't get around to studying for them. Earlier in the semester I was forced to drop my chemistry class. Even when I did study I felt like I was drowning. I usually ended up waiting until two days before an exam and then I started to cram. I guess the trick is to put in some time every day. I've realized that it needs to be quality time, though.

—Stacey Mora

A significant reason for procrastination is the "reward" of not having to face failure: "If I keep avoiding this task, I don't have to admit that I'm having trouble with it. I can protect my self-esteem."

Below, note a task that you have been avoiding and list the reasons why you are procrastinating:

Task:_____

Procrastinating because_____

_____

One thing that helped me a lot was the way we set up our appointment books. The book helped me to get through a huge project that took me about three weeks to complete. Most of the thanks goes to the appointments I made with myself.

—Jacob Brotslavsky

Another strategy for making sure you finish what you need to get done is to turn it into a "game." Here are five sample games:

1. *The Reward Game:* Promise yourself a small reward for accomplishing a task. Rewards might be a quick telephone call, a short walk, or 15 minutes of your favorite music.

2. *The Worst-Scenario Game:* Visualize the worst that could happen if you don't finish this task: you'll get a lower grade, you'll fail the class, someone will be angry with you, you'll be angry with yourself, etc.

3. *The Swiss-Cheese Game:*[2] Imagine that you are like a mouse trying to eat an enormous piece of cheese by nibbling away at it in small bites. Work for a few minutes on the task so that you get a start. Do something else for a while, then come back and do another five minutes' work. You may find that once you get started you'll be willing to go beyond five minutes.

4. *The Partner Game:* Work out a plan with another student who needs to do the same task. Make an agreement to support each other by keeping in touch and setting deadlines when each phase of the task is to be completed.

5. *The Routine Game:* Establish a regular time and place for accomplishing tasks. If you need to study Spanish each day, you may want to go to the language lab or to the library at 3 p.m. every day.

Consider these suggestions for spending your time wisely. Check the items you want to try.

_____1. *Learn to say "no."* Don't use up your time by trying to meet others' needs rather than your own. Remind yourself how much you are worth per hour as a student. When you stop too often to listen to other people's problems and help them when they could help themselves, you are giving away your time and risking bad grades.

_____2. *Limit your study breaks.* You do need to take breaks, but be reasonable. It is okay to take five minutes to stretch, get a drink, circulate the blood. But a half-hour break wastes too much time.

_____3. *Set aside regular times* to study specific courses, just as you set aside specific times to attend classes.

_____4. *Form a study group* to save time when you study outside of class. Make certain that your group sticks to the topic: no wandering off into idle chatter. Excuse yourself from any group that is wasting your time and money.

_____5. *Get a tutor.* A tutor can save you enormous amounts of time as well as frustration and aggravation. Some campuses even offer free tutors.

_____6. *Make a list of sacrifices* you are willing to make until you get your degree.

_____7. *Note the amount of money you are worth per hour in your appointment book for each hour that you study.* Get into the habit of seeing these recorded amounts as "money in the bank."

---

[2] Lakein, 100–101.

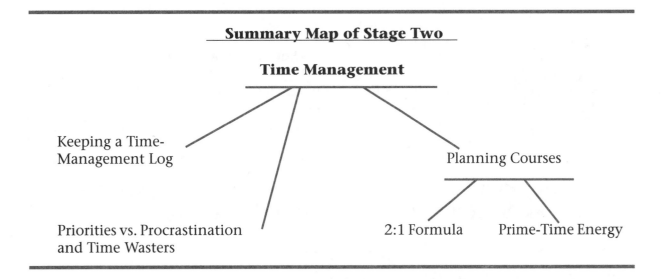

Summary Map of Stage Two

Time Management

Keeping a Time-Management Log

Planning Courses

Priorities vs. Procrastination and Time Wasters

2:1 Formula

Prime-Time Energy

The Self-Contract

An American writer, Marshall Fishwick, paraphrased Socrates when he said, "The uncommitted life isn't worth living." It's up to you to decide what commitment you want to make to your academic life. This commitment will be a specific plan of action with a specific time frame. For example:

I will no longer study in bed for the next two weeks.

For a minimum of one week I will not answer the phone when I study.

I will keep track of my grades in each class for the next four weeks.

I will record my study-time distractions for the next two weeks.

I will add small items to my book bag, starting with a pocket dictionary which I will buy next week.

Signing a self-contract is an effective way to ensure that you will complete what you set out to accomplish. It is your commitment to become a more successful student. At the end of the time period that you specify in your commitment, fill out the Self-Contract Progress Report indicating to what extent you have kept your commitment.

Two sample Self-Contracts follow:

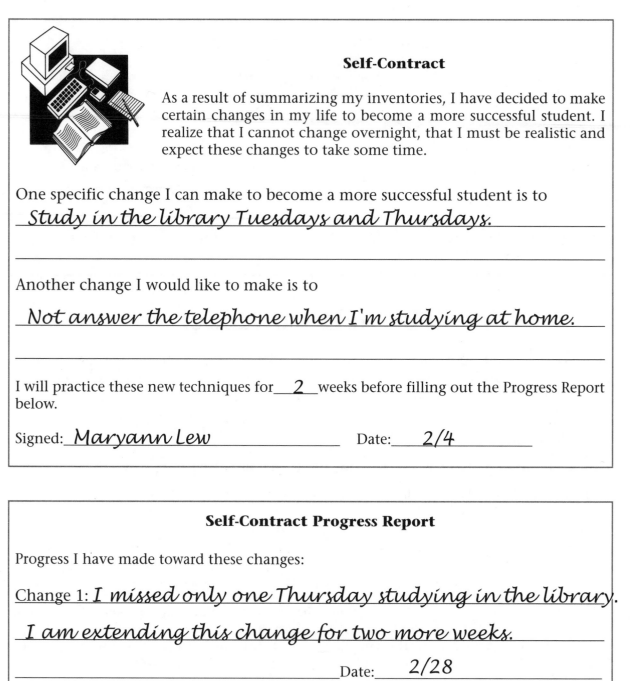

Self-Contract

As a result of summarizing my inventories, I have decided to make certain changes in my life to become a more successful student. I realize that I cannot change overnight, that I must be realistic and expect these changes to take some time.

One specific change I can make to become a more successful student is to
Study in the library Tuesdays and Thursdays.

Another change I would like to make is to

Not answer the telephone when I'm studying at home.

I will practice these new techniques for __2__ weeks before filling out the Progress Report below.

Signed: *Maryann Lew*   Date: 2/4

Self-Contract Progress Report

Progress I have made toward these changes:

Change 1: *I missed only one Thursday studying in the library.*
I am extending this change for two more weeks.
                                        Date: 2/28

Change 2:   *I had to take the phone off the hook during*
study hours because I couldn't tolerate the ringing.
Several times I forgot and answered.
                                        Date: 2/28

Self-Contract

As a result of summarizing my inventories, I have decided to make certain changes in my life to become a more successful student. I realize that I cannot change overnight, that I must be realistic and expect these changes to take some time.

One specific change I can make to become a more successful student is to

Prepare a desk area at home with study

materials available.

Another change I would like to make is to

Ask my family not to disturb me during

my study hours.

I will practice these new techniques for __3__ weeks before filling out the Progress Report below.

Signed:___José Lopez_____   Date:_____9/5_____

Self-Contract Progress Report

Progress I have made toward these changes:

Change 1: I have made a desk area, but need to

add more study materials

_____Date: 9/19_____

Change 2: Sometimes my brothers and sisters

interrupt me when I'm studying. I need to repeat

my need for their cooperation.

_____Date: 9/19_____

Stage Two Journal Entry

We cannot learn without pain.

–Aristotle

Date: _____

Some classes seem painful to take, even though we may be learning. Which class do you anticipate will give you the most trouble? First, freewrite what your attitude is toward this class; include how you feel when you enter the classroom, during class, and when you study for this class. Second, discuss your time management for this course: Do you spend more or less time studying for this course than others? Explain why.

_____

_____

_____

_____

_____

_____

_____

_____

_____

_____

_____

_____

_____

_____

_____

_____

_____

_____

_____

_____

_____

_____

_____

_____

_____

_____

_____

_____

_____

_____

_____

_____

_____

_____

_____

_____

Stage Three
Successful Study Strategies
Step One: Appreciating the Big Picture at College

You simply must have some grasp of the whole before you can see the parts in their true perspective—or often in any perspective at all.
—Mortimer Adler

Objectives

❏ To understand the broad goals of college

❏ To understand different course perspectives

❏ To gain an overview of the main purpose and design of a course and text

Contents

❏ Appreciating the Big Picture at College

❏ Overview of Course and Text Content
   Course Syllabus
   Text Overview
      The Introduction Overview
      The Table of Contents Overview
      The Chapter Overview

❏ Summary Map of Step One

❏ Application Assignments: History Text

❏ Application Assignments: Psychology Text

Key Terms

positive and negative attitudes
syllabus
"helicopter overview"
introduction, foreword, preface
table of contents
headings
subheadings

Self-Awareness Check:
Check the appropriate blanks:

	Often	Sometimes	Rarely
1. I understand why I must take so many seemingly unconnected courses.	___	___	___
2. I enjoy subjects I never studied before.	___	___	___
3. I glance over the table of contents of a new book before I begin to read it.	___	___	___
4. Before studying a chapter, I scan the headings, subheadings, illustrations, introduction, and summary.	___	___	___
5. When I learn something new, I relate it to something from my own observations and experiences.	___	___	___

Appreciating the Big Picture at College

You may wonder why your college requires you to take such a wide variety of courses when you already have a specific career goal in mind. Do you find yourself asking questions such as, "Why consume my energies in fields that don't interest me?" or "Why should I learn information that I may never use?"

Stop and ask yourself if you are approaching your college education with an open mind. Do you have a view of "the big picture"—a long view that includes the rest of your life?

Taking a **positive attitude** toward your course requirements will help you get the most out of your college education. For instance, you may have absolutely no interest in the astronomy course you're taking to fulfill a requirement in science, but after a few weeks you may be surprised to discover an awakening interest in outer space. You may also find that your new knowledge of astronomy gives you a better understanding of the ongoing controversies surrounding the earth's ozone layer and the future of the U.S. space program.

Gaining a broad base of information through your college courses will help you understand and interact more effectively with the world around you. Exploring other disciplines will give you a chance to become more of an expert on life, so why not find out what they have to offer you? And remember, this may be the only real chance you will have in your life to explore so many aspects of people, ideas, nature, and the universe. Put your time to good use!

Exercise 1

The diagram below represents the college curriculum as an opportunity to explore our relationships with ourselves, with other people, with institutions and organizations, and with nature.

Listed on the right are typical courses that help us understand these often complex relationships. Circle the classes you have already taken. If you have completed courses that are not listed, write them in, keeping in mind that courses may belong in more than one category. For example, group dynamics might fall under both Institutions and Others.

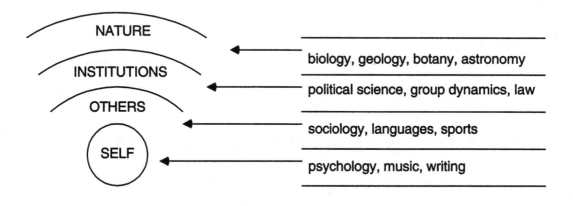

NATURE — biology, geology, botany, astronomy

INSTITUTIONS — political science, group dynamics, law

OTHERS — sociology, languages, sports

SELF — psychology, music, writing

As you take various courses, notice how they are connected. History, for example, is woven into almost every course; e.g., when you study astronomy, you learn about the past theories of the solar system. What you learn in a geography class helps you understand the plants and animals discussed in a biology class. The concepts you study in psychology or sociology can help you understand literary characters in your English class or aid in preparing a speech class assignment.

> *The human mind, once stretched to a new idea, never goes back to its original dimensions.*
>
> —Mortimer Adler

Overview of Course and Text Content

After you have examined the big picture of your college education, the next step is to consider each of your college courses as both a generalist and as a detailer. Look at the overall picture first; then move on to the details that support that view.

Course Syllabus

One of the quickest ways to grasp the big picture of any course is to read the instructor's **syllabus,** which provides a breakdown of course topics by class session as well as information about the textbook, homework assignments, quizzes, tests, and term papers or projects.

The syllabus in the following example not only lists the main topics that will be covered in the course but also outlines everything the student needs to know for effective time management.

Course Outline
Home
Economics II
NUTRITION
Tu–Th   9 a.m.–10:30 a.m.

Instructor: Mercedes Flores, R.D.   Office Hours: 11:00–11:30 M–W
Text: *Nutrition, Concepts and Controversies,* 3rd Edition. Hamilton and Whitney

Dates	Classroom Activity	Homework
2/8–2/17	Introduction, Cultural Influences of Food. Human Body 2/17: Quiz #1 2/17: Class on computations; bring calculator	pgs. xiii–23 pgs. 521–532 3-day food record due
2/22–3/3	First Facts: Foods and Nutrient Needs 3/1: Start scorecards 3/3: Quiz #2 3/3: Energy calculations; bring calculator	pgs. 25–73 Computations due 2/24
3/8–3/17	Carbohydrates and Lipids 3/17: Quiz #3 3/17: Percentages; bring calculator	pgs. 75–144 Scorecards due 3/8 Energy calculations due 3/10
3/22–4/5	Proteins and Amino Acids 4/5: Quiz #4 4/5: Discuss final project	pgs. 147–179 Percentages due 3/22
4/7–4/19	Energy and Weight Control 4/19: Quiz #5 4/19: Contract for final project	pgs. 217–251 Dietary analysis due 4/7

4/19–28	Vitamins 4/28: Quiz #6	pgs. 253–298 pgs. 45–49
5/3–5/10	Minerals and Water 5/10: Quiz #7	pgs. 301–342
5/10–19	Life Cycle—Part I 5/19: Quiz #8	pgs. 397–454 Final project due 5/17
5/19–26	Life Cycle—Part II 5/26: Quiz #9	pgs. 457–520
5/26–6/7	Foods, Labels 6/7: Quiz #10	pgs. 345–395
6/7–9	Oral Reports	
6/10–17	FINAL EXAMS	

Quizzes will be 20 minutes long, no makeups. Two will be dropped—either your lowest scores and/or the one(s) you missed. Quizzes 1–3 need Scan-tron form 882. Quizzes 4–10 need Scan-tron form 888. *Final Exam* will be 2 hours long, comprehensive, using Scan-tron form 884 plus written work.

COURSE PROJECTS

I. Dietary Self-Analysis: See guide sheet—due April 7

II. Final Project: due May 17. Choice of one:

Nutrition Scrapbook—A minimum of 30 articles: 10 from professional nutrition magazines (use those listed as references in your text or on pgs. 581–586), and 20 from the popular press—5 of these should be "incorrect" articles. Use the reading report form—sample given in class—one for each article. If possible, include the original article or a copy of it. Use a wide variety of sources (6 to 8 suggested minimum). Read pages 615–621. As you read each article, look for the "tags" listed on page 10. Read with a critical eye.

Term Paper: Research paper, properly typewritten, footnoted, and referenced. Approximately 10 pages in length. Suggested topics: Nutrition during one stage of the life cycle; food additives; food labeling; vegetarianism; the kidney; the liver; organic farming; farming the oceans; food stamp program; WIC; Title XII; nutritional policies of the U.S.A.; etc. (10–15 hours)

Nutrition Game: Suitable for teaching some nutritional concepts. State 5 goals and objectives in behavioral terms suitable for chosen age group. Must look "professional," i.e., good instructions, boxed, colors, protect surfaces—may adapt old game or start from scratch. (15–20 hours)

III. Grading:

	8 Quizzes	40%
	Dietary Analysis	20%
	Final Project	20%
	Oral Report	5%
	Final Exam	15%

If you understand the general thrust of a course, it is easier to selectively zoom in on specific topics. For example, once you understand that psychology is the study of human behavior, you expect a psychology text to cover such topics as emotions, human drives and motives, and personality theory. We call getting this panoramic take on a course the **"helicopter overview"** study technique. It is similar to getting the big picture of a city by hovering high above it: you can view everything at once and see how the parts of the city relate to each other before descending for a closer look at the details.

Text Overview

The helicopter overview works well with any information that is composed of smaller parts. Every textbook you study can be viewed in this way. Once you gain this overview, you can see the overall framework of the course as well as the textbook. This will greatly facilitate any necessary memorizing.

All textbooks contain the following:

- a preface, foreword, or introduction stating the general viewpoint of the text
- a table of contents that breaks down the big picture into its parts
- chapters, each of which has its own big picture and parts
- sections of chapters

Where and how do you begin your overview? It always helps to start at the beginning; with a textbook, that means looking over the introduction.

The Introduction Overview

Your textbook may actually begin not with an **introduction** but with a **foreword** or **preface** instead. In some texts the introduction is not found until the beginning of the first chapter, and some books have a foreword or preface and an introduction. The preface, foreword, or introduction summarizes the viewpoint, scope, and purpose of the book.

Exercise 2

Turn to the Preface for Students in this book. It begins with, "So you want to be a more successful student?" Reread the entire preface and return to this page.

Without looking back, write what you think is the overall purpose of this book, based on what you read in the preface:

_____

_____

_____

_____

Exercise 3

Read the following foreword from *Our Voices: Essays in Culture, Ethnicity, and Communication*,[1] an anthology for classes in multicultural studies. Underline the words that indicate the purpose of the book.

FOREWORD
Molefi Kete Asante

The appearance of the book *Our Voices: Essays in Culture, Ethnicity, and Communication* is a remarkable achievement in the field of communication. It reflects the evolution of a field that has too long marginalized the voices of African, Asian, Latino, Native, Jewish, and Arab Americans. Because the field of communication has demonstrated a tendency to represent the hegemonic position of white Anglo-Saxon Protestants, the voices of scholars from other traditions have not been heard as often as they might. Indeed, the field has lacked the sustained cultural insights of these intellectuals in any meaningful way.

Our Voices is an innovative contribution to the current dialogue about the nature of communication and a refreshing addition to multicultural studies. It presents an array of original essays by outstanding scholars from various cultures that have been underrepresented in the literature of the field.

Several years ago a friend of mine, a well-known professor in an influential communication department, told me that he felt the field of communication was too narrowly focused. When I inquired about the meaning of his statement, he explained that it needed more scholars who were interested in cultural themes from many perspectives. I believe that the many authors who have produced this volume have applied a pluralistic, nonhegemonic idea to the production of their work. The book comes to us as a projection into the future, to the extent that it broadens the way we see ourselves as communication researchers and as human beings.

Communication is the defining characteristic of contemporary life. We are engaged in communication both as producers and consumers of messages and images. In writing these essays, the contributors have begun the process of providing the basis for a new perspective. The fact that we now have this volume of essays from scholars trained in the field means that we are well on our way toward a new chorus of human voices in communication.

The Table of Contents Overview

To paraphrase philosopher and author Mortimer Adler: The longer you delay in getting a sense of a book's overall plan, the longer you will spend making sense of its contents.[2]

---

[1]Alberto González, Marsha Houston, Victoria Chen, eds. (1994). *Our Voices: Essays in Culture, Ethnicity, and Communication*. Los Angeles: Roxbury Publishing Company.
[2]Mortimer J. Adler and Charles Van Doren. (1972). *How to Read a Book*. New York: Simon & Schuster.

The **table of contents** gives you an immediate sense of a book's big picture. Chapter titles often provide clues about how the chapters relate to the overall subject and purpose of the text. An overview of the table of contents takes only a few moments, but it can save you time later because you will have a better understanding of how all the book's details relate. In other words, you will have another view—a different perspective—of the book's big picture.

Most students skip the table of contents and plow right into the first chapter. While finishing assignments quickly is satisfying, too often students do not do well on tests because they failed to understand the big picture before memorizing details.

Exercise 4

The words you underlined in Exercise 3 (to mark the book's purpose) probably included, *"Our Voices* is an innovative contribution to the current dialogue about the nature of communication and a refreshing addition to multicultural studies," or any other sentence which indicates that the purpose of this book is to add multicultural voices to the field of communications.

Now study the table of contents for this textbook. Note which chapter titles interest you. How do the topics in each chapter relate to each other and to the overall goal of the book?

Contents

Answer the following questions:

The section that looks most interesting to me is_____

I can see that Chapters 8 and 16 are related because

_____

_____

_____

> ***Suggested Activity:*** Compare your answers to Exercise 4 with at least one classmate. Discuss why your answers may vary.

The Chapter Overview

As with the introduction and table of contents, you can gain a better understanding of a book's contents by zeroing in on what each chapter is about. Before you begin studying or reading a chapter of a textbook, take a few minutes and scan the chapter for a quick overview. Be sure to pay special attention to the following:

Chapter Overview

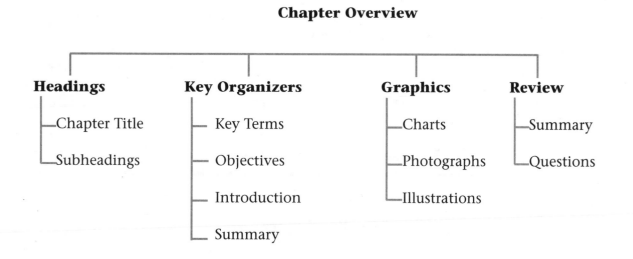

Once you understand the chapter's big picture, you will know what to expect as you begin reading. Your overview gives you the basic outline of the chapter so that when you read you can separate main ideas from supporting details.

Exercise 5

Turn to the beginning of Step 2 on page 83. Quickly scan it for an overview of the chapter, then return to this page.

What is the main purpose of Step 2?_____

What are two key terms that may be important?

1._____   2. _____

Name one study technique covered:_____

To continue practicing overview skills, move on to the application assignments that begin on page 71.

Personal Response Check: As a result of learning about overviewing,

I realize that   (1)_____

(2)_____

Suggested Activity: In a small group, brainstorm the advantages and disadvantages of the overviewing method. Are there other ways to do an overview? Present your lists and suggestions to discuss.

Summary Map of Step One

Get the Big Picture

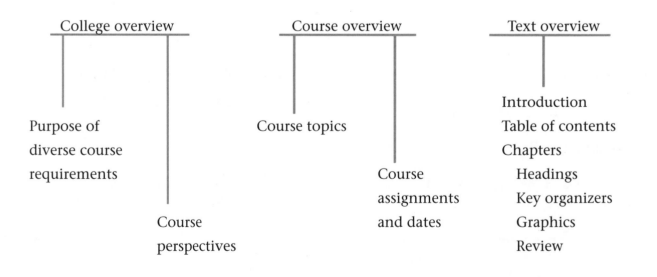

College overview	Course overview	Text overview
Purpose of diverse course requirements	Course topics	Introduction Table of contents Chapters
Course perspectives	Course assignments and dates	Headings Key organizers Graphics Review

Application Assignments: History Text

You are now ready to apply a strategy that uncovers significant detail worth remembering. Specifically you will analyze a chapter titled "American Life in the 'Roaring Twenties,' 1919–1929," taken from the American history text *The American Pageant*. This assignment focuses on a history chapter because research indicates that college social science courses require the most reading.[3]

Performing systematic overviews works best if you have a questioning mind. As you practice, ask questions of the text. Leave nothing to chance. Question the title, the headings, the introduction, and the graphics. Keep a record of your questions by writing them down. The trick is to ask only those questions that you can be reasonably sure are answered in the text. For example, in the title, "American Life in the 'Roaring Twenties,' 1919–1929," you can reasonably expect that the chapter would answer the following:

How would you describe American life in the 1920s?

Why did the author call it the "Roaring Twenties"?

Why use quotation marks around the term "Roaring Twenties"?

What significant events took place between 1919 and 1929?

After preparing study questions for the title, immediately check their usefulness by reading the introduction. If there is no introduction, use **headings** instead. The following applications give practice in using both the introduction and headings.

---

[3]David C. Caverly and Vincent P. Orlando. (1991). "Textbook Study Strategies," in *Teaching and Study Strategies at the College Level* Rona F. Flippo and David C. Caverly, eds., p. 112. Newark, DE: Intercultural Reading Association.

Application 1

Turn to page 312. Read the quote at the top of the page and the first two paragraphs that serve as an intoduction to "American Life in the Roaring Twenties." When finished, return to this page and write a two or three sentence summary which answers the question, "What is the purpose of this introduction?"

_____

_____

Which of the four original questions above was emphasized in the introduction?

_____

_____

Begin your chapter overview by converting all headings into questions. As you practice this technique, you will create your own purpose for reading. (Two questions have been suggested for the first heading.)

The Prohibition "Experiment"

Example: What was the major reason behind Prohibition?
         Why was Prohibition called an "experiment?"

Add your own questions _____

The Golden Age of Gangsterism _____

Monkey Business in Tennessee _____

The Mass-Consumption Economy _____

Putting America on Rubber Tires _____

The Advent of the Gasoline Age _____

Humans Develop Wings _____

The Radio Revolution_____

Hollywood's Filmland Fantasies _____

The Dynamic Decade _____

Armed with questions, you are ready to investigate a chapter. As a check on the validity of your work and the method, skim through the section "The Prohibition 'Experiment'" and determine how quickly you can answer the sample questions. (Check with suggested answers below.*)

*First question: One of the last "spasms" of the progressive movement was pushed largely by women and churches. Question 2: A weak central government cannot enforce what the majority or energetic minority are against.

Application 2

Headings are often accompanied with graphics composed of charts, photographs, and illustrations. Graphics can refer to specific ideas given in the chapter or illustrate supportive detail. To finish an overview, an active reader will question graphics and their captions.

Scan all the graphics in the chapter, "American Life in the 'Roaring Twenties,' 1919–1929," starting on page 312. Read their captions and formulate questions. Question #1 is an example

Heading: Monkey Business in Tennessee

"William Jennings Bryan." This perennial presidential candidate and Christian Fundamentalist was destroyed by biology and Clarence Darrow.

1. Example: How was William J. Bryan destroyed? _____

Heading: The Advent of the Gasoline Age

"Ford Sedan. Automobiles, along with cheap gas, provided quick escape from the confines of the home."

2. _____

Heading: Humans Develop Wings

"Charles Lindbergh. His solo flight across the Atlantic won him the notoriety of a super star."

3. _____

Heading: The Radio Revolution

"Rural Oregonians at the radio. Talking furniture gave new meaning to family life."

4. _____

Heading: The Dynamic Decade

"Measuring a bathing suit. The Charleston, birth control, jazz, and even the length of a bathing suit challenged taboos and shocked the older generation."

5. _____

Application 3

Unless you can transfer your new skills to other textbooks, you will have missed an important part of this course. Practice transferring your new skills to a text you are currently using. As you practice each technique, you will become more adept at discovering how textbooks are organized by questioning introductions, headings, and graphics.

Course: _____

Title of Book: _____

Author(s): _____

1. Read the first paragraph or two of the introduction, and use your own words to capture the main idea of the book.

   _____

   _____

2. Examine the table of contents. Write down two chapter titles that interest you and seem closely related:

   Chapter :_____: _____

   Chapter :_____: _____

   a. How are these chapters related to the title of the book?

   _____

   b. How are these two chapters related to each other?

   _____

   c. I can think of example(s) from my personal experience or observations for

   Chapter :___ : _____

   d. I can see how each chapter relates to the overall idea of the book. For example,

   Chapter_____ , titled, relates to the book's main idea because_____

   _____

3. Do an overview of a chapter by quickly reading the:

- title
- introduction
- all graphics and their captions

- objectives
- headings
- summary or final paragraph

- key terms
- subheadings
- review questions

Return to this page when you are finished.

Title of the chapter:_____

Pages _____ to _____.

Information I found interesting included (use words and phrases):

_____

_____

_____

_____

_____

_____

_____

_____

_____

_____

_____

_____

_____

_____

_____

_____

Application Assignments: Psychology Text

One of the quickest and most effective ways to overview a chapter or section of a text is to ask questions of the headings, keeping in mind that your questions will probably be answered in the text. A questioning mind helps you find the big picture so that you can understand how the parts of a chapter fit together like a puzzle to create meaning. For example, a heading of "Stress and Health" may prompt you to ask such questions as:

How does stress affect our health?
To what extent does stress affect our body?
What kinds of stress threaten our health?

Even if you don't understand a heading, such as "Direct Coping," you can ask the simple question "What is direct coping?" to guide your reading.

Application 4

Before you begin asking questions of the text headings, however, a quick review of the chapter's introduction, or first paragraphs, will introduce the main idea that the headings will explain in depth.

Read the three paragraphs of introduction for *Stress and Health Psychology* on page 330 to overview the main idea or purpose of the chapter. Below write a sentence or two about what you think is the purpose of this chapter. What will the author be explaining to you in the headings?

_____

_____

_____

_____

_____

_____

_____

Are any or all of the original three questions above emphasized in the introduction? If so, place a check mark in front of each question.

Application 5

Continue your chapter overview by converting the headings below into questions. Questions have been suggested for the first two headings, with space provided for you to add your own questions.

Sources of Stress

What are the most common sources of stress?

Add your own questions

_____

_____

Change

Do positive changes create stress as well as negative changes?

Add your own questions

_____

_____

Hassles

_____

_____

Pressure

_____

_____

Frustration

_____

_____

Conflict

_____

_____

Self-Imposed Stress

_____

_____

Coping with Stress

_____

_____

The questions you ask of headings are usually based on healthy skepticism or normal curiosity. This questioning helps you get a clearer focus when reading the text under each heading. Such focus also improves concentration.

Application 6

In addition to asking questions of headings, you can often use an example from your own experience or knowledge of the topic. Even one example for some headings helps you concentrate because you are identifying with the topic, linking what you already know to new information.

Select three of the above headings and write in an example of the topic to the right of the heading. Below are two samples in italics:

Sources of Stress   *Example: Pressure at work*

<u>What are the most common sources of stress?</u>

_____

_____

Change   *Example: I now have a roommate to help pay the rent.*

<u>Do positive changes create stress as well as negative changes?</u>

_____

_____

Application 7: Transfer of Skills

Practice the skills you have learned in this chapter with a textbook from another class by asking questions of headings.

Self-Contract

Now that I know how to get the big picture by overviewing, I plan to:

_____

_____

_____

_____

_____

_____

I will practice these new techniques for at least_____weeks to determine if I want to adopt them as a part of my permanent study strategies. Then I will complete the Progress Report below.

Signed:_____   Date:_____

Self-Contract Progress Report

Progress I have made toward these changes:_____

_____

_____

_____

_____

_____

_____Date:_____

Stage Three, Step One Journal Entry

Very often a change of self is needed more than a change of scene.
—A. C. Benson

Date: _____

Freewrite about why your most difficult class is worth taking despite its problems. Is it possible that the course will help you in the long run (the big picture)? How does this course relate to life, to other courses? Then freewrite about how you can use your learning style preferences to work your way through this difficult or challenging class, or how you can adapt your learning style to meet the needs of this class. Be specific about what changes you must make in order to be successful in this class. You are developing a plan of action that you will monitor in subsequent journal entries.

_____

_____

_____

_____

_____

_____

_____

_____

_____

_____

_____

_____

_____

_____

How do I know what the main idea is?
                                    —David Goldstein

Step Two
Separate Main Ideas From Details

Key Terms

main idea
details
linear and spatial notes
TIPS
linear TIPS
topic
supporting points
summary
spatial TIPS
organizational patterns
sequence
cause and effect
comparison and contrast
classification
analysis

Self-Awareness Check:

Check the appropriate blanks:

	Often	Sometimes	Rarely
1. I can read a paragraph and pick out the main idea.	____	____	____
2. I can decide what information supports the main topic of a paragraph.	____	____	____
3. When listening to a lecture, I can identify the main idea and the information that supports it.	____	____	____
4. I know how to take the kind of notes that allow me to separate main ideas from details.	____	____	____
5. In reviewing for a test, I am confident that I have all the necessary details and facts in my notes to support anticipated test questions.	____	____	____

Like many other students, you may find yourself becoming confused and frustrated when you pick up a book or listen to a lecture because you are unable to identify the **main idea.** Unless you know how to separate a main idea from its details, all data will seem equally important, and you'll end up trying to remember many unnecessary facts. Learning how to distinguish between a main idea and the details that support it will help you understand the big picture before you begin any memory work and is a first step in thinking critically about a topic.

To begin this sorting-out process, let's start with some short exercises that will help you learn how to separate main ideas from details before working with textbook material.

Identifying Main Ideas and Details

Just as every chapter has a main idea, every chapter subsection and paragraph also has a main idea supported by **details** such as facts, reasons, and examples. Once you find the main idea of a reading passage (or lecture topic), you can sort out the details that reinforce or explain this idea. In some paragraphs the main idea is not directly stated. To determine what it is, you may have to reverse the usual process and list the details first.

Exercise 1

For each passage below, underline the phrase that indicates the main idea and draw a wavy line under words that support it. If the main idea of a passage is not stated clearly enough, write the main idea in your own words in the space below the passage.

A. If college students are to achieve academic success, they must learn to be self-directed and use resources effectively. To become self-directed, students must learn how to manage their time, just as successful professionals do. They must also find a suitable study environment and organize it well, so that when they study they are like professionals at work. Students also need to know of every available resource on campus and how to use each one, e.g., library, financial aid, and counseling.

Main Idea:_____

B. The liver is one of the largest organs in the body. It is situated on the right side of the abdomen and is protected by the lower ribs. The liver is like a chemical laboratory with two main functions. It acts in the formation of blood and in the metabolism of carbohydrates, proteins, and fats. The liver creates and then secretes bile, a bitter, alkaline liquid which it sends to the gallbladder for storage.

Main Idea:_____

Linear and Spatial Notes

You can take notes about any topic in one of two forms: **linear notes** or **spatial notes.** Linear notes put information in a sequential order, line by line. Spatial notes look more like a map or a drawing; information is not listed sequentially.

Here are examples of linear and spatial notes for paragraph B in Exercise 1 above:

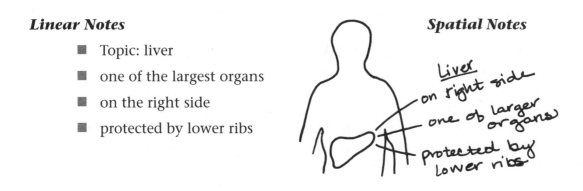

Linear Notes

- Topic: liver
- one of the largest organs
- on the right side
- protected by lower ribs

Spatial Notes

Liver
on right side
one of larger organs)
protected by
lower ribs

Which of these methods appeals to you more? Keep your reaction in mind, as you will be practicing both types of note-taking later on.

The 'TIPS' Technique

Linear TIPS

A quick, easy way to find the main idea of any narrative is through an organizational technique we call **TIPS.** TIPS provides a method to separate information, going from the whole to its parts and then, in the summary, going back to the whole again. It is a first step in thinking critically about a topic because you are beginning a questioning process: What is the main idea of this passage? What are the key points?

The following example based on Exercise 1 shows how the TIPS technique works.

T = **topic** (a word or phrase): *liver*

I = **idea** (the main idea in one sentence): *The liver is a chemical factory.*

P = list of **supporting points** (including facts, examples, reasons, evidence):

> 1. *blood formation*
> 2. *metabolism of food*
> 3. *secretes bile; sends to gallbladder for storage*

S = **summary** (a sentence or short paragraph that briefly synthesizes the TIP items):

> *The liver is a chemical factory that helps form blood and metabolize food; it also secretes bile, which is sent to the gallbladder for storage.*

After developing a TIPS, the next step is to ask questions about it in order to examine the topic and make connections: What is the purpose of this narrative? What is its pattern or structure? What examples or evidence does it present? Is the evidence factual and unbiased? What can I conclude from all these points?

Questions for the above TIPS on the liver might include

What is the purpose of the liver? (Answer is in the points.)

How does the liver help in metabolizing food?

Add your questions about the liver:

_____

_____

_____

_____

_____

_____

Here is another example of a TIPS:

Topic: John Steinbeck's short story "Chrysanthemums"

Idea: The main character's childlessness and boredom with married life cause her to seek personal fulfillment elsewhere.

Supporting Points:

- Elisa Allen is an "earth mother" whose flowers replace the children she doesn't have.

- She finds her farm life boring.

- Her marriage lacks communication and excitement.

- She transfers her emotional and romantic needs to a wandering stranger.

Summary: In John Steinbeck's short story "Chrysanthemums," the main character's childlessness and boredom with married life cause her to find fulfillment elsewhere. Not only is her farm life boring, but so is her marriage, so she lavishes affection on her flower garden. She and her husband no longer communicate well, and they have lost the excitement of early love. When a wandering stranger comes to the farm, she transfers her emotional and romantic needs to him.

Below are some questions that probe this TIPS and lines for you to add your own questions.

What is Elisa's husband like?

What don't they communicate?

What is the universal symbolic meaning of chrysanthemums?

_____

_____

_____

_____

_____

> *By using the TIPS method, I can understand and remember passages without having to go back over them several times. It also helps my mind stay focused when I'm reading.*
> **—Wallace Smithe**

Exercise 2

For the TIPS below, write in "A Student Problem" as the topic. For the main idea, write a sentence explaining a situation that bothers you as a student, such as conflict between work and school, family responsibilities, child care, or financial problems. For the points, give examples of this problem. Then write a summary that includes all the previous TIPS elements: the topic, main idea, and points.

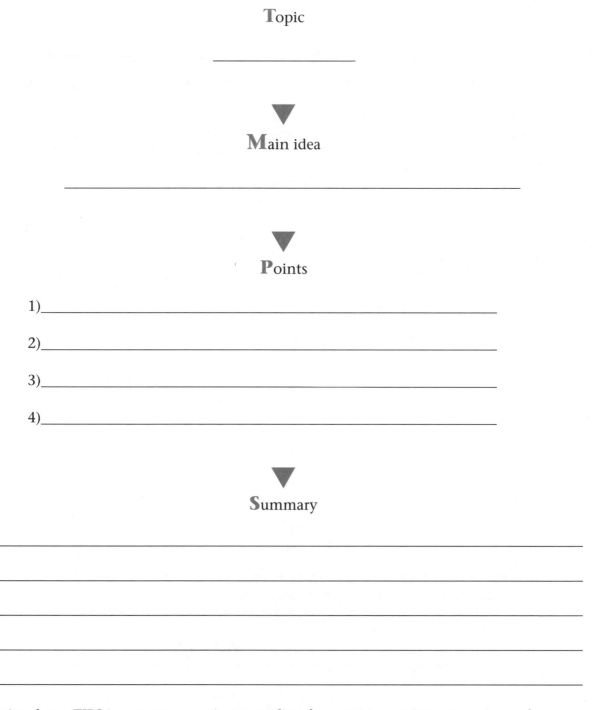

Topic

_____

▼

Main idea

_____

▼

Points

1)_____

2)_____

3)_____

4)_____

▼

Summary

_____

_____

_____

_____

_____

Notice that a TIPS is one way to write an outline for a writing assignment or speech.

Suggested Activity: Compare your TIPS in Exercise 2 with the TIPS of other students in the class. Offer suggestions for a solution to the problem which your classmates did not think of.

Personal Response Check: As a result of practicing with TIPS,

I realize that   (1)_____

(2)_____

Spatial TIPS

As you learned earlier, your note-taking can be either spatial or linear. The same holds true for TIPS; you can use this strategy in either a linear manner or in a spatial format. Below is an example of the linear outline about the liver put into a spatial format:

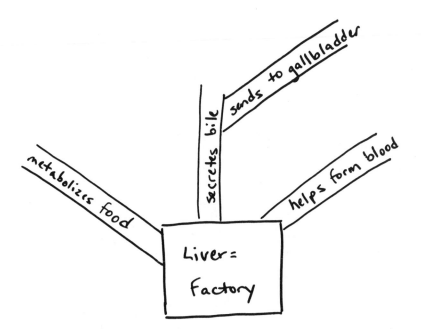

Summary: The liver is a chemical factory that helps form blood and metabolize food; it also secretes bile, which is sent to the gallbladder for storage.

Exercise 3

Use your imagination to outline a spatial TIPS for the following health class topic:

Nutrients in Food

Foods are composed of six types of nutrients: carbohydrates, fats, proteins, vitamins, minerals, and water. These nutrients regulate complex chemical reactions in the cells. They are necessary for growth, cell reproduction, and repair of body tissues. Nutrients also provide energy for muscle contraction.

Questions to probe this TIPS:

1. _____

2. _____

3. _____

> **Suggested Activity:** With three or four classmates, share your respective spatial TIPS so that you can all appreciate the different approaches to creating TIPS.

Exercise 4

Make a linear TIPS for the following passage on ways to improve your listening skills:

Active Listening[1]

Most people take listening for granted. They assume that because they can hear and have listened all their lives that they are adept at it. But how many times do misunderstandings crop up in personal interactions? How often do people fail to understand what others are trying to say, even though they "hear" them? Research suggests that through active listening training, listening skills can be significantly improved.

Communication researchers have developed many different frameworks for improving listening. They suggest that the receiver involve the sender as a participant in the listening interaction. For example, the active listener faces the speaker and maintains eye contact; the active listener also paraphrases the message and formulates questions.

The active listener goes beyond the explicit meaning of the message and seeks an understanding of its emotional connotations as well. He or she approaches the interaction with an open mind and does not tune the speaker out because of a difference of opinion or because the speaker exhibits poor delivery skills. In short, the active listener participates with the speaker cognitively, emotionally, and physically.

T = _____

I = _____

_____

P = _____

_____

_____

S = _____

_____

_____

_____

_____

---

[1] Ellen A. Hay. (1992). *Speech Resources: Exercises and Activities,* p. 25. Los Angeles: Roxbury Publishing Company.

Exercise 5

Below, add your own thoughts and examples about poor listening skills. For example: "When I am bored, my mind drifts" or "Because I daydream, I don't hear half of what my economics instructor says" or "I tune out instructors who state, 'I hear what you are saying, but. . . . '"

1. _____

2. _____

3. _____

4. _____

> ***Suggested Activity:*** In a group, read your thoughts and examples from Exercise 5. Doing so will illustrate the variety of ways you can associate what you are learning about a topic (poor listening skills) with what you already know. By building on your prior knowledge, you will find learning and memorization of new information to be easier.

Exercise 6

Make a linear or spatial TIPS for this textbook explanation for the culture's perception of time:

Native American Perception of Time[2]

The Native American perception of time is different from the dominant Euro-American perception of time (Attneave 1982; Faas 1982; Hanson and Eisenbise 1983; Sanders 1987), which is linear and segmented. For the latter, punctual activities are the norm. In contrast, among the various tribal societies, the perception of time is circular and flexible. The predominant attitude is that the activities will commence "whenever people are ready; when everyone arrives" (Pepper 1976). According to Garrison (1989), "[Native American] people see no need to control time or to let it control them. . . ; the goal is not to limit the time, but to experience and enjoy time as it passes" (122). This consideration of time symbolically reinforces the Native American religious belief of achievement and maintenance of harmony with nature because "nature is allowed to take its own course."

This somewhat "laid back" attitude about time has been jokingly referred to as "Indian time" (Anderson, Burd, Dodd and Kelker 1980; Lockart 1978; Marashio 1982) and has contributed to the development and maintenance of humor in the Native American world. "Indian time" has provided Native Americans unstressed, unpressured time to teach younger generations the "proper way" to greet friends and relatives and to exchange stories and anecdotes. While patiently waiting for cultural festivities to begin, the individual is provided the opportunity to entertain the "audience with his/her talent and flair for the spoken word." For example, according to Steve "Raising" Kane, a Northern Pauite comic orator, a Native American operating on Indian time is an individual who is either early or not so early, but never late (Giago 1990).

---

[2]Charmaine Shutiva. (1994). "Native American Culture and Communication Through Humor," *Our Voices: Essays in Culture, Ethnicity, and Communication*, eds. Alberto González et al. Los Angeles: Roxbury Publishing Company.

Summary: _____

_____

_____

Questions to probe this TIPS:

1. _____

2. _____

3. _____

> ***Suggested Activity:*** After sharing your questions in a small group, share your perception of time. Does it match either the Native American or Euro-American perception?

Rationale for Learning TIPS

When you are reading a textbook or taking lecture notes, use TIPS to organize important material. The act of completing each of the four steps will help you remember the information more efficiently than if you simply read and reread your notes. Why? Because you are not just memorizing by rote but actively engaging in thinking and writing about the information. Any time you take a block of information, break it down, reflect, reorganize, and rewrite it into a summary, you are increasing your memory retention. You have internalized the information. You are an active learner.

This process of creating TIPS may seem very time-consuming, but keep in mind that you shouldn't use TIPS for every paragraph you read—only for important passages. Your TIPS will serve as an excellent review outline for answering both short-answer and essay questions. Generating questions about the TIPS you've done will help you anticipate questions on your next test and, more importantly, it will enhance your ability to think critically, a skill needed in every aspect of life.

TIPS and the Traditional Outline

Making a TIPS is a useful way to organize material for a traditional outline, which has the following structure:

I. Main idea
    A. Subpoint of main idea
    B.
    C.
        1. Support of a subpoint
        2.
II. Main idea

The traditional outline has a very formal structure; there must always be at least two points at each level. For example, a main point (I) must be followed by at least one other main point (II), subpoint A requires at least subpoint B, and so on. Note, however, that it is not necessary for each main point to have the same number of subpoints or any subpoints at all.

Below are examples of traditional outlines based on linear and spatial TIPS:

Role of the Liver

I.   Helps formulate blood
II. Helps metabolize food
III. Secretes bile and sends to gallbladder

Nutrients in Food

I. Six types of nutrients
    A. Carbohydrates
    B. Fats
    C. Protein
    D. Vitamins
    E. Minerals
    F. Water
II. Role of nutrients
    A. Regulate complex chemical reactions in cells
    B. Provide for important functions of the body
        1. Growth
        2. Cell reproduction
        3. Repair of body tissues
    C. Provide energy for muscle contraction

Complete the following:

Native American Perception of Time

    I. Dominant Euro-American perception of time
        A. Linear and segmented
            1. Punctual activities
            2. Need to control time
        B. _____
    II. Native American perception of time
        A. Circular and flexible
            1. Activities begin when people arrive
            2. No need to control time—"nature is allowed to take its own course"
        B. _____

Exercise 7

Convert your Student Problem TIPS on page 90 into a traditional outline, adding subpoints if you wish.

_____

_____

_____

> ***Suggested Activity:*** With classmates, discuss the advantages and disadvantages of the traditional outline compared to the linear and spatial outline.

Identifying Organizational Patterns

An important strategy in separating main ideas from details is to understand that when we talk or write, we organize our thoughts into certain patterns. Once you become aware of the most common **organizational patterns** of thinking, you can cut down on your study time. You may not be aware of it, but you have used these patterns since you were a child. For example, you learned a sequence pattern for eating: breakfast, lunch, and dinner; you learned a cause-and-effect pattern when you burned your fingers on a hot stove. We are not going to teach you anything you do not already know; our aim is to make you conscious of these patterns so that you can spot them readily. This awareness will help you recognize how lecture and book material is organized.

Notice in the following patterns how easy it is to distinguish between the main idea and its supporting details.

1. **Sequence Pattern**: An informative model that shows the steps or timeline of a process, procedure, or series of events (e.g., the photosynthesis process, a chemistry experiment, or the series of events that led to World War II).

   Example: **Golden Age of Gangsterism**

1920	1925	1927	1930
Gangsters compete for profits made from bootleg liquor	Al Capone, the most notorious, tries for complete control	St. Valentine's Day Massacre	Annual income from illegal profits reaches $12–$18 billion year

2. **Cause-and-Effect Pattern**: An informative pattern that specifies how certain events lead to specific results. Depending on the author's style, the cause can lead to the effect (bad study habits often lead to poor grades) or the effect can lead to its cause (Prohibition failed because it was not enforced). Here are some further examples, with the causes underlined.

   Prohibition passed: Corner saloons replaced by speakeasies. Bottles with high alcoholic content easier to hide: Hard liquor consumed in staggering volume. Home brew and bathtub gin became popular: such "rotgut" caused many deaths.

3. **Comparison and Contrast Pattern**: An informative pattern that shows, by comparing and contrasting, how two topics are alike and different (e.g., a comparison/contrasting of two planets, two word-processing programs, or two short stories).

   Example: Antonio's parents in *Bless Me Ultima*

Compare	Contrast	
Both mother and father	Mother	Father
Loved their children	very religious	not religious
Worked hard for their family	down-to-earth	dreamer
Were considerate of elderly people	patient	impatient
Tolerated each other's opinions but held onto own beliefs	believed in security of the land	believed in freedom of the sea

4. **Classification Pattern**: An informative pattern that systematically arranges topical information into groups, types, classes, or categories according to established criteria (e.g., types of accounting systems, urban crimes, or antibiotics).

Example:

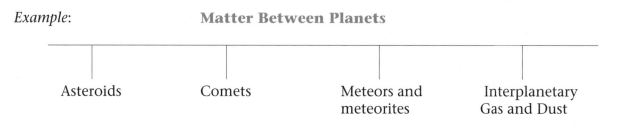

Matter Between Planets

| Asteroids | Comets | Meteors and meteorites | Interplanetary Gas and Dust |

5. **Analysis Pattern**: An informative pattern that separates a whole into its component parts.

Example:

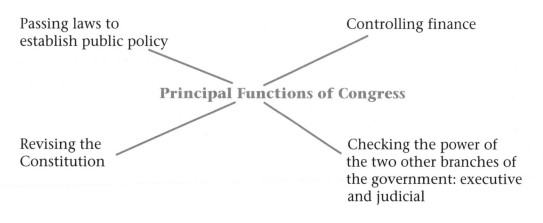

Passing laws to establish public policy

Controlling finance

Principal Functions of Congress

Revising the Constitution

Checking the power of the two other branches of the government: executive and judicial

Exercise 8

Write the name of the appropriate pattern in the blanks.

Sequence   *Comparison/Contrast*   *Cause/Effect*   *Classification*   *Analysis*

_____1.   Our government consists of three branches: the executive, legislative, and judicial.

_____2.   After a bill has been passed by the House of Representatives, the Senate must vote on it; the bill then goes to the president.

_____3.   At election time, we examine the candidate's social, economic, foreign, and domestic policies.

_____4.   If the president vetoes a bill, it cannot become law unless two-thirds of both houses of Congress vote to override the veto.

_____5.   The upper house of Congress, the Senate, consists of two members from each state who serve six-year terms; whereas the lower house, the House of Representatives, consists of members apportioned to the states on the basis of their population who serve two-year terms.

Application Assignments: History Text

Now try practicing each new study technique as follows:

- Apply your new skills to the American history chapter "American Life in the 'Roaring Twenties,' 1919–1929" found on page 312.

- In Application 2 you will apply these new skills to textbooks from your other courses.

Application 1

Read the subheading "The Golden Age of Gangsterism" and make a TIPS.

T = Topic: _____

I = Main idea: _____

_____

P = Points to support main idea:

1. _____

2. _____

3. _____

4. _____

S = Summary

_____

_____

_____

Your own thoughts about what you read:

_____

_____

_____

Personal Response Check: As a result of completing the TIPS in Application 1,

I realize that   (1)_____

(2)_____

Application 2

Select a passage from another textbook and make a linear TIPS.

Title of course: _____

Title of book:_____

Title of chapter:_____

T = _____

I = _____

P = _____

_____

_____

_____

_____

_____

S = _____

_____

_____

_____

_____

_____

_____

Your own thoughts about what you read:

_____

_____

_____

_____

_____

_____

_____

_____

_____

Personal Response Check: As a result of completing the TIPS in Application 2,
I realize that   (1)_____

(2)_____

Application Assignments: Psychology Text

Application 3

Practice making a TIPS with the information under the subheading "Conflict" on page 331.

T = Topic: *Conflict*_____

I = Main idea: _____

_____

P = Points (or examples) to support main idea:

1. _____

2. _____

3. _____

4. _____

S = Summary

_____

_____

_____

_____

Your own thoughts about conflict:

_____

_____

_____

_____

Application 4

Practice making patterns to distinguish between the main idea and its supporting details.

1. **Classification Pattern**: An informative pattern that breaks an idea down into types.

3 Ways of Direct Coping

2. **Cause-and-Effect Pattern**: An informative pattern that specifies how certain events lead to a specific result or results. For the following pattern, select from the text at least one cause that would result in self-imposed stress.

—————————————————————— ⟶ Self-imposed stress

3. **Comparison/Contrast**: An informative pattern that shows how two things are alike and how they are different. Below you will show only how two defense mechanisms are different, knowing that they are alike because they both help us defend ourselves.

Projection   **Identification**

Application 5: Transfer of Skills

Practice the skills you have learned in this chapter with a textbook from another class by making a TIPS and identifying patterns.

Self-Contract

As a result of learning how to separate main ideas from details, I would like to change my study strategies to include:

_____

_____

_____

_____

_____

_____

I will practice these new techniques for at least_____weeks to determine if I want to adopt them as a part of my permanent study strategies. Then I will complete the Progress Report below.

Signed:_____ Date:_____

Self-Contract Progress Report

Progress I have made toward these changes:_____

_____

_____

_____

_____

_____

_____Date:_____

Stage Three, Step Two Journal Entry

The purpose of learning is growth, and our minds, unlike our bodies, can continue growing as we continue to live.

—Mortimer Adler

Date:_____

Not all education takes place inside the classroom. Outside of class, what do you like to learn, and how do you go about learning (for example, a hobby, a sport, or at work)? Give examples of how you have learned. Did you learn mainly (1) visually, (2) auditorily, (3) kinesthetically, (4) as a generalist, (5) as a detailer? Don't forget to describe how your learning process works.

_____

_____

_____

_____

_____

_____

_____

_____

_____

_____

_____

_____

_____

_____

> *Unless detail is placed into a structural pattern, it is rapidly forgotten.*
>
> —Jerome Bruner

Step Three

Learn Study Strategies for Diverse Disciplines

Objectives

- ❏ To examine key organizational patterns for core courses
- ❏ To consider study strategies for these courses

Contents

- ❏ Studying the Social and Behavioral Sciences
    - History
    - Political Science
    - Psychology and Sociology
- ❏ Studying Science and Math
    - Physical and Life Sciences
    - Mathematics
- ❏ Studying Literature
- ❏ Studying a Foreign Language
- ❏ Application Assignments: History Text
- ❏ Application Assignments: Psychology Text

Key Terms

way of knowing
organizational patterns
sequence/timeline
cause-effect
comparison-contrast
vocabulary
definitions
example/case studies
classification
hypothesis-proof
process
problem/solution
conflict
interpretation
stimulus-response

For each discipline there is a specific way of organizing information, its ideas, its **way of knowing.**[1] To understand a discipline's way of knowing, we need to recognize its main **organizational patterns.** Otherwise, we could become overwhelmed by unrelated facts. Successful writers impose order on facts with the patterns that you studied in Step 2. Successful students learn to recognize these patterns.

Following are examples of how some disciplines organize their knowledge. Use these examples to help you understand the organizational systems of different disciplines.

Studying the Social and Behavioral Sciences

History

First, and perhaps most important, history is a story. As such, it is not intended to be a confusing accumulation of miscellaneous facts. That's why the historian is obligated to skillfully select those facts that are significant and organize them into meaningful patterns. These patterns are usually represented as sequence and cause-effect. Finding them is the first step toward understanding history.

Sequence is normally expressed by a timeline. Thoughtfully constructed, a timeline provides "road signs" to aid in recalling specific events. The connection between these events is usually shown through the pattern known as **cause-effect.** It is through such connections that history is transformed into more manageable concepts.

On the following page is a timeline and cause-effect pattern for the actions of one historical figure, the abolitionist John Brown. These patterns help explain what events may have intensified Brown's antislavery beliefs and actions.

---

[1]Jerome Bruner. (1960). *The Process of Education*. Cambridge, MA: Harvard University Press.

Timeline for John Brown's Raid, 1859

Raids by an abolitionist Father	Led massacre of pro-slavery advocates in Kansas	Led slave revolt at Harpers Ferry, Virginia	Hanged: became a martyr to the North
1800	1856	Oct. 16, 1859	Dec. 2, 1859

CAUSES   **EVENT**   **EFFECTS**

- Heavily influenced by father's religious and abolitionist beliefs.

- Raised in Kansas among volatile pro- and anti-slave factions.

- Convinced that slavery was evil and that he could make a difference.

- Led attack on pro-slavery settlement in Kansas; hacked to death five members of one family.

Harpers Ferry Attack, Oct. 16, 1859

John Brown and 22 followers seized federal arsenal. Brown was captured and sentenced to die.

- Hanged on Dec. 2, 1859. He was content to die for "God's eternal truth."

- Northern abolitionists saw Brown as a saint and a martyr.

- The South became more fearful of further slave rebellions.

- Brown was celebrated in song and legend.

The timeline and cause-and-effect chart above suggest that John Brown planned a violent slave rebellion during a period of heightened racial tension, but several different stories could be constructed from the same series of facts. How the story is told will have a significant effect on your study and appreciation of that event and its period in history.

A biographer might emphasize the psychological factors behind John Brown's massacres. A Civil War historian might focus on why the North made Brown into such a hero and martyr. Your history text, however, was probably written by several authors, so it will have a more general viewpoint. Although the text will lead the reader from one event to another to some extent, there will probably not be a strong narrative line to help your understanding. For that reason, recognizing historical patterns becomes all the more crucial.

To study history in any form, begin by constructing your own timeline of events. Rather than starting with an entire chapter, select a more limited topic from a section or subsection. As you read, fill in the who, where, when, and what on the timeline. Then construct a cause-and-effect chart immediately below the timeline. With a little practice, you will be able to recognize patterns that suggest how and why events occurred as they did.

Reading and Research Sources for History

Congressional Record	*Encyclopedia of American History*
Current Biography	*Facts on File*
Current History	*Historical Abstracts*
Dictionary of American Biography	*Historical Statistics of the United States*
Dictionary of American History	*Social Studies Index*

Political Science

Like baseball, complaining about the government seems to be a national pastime. Who among us has not heard from our family, friends, or the media that our government is being run by "corrupt bureaucrats," "the military-industrial complex," or the "far right"? Unfortunately, such simplistic dialogue about complicated issues represents a major portion of the political discourse in today's society. Examining that discourse is only one of the many objectives of political science, the study of governments and how they operate.

As indicated by the word *science,* political scientists are concerned with making their subject more objective. They try to present answers that can be supported by verifiable evidence. For that reason, you will find that basically all texts on government deal with two analytical questions: who holds the power and how is it used?

Government texts typically answer these questions by using historical **comparison-contrast.** For example, researchers studying the origins of democracy will turn to Greece of the fifth century, B.C., where citizens had leisure time to discuss and participate in politics and policymaking. Office-holding was considered not only a coveted prize but a duty required of all Greek citizens. How this ancient belief in political participation began and how it compares with today's voting behavior is the relationship the political scientist seeks.

Turning to the table of contents of any government text, you will probably find the subject divided into general topics such as the "origins of government," "the constitution," "influence of the media," "the electoral process," "civil rights," and "foreign policy." For each topic, ask the political scientist's two vital questions mentioned above: who holds the power and how is it used? For example, fill in the questions that could be asked about the topic "public opinion."

_____

_____

Did you ask who controlled public opinion and to what purpose? If you did, you have grasped two important concepts of political science and formed a framework for studying the text. Along with recognizing analytical writing patterns, finding the answers to the questions of who holds power and to what purpose is crucial to understanding political science.

Studying political science is also a matter of mastering its **vocabulary.** This vocabulary includes both abstract terms, such as *democracy, republicanism, totalitarianism, monarchy,* and *theocracy,* and common words we use in everyday conversation, such as *voting, juries, bureau-*

cracy, polls, nominations, and *deregulation.* These are the words we use to describe and discuss our government, and, more important, to explain our freedoms and define our civil rights.

Reading and Research Sources for Political Science

Congressional Record
Political Handbook and Atlas of the World
Political Science: A Bibliographical Guide to the Literature
Public Affairs Information Service Bulletin
United Nations Documents Index

Psychology and Sociology

Psychology focuses on the behavior of the individual, whereas sociology is concerned with how individuals behave in groups. Both disciplines rely heavily on the organizational patterns of **definitions** and **examples/case studies.** A student must learn many technical words and terms to pass courses in either discipline. When you study the vocabulary for these courses, try to link each term with a concrete example from the text or your own experiences and observations.

In psychology, for instance, the word *rationalization* refers to the common defense mechanism of finding self-deceptive reasons to justify a course of action or explain why something happened. An example is the high school graduate who, when not accepted by the college of his choice, explains to himself and others that he would rather go to the local community college because he didn't really want to live away from home anyway.

In sociology, the term *social norm* refers to a group's unwritten rules of acceptable and unacceptable behavior. For example, a student who constantly interrupts classmates when they are defending a position is defying the social norm of courtesy in classroom debate.

To study both psychology and sociology, concentrate on terms that describe human behavior. Be able to explain the term and provide an example. Whenever possible, use examples from your own experience. The process of illustrating general ideas with concrete examples will help you remember and explain the discipline's key terms and theories when you are taking a test.

Reading and Research Sources for Psychology and Sociology

Journal of Educational Psychology
Psychological Review
Psychological Abstracts
Encyclopedia of Psychology
American Journal of Sociology

Social Research
Social Science Quarterly
Sociological Abstracts
Social Science Index

Studying Science and Math

Physical and Life Sciences

Scientists work in two areas: They seek to explain the known world and to offer hypotheses for the unknown. **Classification** is the main pattern used to organize the known principles and elements of our world. For example, scientists have named and classified animal life. But what is exciting about science is that with new discoveries it is constantly changing, and that includes its classifications.

Below is an example of one way to classify whales:

Whales

(Large sea mammals of the order Cetacea, ranging from 20 or 30 ft. to 100 ft. in length)

Toothless or Whalebone Whales
- Blue Whale
- Finback Whale
- Sei Whale
- Piked Whale
- Humpback Whale
- Gray Whale
- Right Whale
- Bowhead Whale

Toothed Whales
- Sperm Whale
- Bottlenose Whale
- Killer Whale

Although scientists have classified types of whales, they are still exploring many questions about these creatures, such as why some whales seem to deliberately beach themselves, which ultimately causes their death.

The scientific method speculates on the unknown (and reexamines the known) using the organizational patterns **hypothesis-proof** and **process.** When dealing with the unknown, scientists ask two main questions: Why is this so, and how can this be proven? Not only do they want to prove their hypothesis, they want to explain how they proved it. To scientists, the search for an answer is often as important as the answer itself.

To answer these questions, scientists and students work in a laboratory. For courses such as chemistry or physics, the lab is usually a room especially equipped for carrying out experiments. For botany the "lab" may primarily be outdoors; in oceanography, it is often the ocean itself. In science courses, lab notes are as important as, if not more important than, the textbook or lecture notes because they clarify the logic of each step of a scientific process.

In addition to classification, hypothesis-proof, and process, be alert for other organizational patterns used in the sciences, such as cause-effect and comparison-contrast. For example, What causes AIDS? What effect is AIDS having on our society? How does AIDS compare with other sexually transmitted diseases?

As in any other course, determine which patterns appear to be important to your instructor.

Reading and Research Sources for Science

Applied Science and Technology Index
Biological Abstracts
Chemical Abstracts
Current Abstracts of Chemistry and
   Index Chemicus
Dictionary of Physics
Encyclopedia of Earth Sciences

Encyclopedia of Chemistry
Encyclopedia of Physics
General Science Index
Harper Encyclopedia of Science
Physics Abstracts
Science Abstracts
Science Citation Index Medicus

Mathematics

The mathematical "way of knowing" is the organizational pattern of **problem/solution.** Like a story, a mathematics problem has a beginning, middle, and end. The beginning is the problem itself, the middle is the process used to solve the problem, and the end is the solution. Like scientists, mathematicians value the process of solving problems as much as the solution.

Some students have problems with math courses because they lack the necessary prior knowledge. Before attempting to take a difficult math course, you may want to take a prerequisite course or to learn or review basic math principles. Doing so can be especially helpful if you have "math phobia."

Another strategy to help you succeed in a difficult math course is to line up resources before the class begins. Ask former math students to recommend a math instructor; sign up for a course with classmates who are good in math and willing to form a study group; arrange for a math tutor (often campus tutoring is free); locate audio/visual or computer math programs (check the campus Learning Center); find lower-level or alternative math books (at the library or a used book store); purchase an outline review of math (bookstore).

If math is difficult for you, don't take another difficult course at the same time, so you can allow sufficient time for your math assignments. While some students need two hours for a math assignment, you might need three or four. Take breaks when tired to prevent careless errors such as copying numbers wrong. Also, accept the fact that the learning styles and strategies that you use in most courses may not work for math. Be willing to experiment and admit when you are wrong.

Keep up your math homework daily. Math is a sequential, cumulative subject. What you learn in one class is needed to understand the information in the next. If you miss a class, you may become so lost that you'll be tempted to miss another one, but don't cut class even if you are frustrated. Missing more classes will only make the problem worse.

Read the chapter before you go to class so that you'll know the terminology and problem steps, even if you don't understand everything you read. When taking notes, focus on copying the beginning of the problem the instructor writes on the blackboard; then look in your book later for the middle and end steps. **Ask about a step that you don't understand.** Most likely some of the other students won't understand it either and will appreciate your question. For questions that can wait, put a question mark in the margin and ask the instructor or a classmate after class. Clear any questions before you attempt homework assignments. If math tutoring is available, do your homework on campus so that you can get immediate help.

Math is a practical art that can be learned by imitation and practice. Copy sample problems step by step to serve as a pattern for similar problems and solutions. Get a blackboard at home and use it to work out problems. We learn best when we combine speaking, listening, reading, and writing, so as you work on problems, try talking aloud to yourself about them. Test your understanding of a math formula by explaining it to a classmate.

Rework lecture and text problems without looking at the answers or processes to check your understanding of the steps. Some instructors advise that you speculate about what the answer might be before beginning your solution process, using intuition before applying logic. Create variations of a problem and test your ability to solve them.

Ask your instructor for help as soon as you feel that you need it. You should meet the teacher and join a study group during the first week of class. Buy the answer book for the text, if available. This is not cheating. Seeing how the problems are solved, step by step, will help you to understand the solution process.

When taking a test, turn the test paper over before you even read it and jot down formulas you may forget. Use all of the time allowed; it's all right to be the last to turn in your test. The most common mistakes are caused by going through a test too quickly. If you don't understand a math question, ask if the teacher will translate it.

Use returned tests to strengthen your math skills. Find out what steps you missed or what errors you made and redo the problems you missed. This will make you better prepared to move on in the class and help you in reviewing for the next test.

Studying Literature

Whereas most college courses focus on the mass of mankind, literature focuses on the individual. Through an individual's story, we reach a deeper level of understanding and feeling about ourselves and others. Literature goes beyond the intellect and stimulates our emotions, intuition, and imagination. It enables us to suspend disbelief and become immersed in the story being told.

Like history, the main structure of literature is the story, with its sequence of events and **conflict.** Without conflict there is no story. Conflicts themselves often have a pattern, such as the individual in conflict with self, another individual, society, nature, or God. Interpretation of a story or poem often uses a comparison-contrast pattern to examine these conflicts. How do the characters differ in their beliefs, in the way that they react to a conflict? Can their beliefs and reactions be compared in any way?

In addition to understanding sequence and conflict, the literature student needs to know the vocabulary of literature, which includes such terms as *imagery* (mental pictures), *irony* (the direct opposite of what is really meant or expected), *allusion* (an indirect reference to something), and *symbolism* (a representation of something else).

To formulate an **interpretation** of a story or poem for a class discussion or a writing assignment, read closely with pencil in hand, making marginal annotations and underlining strong lines that will help you interpret the story. If a character's behavior reveals conflict, make note of it and compare and contrast it with other characters. Note examples of imagery, allusion, irony, symbolism, and other literary techniques. The marginal notes and underlining for the poem "Remains of My Day" provide some examples.

Remains of My Day

How can I tell them
I can not come out now,
do they not see these eyes
that look in
when they chat about places to go
like Death Valley, "What you haven't been?"
Do I quote Frost
or reflect on my own desert places?

[margin: Who is I? They?]

[margin: What is the symbolism of Death Valley and desert places? (both dry, isolated)]

Or do I feed the cat and brew coffee?
There are appointments to set
messages to answer. Perhaps, I should
clean out another closet, reorganize drawers
see what there is to see
before my salad at one and "My Dinner with André."
Later, I will go to the market
for rosemary, thyme, basil, mushrooms
to make garlic chicken with the lemons
a friend gave me from her garden.

[margin left: allusion to Frost's "Road Not Taken"]

[margin left: catalog of routines]

Meanwhile, the gardener comes on Tuesday
letters are posted, desks cleared
nights return on schedule,
and all the lights go on at once.
Some say it's the best part of the day.

[margin: catalog of routines]

—Carol Lem

[margin: Why is night the best part of the day?]

Often students avoid giving their own literary interpretation because they are unsure of their ability to find the "correct interpretation." Most instructors encourage students to develop their own interpretations, but they do expect these interpretations to be supported with "proof" from the literary work. If an instructor believes that there is only one interpretation, students must choose between feeding back the accepted interpretation or taking the risk of presenting their own.

Some students want to find out how literary critics interpret a work. Before consulting literary critics, develop your own interpretation with sufficient evidence from the writer's own words. Then consult a number of different critics to compare and contrast their interpretations with yours. If you find none that even hint at your interpretation, rethink your position. Do you have sufficient evidence from the work to validate your interpretation? Again, you must consider your instructor's potential reaction. Some will admire an original interpretation, but others may not.

Reading and Research Sources for Literature

Book Review Index
Bullfinch's Mythology
Cassell's Encyclopaedia of World Literature
Contemporary Authors
Dictionary of World Literary Terms
Essay and General Literature Index

Oxford Companion to English Literature
Oxford Companion to American Literature
Reader's Encyclopedia
Standard Dictionary of Folklore,
   Mythology, and Legend

Studying a Foreign Language

Learning a new language requires good listening habits. You must hear how a language sounds—words, sentence order, inflections—before you can practice speaking. The best way to learn a language is to use it, not just in the classroom or reviewing alone, but in as many ways as possible: practicing with classmates and friends on the phone, ordering from a menu in the new language, watching the international channels on television, going to foreign language movies, listening to the language on radio, or talking to others who speak the language.

Using a foreign language is a **stimulus-response** situation, so start by learning typical greetings with appropriate responses and practicing these simple patterns until they come naturally to you. Such repetitive practice is especially valuable because you won't "think" too much while doing it. One of the most common mistakes in learning a new language is the habit of translating. Word-for-word translation makes assimilating a new language difficult because the sentence patterns differ from those of your native tongue. Flashcards encourage word-for-word translation and for this reason are not a good tool for learning a new language. Instead, listen to tapes that ask questions and require you to respond. Also, take the time to make your own tapes so that you can hear how you pronounce the language.

Above all, when you practice phrases and sentences or create your own, be sure to use the patterns recommended by your instructor and the text. If you try to generate your own patterns, you may acquire bad habits. When practicing the familiar pattern, "Here is the _____," you can substitute vocabulary you are learning for such words as *door, window, student, clerk,* or *hotel.* Such pattern practice avoids the temptation to translate and has the added value of breaking the practice into small, manageable units.

The less you "think" and the more you listen and respond, the faster you will learn a new language.

Application Assignments: History Text

Application 1: Writing History from a Timeline

Background

One of the more overlooked presidencies of the twentieth century was the administration of Dwight D. Eisenhower (1952–1960). As one of the most popular commanding generals of World War II, one might expect that Eisenhower would have a rather comfortable time leading a nation that was optimistic about the future. Unfortunately, events during the 1950s grew so tense and divisive that even a well-liked leader such as "Ike" could not escape their formidable consequences. During his term in office, the U.S. and North Korea agreed to end the war, the Soviet Union invaded Hungary, China put pressure on two islands known as Quemoy and Matsu, the U.S. successfully exploded the world's first hydrogen bomb, Egypt seized the Suez Canal from long-time British rule, the Soviets launched Sputnik, *and Fidel Castro took power in Cuba. At home the president had to fight three serious recessions, try to outmaneuver a movement led by Senator Joseph McCarthy that challenged the loyalty of many Americans including top military officials, turn federal responsibility for Native Americans over to the states, and deal with the shooting down of one of our spy planes known as the U-2. Such a cavalcade of problems would be a formidable challenge for the greatest of leaders.*

This account of the events that occurred during Eisenhower's presidency explains little outside of the fact that a president must be well informed and constantly searching for solutions that are in the country's best interest. What is lacking is a story about his decision making. How did he handle the nation's problems? What led him to choose action in some areas and inaction in others? In short, how well did he represent the nation's best interests? Telling a story about these selected events is one way to find answers to these questions.

Examine the following timeline of events with the idea of writing your own narration. Try to discover the connections among the major events that give direction to your story. When you are finished, add your own title.

Timeline

October 1953: Dwight D. Eisenhower appoints Earl Warren as Chief Justice of the Supreme Court. (Eisenhower later recalls this as the biggest mistake he ever made.)

May 1954: *Brown v. Board of Education of Topeka.* (Supreme Court rules that segregation in schools is inherently unequal, thus reversing the 1896 "separate but equal" doctrine of *Plessy v. Ferguson.*)

December 1955: Rosa Parks, an African American seamstress employed in Montgomery, Alabama, refuses to give up her seat on a public bus to whites. (After her arrest, local black officials developed and executed a successful bus boycott and elected Martin Luther King, Jr., as their spokesman.)

November 1956: The U.S. Supreme Court invalidates a Montgomery, Alabama, law that provides for segregation in interstate bus travel.

August 1957: The Civil Rights Commission is established as Eisenhower signs the Civil Rights Act of 1957. It provides penalties for violation of the voting rights of any American citizen.

September 1957: The governor of Arkansas halts a local plan for gradual desegregation of Little Rock's Central High School. (Eisenhower nationalizes the Arkansas National Guard to protect the safety of the children who try to attend the high school. Little Rock's officials close all public high schools in 1959 rather than desegregate them.)

February 1960: Four African American students from North Carolina A & T in Greensboro sit down and order coffee at a department store lunch counter; they are refused service and are subjected to mental and physical abuse. The "sit-in" movement spreads around the country.

October 1960: Martin Luther King, Jr., joins the sit-in movement and is arrested for trying to desegregate an Atlanta snack bar. He faces a four-month sentence at hard labor. He stays in prison until the presidential nominee, John F. Kennedy, persuades a federal judge to release the Baptist minister on bond. (In November, the majority of African Americans cast their votes for Kennedy.)

Application Assignments: Psychology Text

Application 2

Whereas some courses rely heavily on such patterns as cause-effect, sequence, and comparison-contrast, the study of psychology relies very much on definition of terms. Since we remember best what we already know or have experienced, we memorize terms quicker and remember the definitions longer if we add an example from our own memory.

Consulting pages 333–335, for each defense mechanism below, write in a simple definition, an example from the text, and an example from your own experience or knowledge. Although the first term is done for you, add your own example of *denial*.

Defense Mechanisms

TERM	DEFINITION	TEXT EXAMPLE	OWN EXAMPLE
1. Denial	not acknowledging a reality	denying need to study	denying a friend's lack of loyalty
2. Regression			
3. Displacement			
4. Sublimation			
5. Reaction formation			

Application 3: Transfer of Skills

Practice the skills you have learned in this chapter with a textbook from another class to transfer the skill of finding organizational patterns: sequence, cause-effect, comparison-contrast, hypothesis-proof, and process.

Self-Contract

As a result of learning about study strategies for diverse disciplines, I would like to test the following strategies:

_____

_____

_____

_____

_____

_____

I will practice these new techniques for at least_____weeks to determine if I want to adopt them as a part of my permanent study strategies. Then I will complete the Progress Report below.

Signed:_____   Date:_____

Self-Contract Progress Report

Progress I have made toward these changes:_____

_____

_____

_____

_____

_____

_____Date:_____

Stage Three, Step Three Journal Entry

A person needs at intervals to separate himself from family and companions and go to a new place. He must go without his familiars in order to be open to influences of change.
—Katherine Butler Hathaway

Date: _____

Freewrite about the above quotation by reflecting on your going to "a new place" by studying unfamiliar topics. What are examples of topics in your past and present classes that have taken you into new territory and stimulated your thinking?

_____

_____

_____

_____

_____

_____

_____

_____

_____

_____

_____

_____

_____

_____

These are not books, lumps of lifeless paper, but minds alive on the shelves.

—Gilbert Highet

Step Four
Read for Meaning

Objectives

❑ To practice reading

❑ To practice marginal and review notes

❑ To learn concentration strategies

Contents

❑ Read Actively

❑ Three Methods for Marking a Textbook
      Method 1: Highlight or Underline Key
        Words and Phrases
      Method 2: Write Questions in the Margins
      Method 3: Write Key Words in the
        Margins to Summarize

❑ Read Critically

❑ 'Beat the Clock'—A Concentration Game

❑ Summary Map of Step Four

❑ Application Assignments: History Text

❑ Application Assignments: Psychology Text

Key Terms

active versus passive readers
underlining and highlighting key words and phrases
reading critically
summary

Self-Awareness Check:

Check the appropriate blanks:	Often	Sometimes	Rarely
1. When I study, I formulate questions for review.	____	____	____
2. The way I usually mark a textbook is to underline or highlight.	____	____	____
3. When I read, I make notes in the margins.	____	____	____
4. I make review notes when I read the text.	____	____	____
5. When I study I have trouble concentrating.	____	____	____

Read Actively

What is active reading? Consider how the following two students differ in their reading habits:

Student A: Stacy uses the same technique each time she studies. She begins reading a chapter starting with page 1 and continues word after word, page after page. As she reads, she highlights what she assumes are important facts. She does not consciously relate new information to what she already knows or formulate her own questions about what she is reading. When she reviews, she tries to memorize the highlighted information, trusting that her exams will be based on what she has marked.

Student B: Maria varies her reading strategy to fit the subject matter. Depending on the class, she either highlights, writes in the margins, makes a TIPS, or uses flashcards for definitions and concepts. For example, in her biology class she makes flashcards to review scientific words. In her literature class, she annotates in the margins with summary phrases. For her philosophy class, she relies on TIPS to generate questions for densely worded paragraphs. With most of these methods she adds examples of her own to link previous knowledge to new.

Although Stacy reads and highlights regularly, she does not "interact" with the text by consciously relating new information to what she already knows or by formulating her own questions about what she is studying. She is a **passive reader.** In contrast, Maria realizes that she will learn more efficiently if she reaches out for information and does something with it. As an **active reader,** Maria has a better chance of achieving high grades than does Stacy with her limited study method.

Three Methods for Marking a Textbook

There are three methods commonly used by students for marking a textbook. Active readers use all of these techniques.

Method 1: Highlight or Underline Key Words and Phrases

This method has advantages in some courses if you already know what is important. Avoid going to extremes—some students have almost as much highlighting or underlining in their texts than regular print. As a general rule, avoid marking more than 10 percent of a page.

When highlighting, you might try a system of color coding, such as using yellow for main ideas, pink for key terms, and green for supporting details. This technique can make note-taking and review more efficient.

Underlining or highlighting is helpful when you want to memorize exact words and phrases or verify the meaning of text, but they do not require you to "interact" with the material by putting it in your own words or formulating questions about it. Therefore, underlining or highlighting is best used in combination with the two other methods.

Exercise 1: Underlining Practice

Read the following passage taken from a typical biology textbook. Using what has already been underlined as a model, continue underlining key words, main ideas, and their supporting details.

The Nature of Science

Science, biological and other, is a way of seeking principles of order. Art is another means, as are religion and philosophy. Science differs from these in that it limits its search to the natural world, the physical universe. Also, and perhaps even more significant, it differs from them in the central value it gives to observation (particularly to that structured kind of observation called experimentation). Scientists begin their search by accumulating data and trying to fit them into systems of order—conceptual schemes that organize the data in some meaningful way.

These are not two steps, the accumulating and the ordering; they go on simultaneously. Or to put it another way, the accumulation of data is undertaken by scientists as a way of answering a question or supporting or rejecting a hunch or hypothesis. (This is what Einstein meant when he said that it is the theory that decides what we can observe.) The data may be generated by deliberate, planned experiments or may be gleaned retrospectively from one's earlier systematic observation or from verifiable information recorded by others.

When a scientist has collected sufficient data to support a particular conclusion, he or she then reports the results to other scientists; today such a report usually takes place at a scientific meeting. . . or in a scientific publication. If the data are sufficiently interesting or the conclusion important, the observations or experiments will be repeated in an attempt to confirm, deny, or extend them. Hence, scientists always report the methods that they used as well as their results.

When a hypothesis has been sufficiently tested in this way, it is generally referred to as a theory. Thus a theory in science has as somewhat different meaning from the word "theory" in common usage, in which "just a theory" carries with it the implication of a flight of fancy or an abstract notion, rather than a carefully formulated, well-tested proposition. Because the theory of evolution pervades all of modern biology, it has been tested and re-tested, directly and indirectly, for the past 125 years.[1]

> ***Suggested Activity:*** With a group of classmates, compare and contrast what each of you underlined. Discuss any differences, and be prepared to explain why you chose to underline a phrase that another person did not.

Verification: How much of the text did you underline? If you marked more than 10 percent, or approximately 40 words, you were not selective enough. The more you condense the material to its essential ideas and details, the less you will have to remember. If you did not select most of the main ideas underlined by your classmates, you might profit by practicing the following system.

Method 2: Write Questions in the Margins

One way to find important information is to formulate questions based on titles and headings in a text and write them in the margins.

Exercise 2: (Part A)

Assume that in a psychology class you are assigned a reading entitled "Surviving the Breakup: How Children Cope With Divorce." With this title in mind, formulate questions about the topics listed in parentheses below that you would expect the article to answer. The first three questions below are provided as examples.

1. (Scope of problem) *What is today's divorce rate among couples with children?*

2. (Definition) *What does survival mean in this context?*

3. (Custody) *Who ends up with the children?*

4. (Money)

5. (Methods of coping)

6. (Causes of divorce)

7. (Importance of the article)

---

[1]Helena Curtis. (1983). *Biology,* 4th ed., p. 10. New York: Worth Publishers.

> *Suggested Activity:* In groups, compare and contrast the questions asked. Determine which questions relate most closely to the title of the reading.

Asking so many questions based on a title alone may seem excessive, but as you practice questioning what you read, you will become more adept at deriving relevant information from text. For the present, ask as many different questions as you can. The answers you receive will help guide you toward further questions.

Exercise 2: (Part B)

Continue this exercise by asking questions based on headings from the article in Part A.

1. Heading: "California's Children of Divorce"

   Your question: _____

2. Subheading: "Changing Family Circumstances"

   Your question: _____

3. Subheading: "Differing Reactions From Children"

   Your question: _____

4. Subheading: "Importance of Involved Fathers"

   Your question: _____

> *Suggested Activity:* After comparing questions with your classmates, use your prior knowledge and consider the answer to the following question: "Who is more likely to survive a divorce, parents or children?"

Exercise 3 (Part A): Writing Questions from Underlined Answers

Return to the article on science beginning on page 130. Individually or in groups, formulate questions using the underlined information in the text as guidelines and write them in the margins. Below, the first paragraph has been completed for you. *Note:* When you have completed this task, you should have a prepared study guide for personal use.

Example:

How do scientists seek principles of order?

Science, biological and other, is a way of <u>seeking principles of order.</u> Art is another means, as are religion and philosophy. Science differs from these in that it <u>limits</u> its <u>search</u> to the <u>natural world,</u> the physical universe. Also, and perhaps even <u>more</u> <u>significant,</u> it differs from them in the <u>central value</u> it gives to <u>observation</u> (particularly to that structured kind of observation called experimentation). Scientists begin their search by accumulating data and trying to <u>fit</u> them into systems of order—conceptual schemes that organize the data in some meaningful way.

What is the central value of science?

Writing questions from underlined answers works well for texts that emphasize the mastery of specific facts rather than individual interpretation. Texts and supplementary readings that are persuasive, argumentative, or controversial require more interpretation. This is the time to apply all your ability at formulating questions in order to find answers.

Exercise 3 (Part B): <u>Writing Questions and Underlining Answers</u>

When reading, be alert for information that appears incomplete, exaggerated, or doubtful in some way. Such information (generally a claim or assertion) can be translated into a question that may be answered in another part of the text or by your instructor.

For example, read the following paragraph and write questions in the left margin as indicated by the model. Use the topics shown in parentheses and underline answers as you proceed.

Police Use of Deadly Force: Research and Reform[2]

(police power) *How much power does the cop on the street have?*

(judicious use of force)

(force used with great restraint)

When police officers fire their guns, the immediate consequences of their decisions are realized at the rate of 750 feet per second and are beyond reversal by any level of official review. As most police recruits learn in the academy, the cop on the street—who, with the corrections officer, generally can boast of fewer academic and training credentials than any other criminal justice official—carries in his holster more power than has been granted the Chief Justice of the Supreme Court. When used injudiciously, this power has led to riot and additional death, civil and criminal litigation against police and their employers, and the ousting of police chiefs, elected officials, and the entire city administrations. Even when used with great restraint, police deadly force has created polarization, suspicion, and distrust on the part of those who need the police most.

---

[2]James J. Fyfe. (1993). "Police Use of Deadly Force: Research and Reform," *Criminal Justice: Concepts and Issues,* Chris W. Eskridge, ed., p. 91. Los Angeles: Roxbury Publishing Company.

> *Suggested Activity:* In small groups, discuss the questions asked by each class member.

Method 3: Write Key Words in the Margins to Summarize

In Method 3, key words or terms are written in the margins instead of questions. Key words summarize the main ideas of paragraphs and their supporting points and lead you to essential information within the text. Instead of rereading underlined or highlighted sections to review, you can skim through your key word column and turn the words into questions for quizzing yourself. Key words are also useful when you are writing a term paper or searching for information during an open-book exam.

Note: As you will probably recognize, when you summarize ideas and their supporting points, you are using a variation of the TIPS procedure described in Step 2.

Exercise 4

Read the following passage typical of many political science texts. In addition to underlining and highlighting, write key words in the margin. The questions in parentheses are similar to ones you ask yourself as you read the key words.

Majority Rule and Minority Rights

public policy (What determines public policy?)

popular government (What two problems face all popular governments?)

It is the will of the people, not the dictate of a ruling elite, that determines public policy in a democracy. But defining and determining the popular will are two problems that face all popular governments. To solve these problems, democracy requires some agreed-upon standard in order to make public policy. The only adequate device democracy submits is majority rule.

Democracy can be described as an experiment designed to find satisfactory ways to control or order human relationships. It does not claim that the majority is always right but that it will always arrive at the best of all possible decisions on public matters. Indeed, the democratic process, that is, the process of majority rule, does not intend to come up with either "right" or "best" answers. Instead, the democratic process is one that searches for satisfactory solutions among many competing ideas in the public arena.

While admitting the possibility of error, democracy insists that the majority's decision will, more often than not, be satisfactory. Furthermore, democracy recognizes that seldom is any solution to a public problem so satisfactory that it cannot be improved upon. Circumstances surrounding the original decisions plus the passing of time can alter the standards by which democratic decisions were made. Therefore, the process of experimentation, of seeking answers to public questions, is a never-ending one.

Majority Rule and Minority Rights (continued)

Unquestionably, a democracy cannot function without the principle of majority rule. Unchecked, however, a majority can crush all opposition, and in the process, destroy the idea behind democracy . Therefore, democracy acknowledges that its existence depends on majority rule checked or restrained by minority rights. Fundamental to these impediments is the recognition that through lawful means, minorities may become majorities. Accordingly, it is imperative that the majority listens to the minority's arguments, hears its objections, bears its criticisms, and welcomes its suggestions. To do otherwise is to contradict the essential meaning of democracy itself.

Suggested Activity: Review and compare your key words within your group. Try to resolve differences by citing evidence from the article. There are several possible interpretations from which to extract key words, but there should be enough agreement to enable you to write a one- or two-sentence summary of the article below, using the key words.

_____

_____

_____

_____

Now formulate questions based on the summary. Write one question based on factual information in the article and one that challenges the author.

1. _____

   _____

2. _____

   _____

Suggested Activity: Within your group, discuss the differences in your questions and challenges to the author's points.

Another technique for using the margins of a page is to write a brief **summary** at the top or bottom of that page. Reading these summaries from the first page to the last will give you a quick overview of the chapter's main points. An effective review strategy is to read the page summaries to review the chapter before testing yourself on the questions and key words written in the side margins.

Comparison of Three Methods for Marking a Textbook

The three methods for marking a textbook described here have both advantages and disadvantages.

The main advantage of highlighting or underlining (Method 1) is its ease and speed for marking key words and passages. Color coding can also provide a quick review. This method may serve your study purposes if you are already able to master the subject without much effort. Its major disadvantage is that it requires minimal active thought.

Writing questions in the margins (Method 2) requires you to find answers in the text. It also provides practice in anticipating questions your instructor will ask. More important, questions that you are unable to answer may help you identify ideas or concepts that you do not yet understand.

Writing key words in the margins (Method 3) takes more time than marking text or writing questions but has the advantage of compelling you to interact with the material. You cannot simply skim over paragraphs. Your mind has to process information in order to reduce it to key words. This method increases retention because you are reading more actively.

Methods 2 and 3 lead you to the next section, which shows you how to record your active involvement with text.

'Beat the Clock'— A Concentration Game

Like most students, you probably have difficulty concentrating for very long, especially when studying a subject that you're not very interested in. You can improve your concentration by playing a game of 'Beat the Clock' when you read or study. Before beginning a task, estimate how long it will take and then try finish within the limits you have set. Record the times you start and finish so you know how long you actually took to complete the work. Also, since the average attention span is only 15 to 20 minutes at its peak, you will do best if you divide your work into small segments that can be done in 10 to 15 minutes.

I always remember more when I'm reading under a time limit. It just makes me understand and retain the material better. Being under pressure, especially for a test, helps me concentrate. Setting a goal helps too.

—Tracey Schneider

Read Critically

Reading actively also means **reading critically.** Selecting important words and phrases, asking probing questions, and summarizing key ideas are characteristic of those who read critically. Critical readers do not simply accept the messages given in text at face value; they doubt claims, challenge assertions, and separate the trivial from what is relevant or significant. These are aptitudes we all have and can develop but that we too rarely use.

The following two exercises will give you an opportunity to practice your natural ability to read critically. To help focus your attention, play 'Beat the Clock,' the game of concentration described on page 136, by entering the times indicated below:

	Example:	*Exercise 1*
Estimated Time of Task:	*15 minutes*	_____
Starting Time:	*8:05 pm*	_____
Finishing Time:	*8:30*	_____
Time Spent:	*25 minutes*	_____

Critical Reading Exercise #1

Read the examination of the communication styles of two cultures. As you read, write questions or key words in the margin. Be alert for statements that you disagree with or for which you would like more proof.

The Rhetoric of *La Familia* Among Mexican Americans[3]

"You are going out so soon? At what time will you be back, *hijo?*" the mother asks as she approaches her son and fixes the collar of his shirt. She touches his cheek with the palm of her hand while looking at him with love and pride. Manuel, a six-foot-tall, 25-year-old man, checks the rest of his attire then embraces his mother and kisses her farewell on the cheek.

"I will be back soon, no later than eleven," he replies. "Jenny and I are going to the movies. And, yes, *Mami,* I left the money for the rent on your night table, where Cristina left the money for the food."

As he departs, his sister Cristina enters the apartment. "Have fun, Manuel," she says and turns around to kiss her mother on the cheek. *"Hola, Mami.* What are we having for supper? Is Dad still at work? Where is Uncle Beto? Is Grandma asleep?" She sits on a couch.

"Cristina," the mother says without answering any of her questions, "when are you going to get married to Joe? He is four years older than you; you are 22, and you will be graduating from college this year. We will help you get started and help you along. Joe is a good, hard-working young man."

"I don't know, sounds all right, but . . . " Cristina sighs. "We have only known each other for a couple of months, and, you know how it is, he wants to have everything clear and organized before we even talk about marriage. He will have to move out of his parents' house, and there are still younger kids in the family, they need support. . . ."

If this same episode had transpired in an Anglo family, the dialogue would most likely have been different.

"See you, Mom," Tom says as he opens the door to leave. Noticing that his sister Cary has arrived, he adds, "I better leave, she's back!" Cary glares at him as he goes by. As she walks in, she says, "I have a lot of work to do, Mom." She marches off to her bedroom and closes the door. Throughout this exchange, the mother does not take her eyes off what she is doing, nor does she respond to her children's statements.

Two typical households, one Mexican American and the other Euro-American, reflect two very different underlying values and assumptions of what a family is and what it provides for its members. The communication of the Mexican American family in the above episode points to the continued interdependence of its members across generations. It also makes explicit that sharing time in conversation is a valued form of family interaction. Touch, affection, and greeting rituals are means of affirmation. In contrast, the communication in the Anglo family points to some basic assumptions about the value of individualism and the need to maintain it through more restricted communication and contact. In the Mexican American family, the formality given to greeting rituals is intended to keep both familiarity and distance. In the Euro-American family, cultural valuations seem to limit interdependence and affiliation to the family, so as to make the children leave the "nest" and form other independent, nuclear families. In my opinion, the Euro-American family rarely uses touch in its casual interactions and even less so with grown children. The cultural perception of touch for Euro-Americans seems to work as (1) a means of control and preventing any tendency towards individualism and (2) a communicative device reserved mainly for sexual encounters. The need for independence and individualism apparently fosters an emotional distance between the generations that severely impairs significant bonding among family members.

The Mexican American family is the source of many of the cultural values, attitudes, and assumptions that Mexican Americans carry with them into their interactions with mainstream society. This composite of cultural elements that influence the Mexican American character is what Mexican Americans call *la familia* (the family). Consequently, the analysis of the rhetoric that frames Mexican American family values and activities will facilitate Euro-Americans' understanding of Mexican Americans. Moreover, awareness of the Mexican American valuation of the family provides a model for society of such productive attributes as community, solidarity, respect, and discipline.

[3]Margarita Gangotena. (1994). "The Rhetoric of *La Familia* Among Mexican Americans." *Our Voices: Essays in Culture, Ethnicity, and Communication,* Alberto Gonzlez, Marsha Houston, and Victoria Chen, eds., pp. 69–70. Los Angeles: Roxbury Publishing.

Suggested Activity: Compare your marginal notes with those of other students.

Personal Response Check: As a result of playing 'Beat the Clock,'

I realize that (1)_____

(2)_____

Critical Reading Exercise #2

Fill in the blanks below with the amount of time you estimate you will need to complete the four tasks listed. When you finish the task, figure out how much time you actually took. As you will notice, this exercise involves TIPS. You may want to review the TIPS procedure explained on page 87.

Tasks:

1. Read the passage on the next page. Write questions or key words in the margin.

2. Make a TIPS following the article.

3. Use your TIPS to write a summary of approximately 25 words.

4. Write one or two questions unanswered in the passage.

Estimated Time of Task:_____

Starting Time:_____

Finishing Time:_____

Time Spent:_____

Asians and Jews[4]

Comparing the social success of Asian-Americans with that of Jews is irresistible. Jews and Asians rank number one and number two, respectively, in median income. In the Ivy League they are the two groups most heavily "over-represented" in comparison to their shares of the population. And observers are quick to point out all sorts of cultural parallels. As Arthur Rosen, the chairman of (appropriately) the National Committee on United States–China Relations, recently told *The New York Times,* "There are the same kind of strong family ties and the same sacrificial drive on the part of immigrant parents who couldn't get a college education to see that their children do."

In historical terms, the parallels can often be striking. For example, when Russian and Polish Jews came to this country in the late nineteenth and early twentieth centuries, 60 percent of those who went into industry worked in the garment trade. Today thousands of Chinese-American women fill sweatshops in New York City doing the same work of stitching and sewing. In Los Angeles, when the Jews began to arrive in large numbers in the 1880s, 43 percent of them became retail or wholesale proprietors, according to Ivan Light's essay in *Clamor at the Gates.* One hundred years later, 40 percent of Koreans in Los Angeles are also wholesale and retail proprietors. The current controversy over Asian-American admissions in Ivy League colleges eerily recalls the Jews' struggle to end quotas in the 1940s and 1950s.

In cultural terms, however, it is easy to take the comparison too far. American Jews remain a relatively homogeneous group, with a common religion and history. Asian-Americans, especially after the post-1965 flood of immigrants, are exactly the opposite. They seem homogeneous largely because they share some racial characteristics. And even those vary widely. The label "Chinese-American" itself covers a range of cultural and linguistic differences that makes those between German and East European Jews seem trivial in comparison.

The most important parallels between Jews and the various Asian groups are not cultural. They lie rather in the sociological profile of Jewish and Asian immigration. The Jewish newcomers of a hundred years ago never completely fit into the category of "huddled masses." They had an astonishingly high literacy rate (nearly 100 percent for German Jews, and over 50 percent for East European Jews), a long tradition of scholarship even in the smallest shtetls, and useful skills. More than two-thirds of male Jewish immigrants were considered skilled workers in America. Less than 3 percent of Jewish immigrants had worked on the land. Similarly, the Japanese, Korean, Filipino, and Vietnamese immigrants of the twentieth century have come almost exclusively from the middle class. Seventy percent of Korean male immigrants, for example, are college graduates. Like middle-class native-born Americans, Asian and Jewish immigrants alike have fully understood the importance of the universities, and have pushed their children to enter them from the very start.

Thomas Sowell offers another parallel between the successes of Asians and Jews. Both communities have benefited paradoxically, he argues, from their small size and from past discrimination against them. These disadvantages long kept both groups out of politics. And as Sowell writes in *Race and Economics:* "Those American ethnic groups that have succeeded best politically have not usually been the same as those who succeeded best economically . . . those minorities that have pinned their greatest hopes on political action—the Irish and the Negroes, for example—have made some of the slower economic advances." Rather than searching for a solution to their problems through the political process, Jewish, Chinese, and Japanese immigrants developed self-sufficiency by relying on community organizations. The combination of their skills, their desire for an education, and gradual disappearance of discrimination led inexorably to economic success.

---

[4]David A. Bell. (1985). "The Triumph of Asian-Americans." *The New Republic.*

T = _____

I = _____

P = _____

         _____   _____

         _____   _____

         _____   _____

Summary: _____

_____

_____

_____

Questions: _____

_____

_____

_____

Personal Response Check: As a result of making a TIPS and playing 'Beat the Clock,'

I realize that   (1)_____

                 (2)_____

Suggested Activity: Discuss with your classmates the advantages and disadvantages of playing 'Beat the Clock.'

Summary Map of Step Four

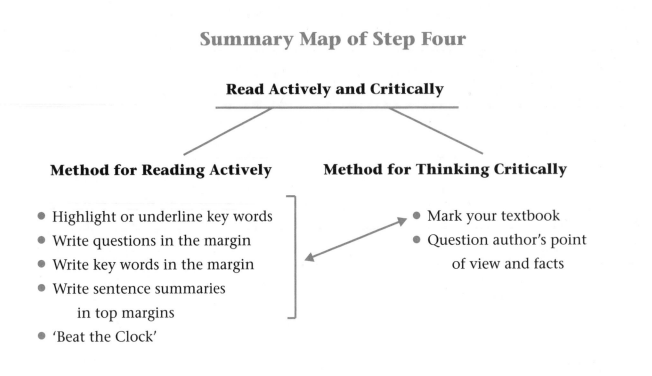

Read Actively and Critically

Method for Reading Actively

- Highlight or underline key words
- Write questions in the margin
- Write key words in the margin
- Write sentence summaries
     in top margins
- 'Beat the Clock'

Method for Thinking Critically

- Mark your textbook
- Question author's point
     of view and facts

Application Assignments: History Text

Application 1 (Part A)

Practice taking textbook notes using the question-and-answer format and playing 'Beat the Clock' for "American Life in 'The Roaring Twenties,' 1919–1929." Turn to the heading "Monkey Business in Tennessee" on page 314. For this exercise, the question and answer columns are partially filled in. Complete both columns by filling in missing questions and answers.

Estimated Time of Task: _____

Starting Time: _____

Finishing Time:_____

Time Spent: _____

Monkey Business in Tennessee

Question Column	Answer Column
1. In what ways did education improve in the 1920s?	1._____ _____
2._____ _____	2. Students should "learn by doing" and teachers should be educating for life outside of school.
3. In spite of advances in education and science, why did Fundamentalists object to the teaching of evolution?	3._____ _____
4. What was the decision rendered in the "Monkey Trial" held in Dayton, Tenn., in 1925?	4._____ _____
5._____ _____	5. Bryan was made to appear foolish by Clarence Darrow.

You have prepared a review sheet that can be used in a unique way. Test yourself by folding your paper length-wise. Look only at the side that has the answers. By looking at the answer, see if you can recall the orginal question. If you can, you can probably remember the information for the exam.

Suggested Activity: With a small group of classmates, compare and contrast how each of you filled in the answer column. Add any relevant points to your own list of answers.

Application 1 (Part B)

For the section titled "The Mass-Consumption Economy," on page 315, use the question-answer format below. First read the passage and study the sample notes in the answer column. Complete the notes and fill in the question column.

Estimated Time of Task: _____

Starting Time: _____

Finishing Time: _____

Time Spent: _____

The Mass-Consumption Economy

Question Column	Answer Column
1._____ _____ _____	1. World War I Treasury Secretary Andrew Mellon's tax policies, new machines powered by abundant oil, and the assembly line.
2._____ _____	2. Electrical power and the automobile (Americans owned 30 million by 1930) become giant businesses.
3._____	3._____
4._____	4._____
5._____	5._____
6._____	6._____
7._____	7._____

Application 1 (Part C)

For the section titled "Putting America on Rubber Tires," on page 316, create a question-answer chart. Read the entire headed section and write a summary. Then reread to write questions and answers in the Q/A box. When done, determine whether you wish to change your summary based on a more complete reading. Time yourself to help your concentration.

Estimated Time of Task: _____

Starting Time: _____

Finishing Time: _____

Time Spent: _____

Putting America on Rubber Tires

First Summary:

Question Column	Answer Column
1._____	1. Represented the most amazing industrial development of the 1920s based on the assembly line and mass-production
2._____	2._____
3._____	3._____
4._____	4._____

Second Summary:
(Include the reasons for Henry Ford's success.)

> ***Personal Response Check:*** As a result of practicing different ways of taking notes, asking and answering questions, and writing summaries,
>
> I realize that   (1)_____
>
> (2)_____

Application Assignments: Psychology Text

Application 2

Practice taking textbook notes using the question-answer format and playing 'Beat the Clock' for the introduction to this chapter on stress and health and the section "Sources of Stress," pages 330 to 331. As you read and take notes, you are anticipating questions the instructor may ask on a test.

For this exercise, the question and answer columns are partially filled in. Complete both columns by filling in missing questions and answers. The last item is for you to determine a question and answer.

Practice timing yourself by estimating the time you think it will take you to do the exercise on the following page.

Estimated Time of Task: _____

Starting Time: _____

Finishing Time: _____

Time Spent: _____

Sources of Stress

Question Column	Answer Column
1. What is one definition of stress?	1._____ _____
2._____	2. Facing two or more incompatible de-mands, needs or goals
3. What are three basic choices for cop-ing directly?	3._____ _____
4._____	4. Example: Rather than accept a pro-motion that requires moving to an-other state, the person quits and takes another job.
Create your own question and answer below: 5._____ _____	5._____ _____

Self-Contract

As a result of learning about reading actively and critically, I would like to test the following strategies:

_____

_____

_____

_____

_____

_____

I will practice these new techniques for at least_____weeks to determine if I want to adopt them as a part of my permanent study strategies. Then I will complete the Progress Report below.

Signed:_____   Date:_____

Self-Contract Progress Report

Progress I have made toward these changes:_____

_____

_____

_____

_____

_____

_____Date:_____

Stage Three, Step Four Journal Entry

Great ability develops and reveals itself increasingly with every new assignment.

—Balthasar Gracian

Date:_____

In the preceding steps, you have given yourself assignments by writing a self-contract to make changes. First, reread your self-contracts in Stage Two for time management and at the end of Steps 1 through 3 in Stage Three. Freewrite about the contracts you have made so far: What percentage of the contracts have you kept? What actions have you taken? What have been the results? How has your ability to study improved? What strategies that you tried have not worked well for you? Explain a new learning strategy you would like to try.

_____

_____

_____

_____

_____

_____

_____

_____

_____

_____

_____

_____

_____

_____

The beginning of wisdom is the definition of terms.
—Socrates

Step Five
Develop Your Vocabulary

Key Terms

vocabulary
definitions
glossary
dictionary
inferences
context
flashcards
spatial maps

Self-Awareness Check:
Check the appropriate blanks:

	Often	Sometimes	Rarely
1. My courses include unfamiliar words and terms.	____	____	____
2. Tests in these classes assume I understand certain key terms.	____	____	____
3. I use flashcards to review new vocabulary.	____	____	____
4. I practice using new words in sentences.	____	____	____
5. When I do not do well on a test item, it is because I do not know the vocabulary.	____	____	____

There are those who say that a large vocabulary is not all that important because in everyday life people use only one or two thousand "ordinary" words to communicate their needs and to understand each other. Such a contention is accurate if we limit our scope to ordinary conversation.

However, in most college classes you need a large reading and listening vocabulary to understand the meaning of texts and lectures. Lack of vocabulary will break your concentration every time you encounter a word that you do not know. Here is an example:

We were safe until crepuscule, when the lions began their hunt.

Unless you know that *crepuscule* means twilight, you won't fully understand this sentence. When reading a passage that contains a number of unfamiliar words, you'll stumble over a word, begin again, stumble over another word, and try in vain to pick up the main idea. By the end of a paragraph, you may not understand much of what you have read.

There are, however, ways to avoid the frustration of encountering unfamiliar words. These include guessing the meaning of words from context, using vocabulary flashcards, and creating spatial maps to help you remember new words and terms.

Develop Your Vocabulary

Any student can learn biology; the biggest brick wall toward understanding is lack of vocabulary.

—Terry Augustine

Each academic discipline or subject-matter area has its own special **vocabulary.** For example, *osmosis, chromosome,* and *protoplasm* are terms used in biology; *circumference, hypotenuse,* and *apex* are words used in geometry; and *stanza, meter,* and *rhyme* are terms used in describing poetry. Specialized words and terms such as these will be explained in your text. In addition, most textbooks include a variety of aids to point out and explain technical terms. For example, words may be highlighted with **boldface type,** underlining or *italics,* and **definitions** may be provided in the margins or at the beginning or end of chapters. Texts in disciplines such as psychology, sociology, and economics often include a **glossary**, or mini-dictionary.

Check one of your textbooks for its "vocabulary friendliness" by answering the following questions. If the answer to a question is yes, put a check mark in the blank beside it.

_____1.   Does your book have a glossary?

_____2.   Does each chapter have a vocabulary preview or review?

_____3.   Are technical terms underlined, *italicized,* or in **bold print**?

_____4.   Are these terms also defined in the glossary?

_____5.   Are terms defined in the margin?

Guessing From Context

In your course work you will probably encounter a number of unfamiliar words in addition to technical vocabulary, and you will need to determine their meaning. Contrary to the advice often given by parents and teachers, it is not productive to stop reading and look up every word you don't know in a **dictionary.** Not only does it take time and disrupt your train of thought, but when several definitions are listed for the same word, you may not be able to decide which one applies.

A better method for discovering the meaning of unfamiliar words is a technique called "guessing from context." It should be noted, however, that in this case the word *guessing* is a misnomer, an inaccurate term for what is actually a complex process of deduction. When you encounter words that you don't recognize or understand, you may be able to deduce their meaning in many instances because there is a lot of repetition in the English language.[1] For example, you may not know the meaning of the word *misnomer* in the second sentence of this paragraph, but later in the same sentence it is clearly defined as an "inaccurate term." Authors often use such direct clues to assist understanding.

---

[1] Jo-Ann Lynn Mullen. (1987). *College Reading and Learning Skills,* p. 200. Englewood Cliffs, NJ: Prentice-Hall.

If there are no direct clues to a word's meaning, you must deduce, or infer, what it means from its context and the way in which it is used. Fortunately, we all have the ability to infer and, in fact, are continually drawing **inferences,** both consciously and unconsciously. We infer displeasure from a frown, happiness from a smile, ignorance from poor spelling, politeness from good table manners, and so on. Inference is as natural an activity for human beings as eating or sleeping.

Studies indicate that guessing from context adds more words to your vocabulary than direct instruction. Since vocabulary knowledge is the single most important factor in predicting reading success, the efforts you make to expand your knowledge of words will be well rewarded.[2]

Exercise 1

Read the stories under the headings "The Advent of the Gasoline Age" and "Humans Develop Wings," beginning on page 318. As you read, list words that are unfamiliar or that you believe are important to the topics.

_____   _____   _____

_____   _____   _____

_____   _____   _____

_____   _____   _____

_____   _____   _____

_____   _____   _____

Finding the meaning of essential vocabulary leads to full comprehension of text. The most efficient method of discovering such meanings is through a word's **context**—that is, how it is used in a sentence, several sentences, or a paragraph.

---

[2] Harry Singer. (1964). "Substrata Factor Patterns Accompanying Development in Power of Reading, Elementary Through College Level," in E. Thurston & Hafner, eds., *Philosophical and Sociological Basis of Reading.* Fourteenth Yearbook of the National Reading Conference, 14:41–45.

Sometimes, words are compared or contrasted as in the following:

> *New industries boomed* <u>*lustily*</u>*; older ones grew sickly.*

If you know that an industrial boom produces great excitement as well as great wealth, then you already have a strong hint that industry was having great success. If you recognized that *lustily* was being compared with *sickly,* you could reach a similar conclusion.

Other times, words come in "bunches," and your detective powers are put to the test:

> *Virtuous home life partially broke down as joyriders of all ages* <u>*forsook*</u> *the ancestral hearth for the wide-open spaces.*

In this example, understanding several key terms can be used in understanding context. *Virtuous* and *joyriders* are two of them. In other words, the teachings learned at home were being eclipsed by the joys of riding around the countryside. Tried and true lessons were exchanged for entertainment. Consequently, something valuable was being lost to something more superficial. If the joyriders reject valuable lessons for the wide open spaces, then the meaning of *forsook* (past tense of *forsake*) becomes clear.

Often, the meaning of a target word is explained in a sentence immediately following.

> *Autobuses made possible the consolidation of schools and to some extent of churches. The sprawling suburbs spread out still farther from the urban core.*

Sprawling suburbs suggests that people are losing contact with each other as well as the center of the city. In order to reunite or join units that are more readily identified and controlled, "consolidation" becomes a convenient tool.

As a practice exercise, test your powers of deduction with the following sentence:

> *Zooming motorcars were agents of social change. At first a luxury, they rapidly became a necessity. Essentially devices for needed transportation, they soon developed into a badge of freedom and equality—a necessary prop for self-respect. To some,* <u>*ostentation*</u> *seemed more important than transportation.*

What clue or clues indicate the meaning of *ostentation* in the previous sentence? _____

_____

What is your best guess about its meaning? _____

_____

Exercise 2: Practice Makes Perfect

Read the passages below and write your definition of the underlined words.

1. New industries boomed <u>lustily</u>; older ones grew sickly.

   _____

2. The public was made increasingly air-minded by unsung heroes—often <u>martyrs</u>—who appeared as stunt fliers at fairs and other public gatherings.

   _____

3. The automobile contributed notably to improved air and environmental quality, despite its later <u>notoriety</u> as a polluter.

   _____

4. Fed up with the <u>cynicism</u> and debunking of the jazz age, they [Americans] found in this wholesome and handsome youth [Lindbergh] a genuine hero.

   _____

5. From the section "Humans Develop Wings," write the sentence in which you find the word *debunking* on the lines below. Then write its meaning.

   Sentence: _____

   _____

   Meaning: _____

   _____

Using Vocabulary Flashcards

When learning vocabulary, you need a systematic method for recording and remembering specialized words and terms. All the practice in the world is no substitute for a system tailored to your individual needs. This is especially true for vocabulary-heavy courses such as psychology, economics, engineering, political science, and computer science. The following flashcard system provides a method for processing key words while compiling a personal glossary for reference and review.

To begin, suppose that in a music class you encounter a word that is new to you, such as *theme*. Write the word in the upper left corner of a 3 x 5 card, and in the upper right corner write the topic it is related to—in this case, *music*. Underneath this information, copy the sentence in which you found the word. Then write your guess as to what the word means. The front of your card will look something like this:

Front of Card

Word and Topic	theme music
Sentence and Source	"Mozart's music adds an element of danger as he develops his theme." (Music Appreciation)
Guess	The subject of a musical composition

If the context does not present enough clues for a confident guess, you can include the glossary or dictionary definition on the reverse side of the card. Do not write the word itself on the back of the card. Instead, leave a blank in the definition where the word should go. Then write your own sentence using the word correctly, again leaving a blank, for later review.

Back of Card

Glossary or Dictionary Definition	A melody forming the basis for variations of a musical composition is called____
Your Sentence	The _____ of *The Star-Spangled Banner* is meant to stir the emotions.

Guessing the meaning of a word before looking it up in a dictionary will develop your ability to identify unfamiliar words. This is an important skill, as there will be situations in which a dictionary is unavailable or not permitted (such as in an exam). Given practice, you will be surprised at how accomplished you become at outguessing the dictionary.

Write your own sentence for the flashcard in the example below:

Front of Card

Word and Topic	repression defense mechanisms
Sentence and Source	"You might be angry at the way your parents treated you as a child. But you don't feel comfortable confronting them, so you suppress your feelings." (Psychology)
Guess	To deny one's feelings by hiding them.

Back of Card

Glossary or Dictionary Definition	_____ is forcing thoughts and feelings out of our consciousness by forgetting a painful or significant experience.
Your Sentence	

Flashcards are a useful tool for review. Before looking at the front of the card, mentally fill in the blanks on the back. When you can remember the meaning of a word from its context, you understand it. When you begin to use the word in conversation or writing, you have made it yours.

If you accumulate a large number of flashcards, don't try to master them all at once. Instead, divide them into stacks of ten; by working with ten cards every day, in five days you can easily master 50 words.

Using Spatial Maps to Remember Word Meanings

As an alternative method for remembering word meanings, it can be helpful to create **spatial maps** that organize terms into groups that relate to an overall topic in some way.

Suppose that you are taking an economics course. Your instructor emphasizes that all economic systems are based on factors of production, which include *land,* a term for natural resources; *labor,* the ability to produce goods and services; *capital,* or wealth, goods, and services; and *entrepreneurs,* who organize all of the other factors in order to produce goods and services.

A spatial map illustrating the factors of production of the United States' economic system might look like this:

U.S. ECONOMIC SYSTEM

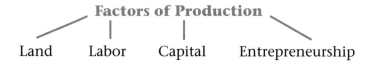

In this spatial map, the words are organized like an upside-down tree, moving from the general to the specific. Factors of production are the basis of all economic systems. *Land, labor, capital,* and *entrepreneurship* are the specific factors or elements that make up the economic system of the United States.

Here is another example. Assume that the topic in a political science class is *gerrymandering.* Gerrymandering is a political strategy used by political parties and their incumbents to change district boundaries for their own benefit. They redistrict a ward to include a greater or lesser number of constituents of a particular political, economic, or ethnic persuasion.

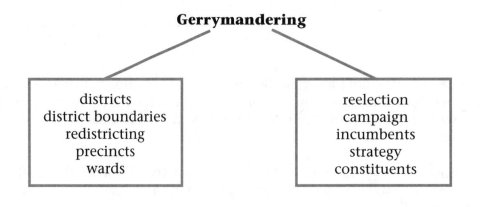

In this type of spatial mapping, you first write down words you already know, such as *district* and *reelection.* Then, underneath, you list new words and key terms that relate to these familiar words. For example, you list *incumbents* and *constituents* under reelection because they are related to reelection.

The advantage of using spatial maps to memorize is that you can connect the words to a topic (in this case, reelection, which in turn relates to the overall subject of gerrymandering), instead of trying to memorize a list of isolated definitions.

Exercise 3

The following paragraph is typical textbook material for a literature survey course. Underline key words and then map the ones relating to the topic of characterization.

> Characterization involves both major and minor characters. Major, or "round," characters are usually three-dimensional, fully developed, complex people who struggle with internal and external problems toward a better understanding of themselves and their environment. Minor, or "flat," characters, however, usually reveal only superficial traits. They serve an author's specific purpose, such as an alter-ego for the main character or a stock character (the butler or next-door neighbor).

> Characters can be either dynamic or static. Dynamic major characters change and evolve through the story's conflicts. At the end, they are no longer the same people they were at the beginning. In contrast, static characters (usually minor) remain the same throughout.

Create your map here:

> ***Personal Response Check:*** As a result of studying how to guess from context, use flashcards, and create spatial maps to learn vocabulary words,
>
> I realize that   (1)_____
>
>   (2)_____

Application Assignment: History Text

Application 1

Turn to the heading "The Radio Revolution" on page 320 to practice more guessing from context. As you read, locate the words listed below and write the sentence in which the word appears. Guess its meaning, then check your answer in the glossary or dictionary.

1. *sustained*

   Sentence: _____

   _____

   Guess: <u>bolstered or supported by</u>_____

   Definition: _____

2. *drabber*

   Sentence:_____

   _____

   Guess: _____

   Definition: _____

3. *perennial*

   Sentence:_____

   _____

   Guess: _____

   Definition: _____

4. *medium*

   Sentence: _____

   _____

   Guess: _____

   Definition: _____

5. *gospel*

   Sentence: _____

   _____

   Guess: _____

   Definition: _____

Suggested Activity: With a classmate, discuss which clues helped you infer meaning for the vocabulary in this exercise. Are there different meanings for some of these words outside of American history? Quiz each other on the words you have learned.

Self-Contract

As a result of studying about how to develop my vocabulary, I would like to change my study strategies to include:

_____

_____

_____

_____

_____

_____

I will practice these new techniques for at least_____weeks to determine if I want to adopt them as a part of my permanent study strategies. Then I will complete the Progress Report below.

Signed:_____   Date:_____

Self-Contract Progress Report

Progress I have made toward these changes:_____

_____

_____

_____

_____

_____

_____Date:_____

Stage Three, Step Five Journal Entry

People can be divided into three groups: those who make things happen, those who watch things happen, and those who wonder what happened.

—John W. Newburn

Date: _____

Discuss how vocabulary plays a role in the courses you are now taking. Which courses have the most demanding vocabularies? Which tests use vocabularies that you find difficult? What are your strategies for learning a difficult vocabulary? Are these strategies successful?

_____

_____

_____

_____

_____

_____

_____

_____

_____

_____

_____

_____

_____

_____

_____

How do I know what the main idea is?
—David Goldstein

Step Six
Improve Your Lecture and Textbook Notes

Objectives

❏ To understand what to do before, during, and after lectures and text readings
❏ To practice telegraphic note-taking methods
❏ To learn different lecture and note-taking styles and strategies

Contents

❏ Lecture Notes
❏ Evaluation of Lecture Classes
❏ Steps in the Lecture Note-Taking Process
❏ Questions Students Frequently Ask About Lecture Note-Taking
❏ Telegraphic Note-Taking: Sentence Fragments and Abbreviations
❏ Question/Answer Lecture Note-Taking Method
    Linear Note-Taking Method
    Mapping Note-Taking Method
❏ Combination of Linear and Spatial Notes
❏ Organization of Disorganized Notes
❏ Combined Text and Lecture Notes
❏ TIPS and the Traditional Outline
❏ Steps in the Textbook Note-Taking Process
❏ Summary Map of Step Six
❏ Application Assignments: History Text

Key Terms

active listener
auditory, visual, and kinesthetic learners
objective and subjective
organizational patterns
telegraphic note-taking
linear and spatial note-taking methods
mapping method

Self-Awareness Check:

Check the appropriate blanks:	Often	Sometimes	Rarely
1. I can keep up with my instructors' lectures.	____	____	____
2. I avoid using full sentences to take notes.	____	____	____
3. I make textbook review notes.	____	____	____
4. I highlight my notes and write questions based on them.	____	____	____
5. I use several different methods of lecture and text note-taking.	____	____	____

Lecture Notes

As described in Step 4, when you take notes, you are in a sense "writing" your own textbook. Therefore, it is helpful to keep notes that are as complete as possible. Use the same study method for your lecture notes as you would for a text, with a question column anticipating what your instructor might ask. Taking notes in class forces you to concentrate as an **active listener,** processing the information your instructor is providing—instead of passively sitting back and listening.

The amount of note-taking you do during a lecture will depend on your learning style. Most people are **visual learners.** They tend to take more notes than **auditory learners,** who learn and remember primarily by listening. **Kinesthetic learners** learn best by using their muscles, so note-taking enhances their learning process.

The quotation "Genius is the ability to reduce the complicated to the simple" certainly applies to the skill of note-taking. Good note-takers listen to complicated lectures and reduce them to simple phrases and sentences so that later they can remember the main ideas. Lecture note-taking is like an auditory TIPS: You listen for a topic and its main idea, then add supporting details.

Unfortunately, too many students daydream during lectures. A study of 85 college sophomores at Wayne State University[1] indicated that students' minds tend to drift during a lecture: 20 percent of the students thought about sex, 20 percent about old memories, and 40 percent about miscellaneous matters such as lunch and errands to do. Only 20 percent were actually listening to the lecture, and of that 20 percent only 12 percent were listening actively.

---

[1] *San Francisco Examiner and Chronicle,* September 1, 1968.

Students often let their minds drift because they think much faster than their instructor can lecture. To help you concentrate on what your instructor is saying, take careful notes and try to anticipate what he or she will say next.

Every course is different, and your interest will naturally vary. In some classes, you will have no problem listening actively. Use the following evaluation form to analyze three of your lecture courses.

Evaluation of Lecture Classes

Evaluate your present courses to decide the kind and the amount of lecture notes you should be taking.

Course 1:   Title: _____ Instructor: _____

Into which group does the lecture fall?

_____1. Lecture follows text closely.

_____2. Lecturer uses text as a base only.

_____3. Lecturer pays little or no attention to text.

_____4. A combination of _____ Describe:_____

What percentage of tests will come from: lecture _____% text_____%

What kind of test will be given: objective _____ essay _____ short answer _____

     combination _____ other:_____

Problems I have in taking notes for this class:_____

_____

Course 2:   Title:_____ Instructor: _____

Into which group does the lecture fall?

_____1. Lecture follows text closely.

_____2. Lecturer uses text as a base only.

_____3. Lecturer pays little or no attention to text.

_____4. A combination of _____Describe:_____

What percentage of tests will come from: lecture _____% text _____%

What kind of test will be given: objective _____ essay_____ short answer_____

combination _____ other: _____

Problems I have in taking notes for this class: _____

_____

Course 3:   Title: _____ Instructor: _____

Into which group does the lecture fall?

_____1.   Lecture follows text closely.

_____2.   Lecturer uses text as a base only.

_____3.   Lecturer pays little or no attention to text.

_____4.   A combination of_____Describe:_____

What percentage of tests will come from: lecture _____% text _____%

What kind of test will be given: objective _____ essay_____ short answer_____

combination _____ other: _____

Problems I have in taking notes for this class:_____

_____

Steps in the Lecture Note-Taking Process

The First Week of Class

Find out as much as you can about the kinds of tests your instructor will give. Will the questions be **objective** (true/false, multiple choice, matching, completion), **subjective** (short answer and essay), or a combination of both?

Before a Lecture

Skim through the topic of the lecture in your textbook to gain a general idea of what the instructor will be talking about. Doing so will familiarize you with some of the terms, names, and ideas that may be included. You'll also know how to spell difficult words and where to concentrate your note-taking. If you do not know what the instructor will lecture on, simply ask in advance. Most instructors are impressed when a student cares enough to read ahead.

During a Lecture

Leave extra space in your notes when something is not clear or if you can't keep up. Put a question mark in the margin as a reminder to obtain this information from a classmate, your instructor, or a book. Do not outline unless the lecture is so organized that outlining comes easily. Concentrate on listening for main ideas and supporting details. When you hear something that reminds you of an example from your own experience, jot down "EX" and a note to trigger your memory.

If you have determined that you will be tested with objective questions, make sure to note specific information as well as general ideas. If you will be asked subjective questions, concentrate on general ideas with supporting points, but skip very detailed information. If there will be a mix of objective and subjective questions, do the best you can with both general ideas and specifics, remembering that if you jot down key words, you can always look up definitions and details later.

If your instructor follows the text closely, you need only jot down key words if you already know that full explanations are in your text. Listen mainly for indications of what your instructor considers important. If, on the other hand, your instructor uses the text as a base only, concentrate on new information that supplements your text.

Some instructors do not lecture on what is in the text because their students can read that information on their own time. Instead, these instructors provide almost completely new material. For these lectures, take especially careful notes, marking key words that you need to look up later.

Watch for instructors' clues that something is important. Examples: the instructor pauses before introducing a new topic, speaks more slowly, repeats a phrase, writes on the board, or uses emphatic body language.

At the End of a Lecture

Before you leave your seat, quickly skim over your notes (for one to two minutes at the most). Add points, ideas, and question marks while your memory is still fresh.

After a Lecture

Within a few hours, read over your notes, fill in missing information, and decide whether they need to be reorganized. If your notes are disorganized, use the margin or a separate page to reorganize them. Place your topic for the lecture at the top, sift through your notes to find main ideas, and then look for points that support each main idea.

As your next step, use the Q/A (question and answer) format you learned in Step 4 to anticipate what questions your instructor may ask. You cannot formulate a question unless you understand the material, so this will help you spot areas that you need to work on.

Within 24 Hours

Quiz yourself with your Q/A notes. It is important to read your Q/A aloud so that you can hear yourself answer the questions. This may strike you as odd, but when you listen to yourself, you can better spot questions that you have not adequately answered. Also, auditory learners tend to absorb information best from hearing their answers.

At the Beginning of the Next Class

Arrive a few minutes early and find a classmate who takes good notes. Ask for any information that you are missing. You may also want to team up with a classmate to exchange sets of notes at the end of each class. Use carbon paper to make an extra set. (This is much easier than constantly making photocopies and certainly much cheaper.) Get into the habit of studying, exchanging notes, and cooperating with classmates. However, do not depend on someone else's notes as a substitute for your own.

Questions Students Frequently Ask About Lecture Note-Taking

Before reading the answers below, try to answer the questions yourself.

How can I become a better listener?

- ■ Attend every lecture so that you do not lose track of topics covered.

- ■ Skim over the lecture topic in your text before the lecture (see above).

- ■ Sit toward the front of the room, where there are fewer distractions.

- ■ Listen for signal words that indicate the **organizational pattern** your instructor is using to explain class material. Examples:

  - • Sequence (*first, second, third, in conclusion*)

  - • Comparison (*this is similar to, this is also an example of, similarly*)

  - • Contrast (*however, in contrast, unlike this*)

  - • Causes (*one reason, another cause*)

  - • Effects (*this results in, another effect*)

  - • Classification or types (*one group is. . . another type is. . .*)

  - • Problem solution (*the problem includes several possible solutions*)

  - • List (*there are five basic food types; let's discuss three examples*)

- ■ Listen for signal words that indicate the instructor is changing topics (*now let's look at, we must also consider, another important issue is*).

- ■ Listen for examples that support points (*one example is, to illustrate, one case study points out*).

> *Suggested Activity:* Brainstorm other ideas for becoming an active listener.

Should I write on both sides of a page in my notebook?

No. Save the back sides so that you can make outlines, write TIPS, make Q/A sheets, or add information from other students' notes or your text.

Should I use pen or pencil to take notes?

Use a pen for most courses. You can write faster, read better, and avoid pencil smudges. If you make an error with a pen, just cross it out.

Should I use a tape recorder to take notes?

The problem with using a tape recorder is that you may come to depend on it rather than on improving your note-taking skills. Also, consider the time you will spend listening to the tape. You have already devoted an hour in class, and now you will need to spend another hour listening to the lecture again—and more time to transcribe your notes.

However, there are certain situations where using a tape recorder is advisable. For example, if you have an instructor who talks so rapidly that you cannot keep up, or if you are an extremely poor note-taker and can't find a classmate willing to share notes, then you may want to use a recorder as a backup to note-taking. If you use a tape recorder with a counter, record the counter number every few minutes in the notes that you are taking. When you clean up your notes, you can quickly find missing information on your tape. But avoid using the tape recorder as a "crutch."

Should I highlight my lecture notes the same way as I do my textbook notes?

Yes, but sparingly. Most students tend to highlight so much that the result is meaningless. If you highlight more than about 10 percent of a page, you have probably defeated your purpose.

Should I use a spiral notebook or a three-ring binder?

The three-ring binder has far more advantages. You can change the order of your notes and insert handouts. You can leave the notebook at home, where it will not be lost or stolen. Take extra paper with you to school, and at the end of the day insert that day's notes. Also, at the conclusion of the course, you can file your notes so that you can reuse the binder and any extra paper.

How can I take notes in a dark room when the instructor is showing slides or a movie?

Purchase a pen with a small built-in flashlight. If you can't find one, use a "penlight" flashlight. First, however, you may want to ask the instructor if taking notes is necessary.

What should I do when a classmate wants to borrow my notes?

Never let your notes out of your sight. A classmate who wants to borrow them to copy may lose them. However, you can still be helpful to a classmate by offering to walk to the nearest photocopy machine.

Suggested Activity: In a class discussion, seek possible answers and solutions for other note-taking problems.

Personal Response Check: As a result of learning about note-taking,

I realize that   (1)_____

(2)_____

Telegraphic Note-Taking: Sentence Fragments and Abbreviations

One of the reasons you may not be taking thorough notes is that you are trying to write in complete sentences—attempting to transcribe verbatim almost everything the instructor says. To increase your speed, use **telegraphic note-taking** (i.e., incomplete sentences) and abbreviations as much as possible. Develop your own form of shorthand, but make sure that you will be able to read it at a later date. Consider the following sentence and the important underlined words.

> Vincent <u>Van Gogh</u> was a <u>Dutch artist</u> who painted his famous <u>Starry Night</u> to show the <u>energy of nature.</u>

Rather than write down this entire sentence, you might jot down:

> *Van Gogh — Dutch painter — Starry Night* = nature is energy

Exercise 1:

For the following sentences from an art history lecture, first underline the key words, then write telegraphic notes.

1. Vincent Van Gogh's *Starry Night* impresses us because of the painting's powerful sense of movement and vitality.

2. This painting depicts the universe as overwhelming compared to the insignificance of man.

3. Van Gogh's canvas is alive with swirling light patterns and trees that reach toward the heavens.

Suggested Activity: Take turns with a classmate practicing telegraphic note-taking. (One person dictates a sentence while the other writes down key words.)

Exercise 2:

One of the best ways to break the habit of taking notes in sentence format is to practice taking notes during a TV or radio news program. There is no way that you can keep up with a news reporter unless you resort to telegraphic note-taking.

In this exercise, take notes as you listen to five minutes of news, and record at least five news items. Study the following example of one news item below before beginning the assignment.

Example

Topics	*Points*

Downtown Fire	- Tues 6pm
	- 4th & Main
	- old hotel
	    -68 escaped
	    - 2 injured
	        -1 old man
	        -1 child
	    - fire trap
	    - bldg. destroyed

Now begin the assignment. To record five new items, you may need to use additional paper.

Topics	Points

Using Abbreviations

Are you using abbreviations whenever possible? The common abbreviations below may include some that you already use:

&	=	and	w/	=	with
#	=	number	w/o	=	without
%	=	percent	w/n	=	within
=	=	equals	<	=	less than
$	=	money	>	=	more than
@	=	at	+	=	plus
~	=	approximately	s/b	=	should be

Two helpful shorthand abbreviations are the dot (.) to replace *ing* and the slash (/) for *ed*. The dot goes below the word so that it doesn't look like a period.

For example: painting = paint   painted = paint

Exercise 3:

Practice using the dot for *ing* and the slash for *ed:*

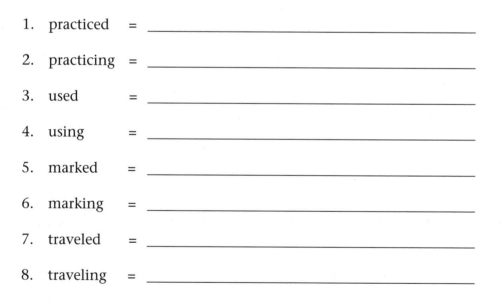

1. practiced   = _____

2. practicing = _____

3. used   = _____

4. using   = _____

5. marked   = _____

6. marking   = _____

7. traveled   = _____

8. traveling   = _____

Another technique is to omit vowels to shorten a word. Can you read these sentences?

1. *U cn sv tme if u lrn to tk ntes.*

2. *We r lrn that we have us/ too mch effrt in nte-tk*

Make a list of words you use frequently in a particular class and insert abbreviations for them. For example, in an art history class, the following words are often used:

artist   (artst)
abstract   (abstrct)
chromatic   (chrmtc)
classic   (clssc)
color   (clr)
painting   (pnt)
brush   (brsh)

Suggested Activity: With a partner, take turns talking about what each of you has learned from this course. While one partner talks, the other should take notes using some of the techniques suggested above.

Exercise 4

For a class you are taking, list five words you hear often in lectures. Then write them in abbreviated form, omitting vowels and using dots and slashes.

Class: _____

1. _____   (_____)

2. _____   (_____)

3. _____   (_____)

4. _____   (_____)

5. _____   (_____)

Personal Response Check: As a result of practicing telegraphic note-taking techniques,

I realize that   (1)_____

(2)_____

Question/Answer Lecture Note-Taking Method

Linear Note-Taking Method

In Step 4 you learned about the Q/A format. Taking lecture notes with question/answer columns is actually a TIPS approach. Your topic (T) is a heading for your notes; questions in the left margin are the main ideas (I) about the points (P) you jotted down during the lecture in the right column. Summaries (S) are optional but help prepare for short answer and essay test questions. (Write your summaries in a different colored ink for easy retrieval during reviews.) The summary and questions are written after the lecture.

The following **linear lecture notes** for an art course demonstrate the Q/A method, based on the Cornell note-taking system.[2] The letters in parentheses reflect how the Q/A format relates to TIPS.

<table>
<tr>
<td colspan="2" align="right">Art 101/Date</td>
</tr>
<tr>
<td colspan="2" align="center">**Paolo Soleri's Arcology (T)**</td>
</tr>
<tr>
<td align="center">**Questions (I)**</td>
<td align="center">**Answers (P)**</td>
</tr>
<tr>
<td>Who is Paolo Soleri?</td>
<td>- Paolo Soleri (1919-   )
   - visionary and utopian architect
   - student of Frank Lloyd Wright
   - rebelled against Wright's theories</td>
</tr>
<tr>
<td>What is arcology?</td>
<td>- arcology = ecological architecture, making good use
   of land, eliminating sources of pollution</td>
</tr>
<tr>
<td>What is Soleri's vision?</td>
<td>- large cities under one roof: handle all man's needs
   Ex: a structure to house 1 million people under 1 roof
     - 300 stories high, 14 sq. acres</td>
</tr>
<tr>
<td>What are the benefits of arcological structures?</td>
<td>- Benefits:
   - economic use of land
   - freedom from pollution
    - Ex: no cars</td>
</tr>
<tr>
<td>*Summary:* (S)
(in different colored ink)</td>
<td>Paolo Soleri is a utopian architect who rejects Frank Lloyd Wright's theories and advocates "arcology," using ecology and architecture to design mammoth cities under one roof to serve all man's needs. This makes more economic use of land by having 1 million people in a 300-story high-rise, under one roof. Also eliminates most pollution; e.g., no cars.</td>
</tr>
</table>

[2] Adapted from Walter Pauk's Cornell Note-Taking System. (1989). In *How to Study in College*, pp. 144–153. Boston: Houghton Mifflin.

Mapping Note-Taking Method

The linear note-taking method does not match every student's learning style. The **mapping method** is one alternative to consider. This system uses the same spatial format you have studied earlier in this book.

As your instructor lectures, draw lines and insert words and phrases, subdividing major and minor points like the branches of a tree. Do not try to put too much information on one map. (See the example that follows.)

You can still create a question column on the same page or on the opposite page. Unfortunately, this system does not allow for each question to be directly opposite its answer. Another disadvantage is that you are limited to very few words: avoid putting too much information on one page or you will defeat the purpose of a clear map. Start a new map for each new idea in the lecture.

Lecture Topic: Consumers

Steps in the Buying Process

Desire ⟶ Recognition ⟶ Search ⟶ Purchase Decision ⟶ Product use and evaluation

Consumer Satisfaction

Product benefits	=	Economical Efficient Pleasurable
Product purchase	=	Budget constraints Brand loyalty (Ex: toothpaste) Advertising influence
Consumer profile	=	Perceptions Preferences Lifestyle (Ex: student) Geographic factors Demographic factors Income (Ex: student loans)

Summary: _____

_____

_____

Questions:

1. What are three aspects that lead to consumer satisfaction?

2. What are four factors of a customer's profile?

3. Name three influences that can lead to the purchase of a product.

Combination of Linear and Spatial Notes

Many students prefer to combine linear and spatial note-taking methods, demonstrated by the following example.

Psychology 102

Lecture Topic: Maslow's Theory of Self-Actualization

Different theories on how motives originate and operate:
      1. Behaviorist psychologist = <u>learned systems</u>
                                           biological drives
      2. Cognitive psychologist = mental process to make decisions
                                        brain = executive
      3. Humanistic psychologist = humans seek development of their potential

Maslow's Theory of Self-Actualization

Optimal

Self-Actualization
*Ex: Using my talents and skills
to reach full potential*

Esteem
Ex: Recognizing my talents and skills

Feeling loved and sense of belonging
Ex: Being loved by my family

Safety
Ex: Living in a crime-free area

Basic need

Physical satisfaction
Ex: Having food and shelter

Summary: Before we can reach our full potential, we must have food and shelter to meet our basic needs, must feel we are safe and loved, and must feel good about ourselves.

Questions: _____

_____

_____

Organization of Disorganized Notes

Open up your binder or notebook so that it is lying flat, with the back of the previous page on the left side and the front of a new page on the right. If you take notes only on the right, then you have the left free for making outlines, mapping, writing questions or summaries, and adding other supplemental information. The back (i.e., the left-hand page in the example below) is also useful for reorganizing jumbled lecture notes—preferably in a TIPS format like this example.

Example on Heart Disease

	Health/Date
Back of Last Page (Left Side) (Notes Organized After Lecture)	Front of Next Page (Right Side) (Disorganized Lecture Notes)

Topic: the heart
 	
■ <u>Statistics</u>
      - 1991: over 800,000 died
      - recent decline but still #1 killer
      - more young dying
 	
■ <u>The Heart</u>
      - size of fist
      - adult size, about 11 oz.
 	
■ <u>Make-up</u>
      - cardiac muscle largest
         involuntary muscle
      - lined w/ layers of cells & muscle
      - outside: protective sac of fluid
 	
<u>Summary:</u> Heart disease is still #1 killer and more young are dying. 1991: over 800,000 died, although recent decline. Heart in adult is size of fist, about 11 oz., lined with layers of cells and muscles, outside protected by a sac of fluid. Body's largest involuntary muscle.
 	
Questions:_____
 	
_____
 	
_____
	Topic: the heart
	
	      - lined w/ muscle
	      - 1991
	      - over 800,000 died
	      - recent decline
	      - lined w/ layers of cells
	      - size of fist
	      - outside—protective sac of fluid
	      - still #1 killer
	      - adult heart ~ 11 oz.
	      - largest involuntary muscle
	      - more young dying
	
	Note: These disorganized notes on the right provide points that are not grouped. The organized notes on the left divide the points into three main points and suggest the main idea in the first sentence of the summary.

Combined Text and Lecture Notes

Another variation is to use the left side of a page for textbook notes that relate to lecture notes on the right side. The purpose is to combine information in one place for easier studying. This variation also includes marginal key terms that can be mentally turned into questions. For example, the marginal phrase *personal life* can become the question *How did Emily Dickinson's personal life influence her poetry?*

Example of Combining Text and Lecture Notes on Poet Emily Dickinson

| Left Side (Text Notes) | Emily Dickinson | Eng. 1B/Date |
	Right Side (Lecture Notes)	

- father:
  strong Calvinist, dominated
    daughter
- enjoyed intense intellectual
  friendships:
  - Benjamin Newton, law
    student who encouraged
    her as a poet
  - Rev. Charles Wadsworth left
    for California; supposedly
    the "lover" in her poems
  - T. W. Higginson, wrote for
    The Atlantic, encouraged
    her writing
	personal life
	
	intellectual
	friendships
	
	characteristics
	of her poetry
		- dominated by father
		- lived at home, last 25 yrs,
		    secluded
		- composed almost 1000 brief
		    poems on scraps of paper
		- beat influenced by hymns
		- impudent with God
		- intrigued by death in
		    "graveyard" poems
		- only a few poems published
		    while she was alive, w/o
		    her consent

TIPS and the Traditional Outline

A linear or spatial TIPS is an effective method for organizing material in traditional outline form. A discussion and examples of this approach can be found in Step 2 on pages 87 and 91.

Steps in the Textbook Note-Taking Process

As they read, most successful students also take notes as a supplement to their marginal questions and key words. Keeping a record in a notebook of what you have studied is like having your own database, a personal retrieval system that makes knowledge your own. When you take notes for a chapter, you are in effect creating a "minichapter" that is both simple (in words that you can understand) and brief enough to capture the main ideas and selected details.

Taking notes from your textbook is worth the effort if:

- Your instructor does not lecture on text material and you need text review notes.

- You want to translate text material into visual aid summaries, such as spatial maps, diagrams, charts, and illustrations.

- You want to add text notes opposite your lecture notes.

- You are a kinesthetic learner, and taking text notes aids your memory.

- You want to review text chapters without having to carry the book with you.

- You become overwhelmed by so much text material and need an outline or summary of the main ideas.

Your first step in taking textbook notes should be to skim the chapter to understand what it is about; then read more slowly, marking the text with highlighting, questions, and/or marginal key words.

Next, determine what text information you may be tested on that is difficult for you to remember. This is the information to record in your review notes, not everything in a chapter or subsection.

Your next decision is how and where to record these text notes—in linear or spatial form, or a combination; on notecards; in a separate binder; on the back of or opposite related lecture notes?

The following examples illustrate several possible formats for text note-taking. The Q/A format[3] mentioned on page 181 of this chapter works well for text notes. Divide your paper into two columns and list notes from the text on the right and questions your instructor might ask on the left. Your notes should follow the same structure as the headings and subheadings of the chapter, in effect creating an outline.

---

[3] Pauk, 144–153.

Below is a sample of a typical literature text chapter with a title, headings, and subheadings.

Chapter 1: Reading Fiction

Definition of Fiction
Types of Fiction
Elements of Fiction
    Plot
    Point of View
    Character
    Setting
    Theme
    Tone and Style
    Symbolism

Review notes for this chapter in the Q/A format might look like this:

Reading Fiction	Eng. 1B/Ch.2
What is the definition of fiction?	■ Word comes from Latin word meaning "to form." ■ Stories at least partially imagined, made up. May be based on fact but not entirely true (Example: Norman Mailer's *The Executioner's Song*).
What are types of fiction?	■ Two main forms: short story and novel.
What is plot?	■ Plot = progression of events in the story.

You may prefer the TIPS format, which includes **T**opic, **I**dea, **P**oints, and **S**ummary:

T =   Reading Fiction

I =   Fiction: stories (imagined or at least partially imagined)

P =
- may be based on fact, not entirely true
(Ex: Mailer's *The Executioner's Song*)
- the word *fiction* comes from Latin word "to form"
- two types of fiction:
  - short story
  - novel
- plot: progression of events in the story

S =   Fiction, from a Latin word meaning "to form," consists of stories, imagined or at least partially made up. Fiction has two main forms, the short story and novel. One element of fiction is plot, the progression of events in the story.

Both the Q/A and TIPS formats separate main ideas from supporting points; however, one emphasizes questions and the other a summary. If you are taking an objective test, you may prefer the Q/A format for review notes, while TIPS may be more effective for short answer and essay exams.

The following is an example of spatial text notes:

English 1B

Comparison/contrast of two characters in John Updike's short story "A & P"

As you have seen, there are many different ways to take notes. What is most important is the relationship between your note-taking methods and your test results. If your test scores

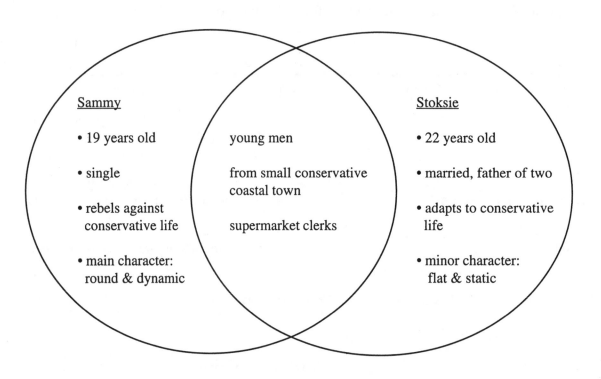

are low because your notes are incomplete or ineffective, consider trying some of the ideas in this chapter.

If your notes seem to be complete, the problem may be your review technique. Many students find that they absorb material better if they explain it to someone else, using their notes for reference. This approach is helpful even when you are alone, because by acting as both lecturer and listener, you move from a visual to an auditory memory system. As you talk aloud about material you're reviewing, you can add details and ideas that are meaningful to you and thus make it easier to remember. This review technique proves the adage that "we learn best what we teach to others."

How much you benefit from note-taking will largely depend upon your learning style and your desire to improve your grades.

Summary Map of Step Six

Improve Your Lecture and Textbook Notes

Lecture Notes

Steps in lecture note-taking

- Evaluation of lecture class
- Before a lecture
- During a lecture
- End of lecture
- After lecture
- Within 24 hours after lecture
- Beginning of next class

Questions students ask about note-taking

Telegraphic note-taking shortcuts
  Fragments
  Abbreviations

Text Notes

Combine text and lecture notes

Organize disorganized notes

Use TIPS and Q/A
    Linear notes
    Spatial map
    Traditional outline

Application Assignments: History Text

Application 1

Turn to the heading titled "Hollywood's Filmland Fantasies" on page 321. Skim over the reading and decide which note-taking method will produce the best results (i.e., linear or spatial). To check your decision, choose a partner to read the section aloud to you while you take notes. Please keep in mind that quality in note-taking is not measured in quantity but in how useful the notes are in the future.

Use the space below and additional paper if necessary. Provide at least three questions and a summary of about 25 words.

Class: _____ Date: _____

Title: _____

_____

_____

_____

_____

_____

_____

_____

_____

_____

_____

_____

_____

_____

_____

Application 2

Take notes in one of your other classes, using either the linear or the mapping method. After class, add questions, a summary, and textbook notes if appropriate. Attach your set of notes or a photocopy to this sheet when you turn it in to your instructor.

Personal Response Check: As a result of studying about and practicing note-taking methods,

I realize that   (1) _____

(2) _____

Self-Contract

From my practice using lecture and text note-taking methods, I would like to adopt the following study strategies:

_____

_____

_____

_____

_____

_____

I will practice these new techniques for at least_____weeks to determine if I want to adopt them as a part of my permanent study strategies. Then I will complete the Progress Report below.

Signed:_____ Date:_____

Self-Contract Progress Report

Progress I have made toward these changes:_____

_____

_____

_____

_____

_____

_____Date:_____

Stage Three, Step Six Journal Entry

I am part of all I have read.

—John Kiernan

I know of but one freedom, and that is freedom of the mind.
—Antoine de Saint-Exupéry

Date: _____

One way for what you have read to become a part of you is to record words and their ideas by taking notes. Discuss any note-taking problems you have. Include at least one note-taking strategy you intend to try.

Now freewrite about where you stand in each of your classes. How does note-taking relate to your grades? How satisfied are you with your grades?

What are some of the interesting ideas you have learned in each class? For each class, what more do you want to learn? What questions do you have about each subject that are still unanswered? How have you changed or grown by taking these courses?

The art of remembering is the art of thinking. . . . Our conscious effort should not be so much to impress or retain [knowledge] as to connect it with something already there.

—William James

Step Seven
Review and Memorize

Key Terms

checkmark review method
study group
association
visual memory system
auditory memory system
kinesthetic memory system
grouping
repetition
pocket learning
distributed learning
mnemonic techniques

Self-Awareness Check:

Check the appropriate blanks:	**Often**	**Sometimes**	**Rarely**
1. I begin reviewing within 24 hours of reading.	___	___	___
2. I mark passages that I do not understand.	___	___	___
3. I use alternate sources in addition to my texts and lecture notes.	___	___	___
4. I know four mnemonic study techniques.	___	___	___
5. I use a study group to prepare for tests.	___	___	___

The Reviewing Process

My study system is simple:
1. *Budget time.*
2. *Study away from home.*
3. *Carry study materials every day (books, pens, reference materials, etc.) so I can study in case an instructor doesn't show up or dismisses class early.*
4. *Review, review, review.*

—**Rebecca Thure**

Using the Checkmark Review Method

A key to earning better grades is developing a systematic way of reviewing. Too often students decide randomly what to study, when to study, and how to study. Their hit-and-miss approach misses more than it hits. Human nature seeks pleasure, not pain; therefore, when students review, they tend to ask themselves questions to which they already know the answers.

The **checkmark review method**[1] protects you from yourself—it forces you to concentrate on what you do not know rather than on material you have already mastered. It also offers an element of challenge and the reward of accomplishment, taking the drudgery out of studying.

---

[1] This method was suggested by Dr. Phoebe Helm, Truman College, River Grove, Illinois.

In this method, you will be in competition with yourself: the goal is to eliminate (after three checks) questions you know how to answer.

Here is how the checkmark review method works.

Step 1: Quiz yourself by reading aloud the questions you have written in your notebook and textbook question columns. Then determine how well you answered the question. You may have to reread the answer to judge. If you answered correctly, put a check (✓) under the question.

If you did not answer correctly, put an X under the question and then immediately take time to reread the material so that you will know the answer the next time.

Step 2: Review again within 24 hours. Follow the same procedure, putting a ✓ or X next to the previous mark. Take time to restudy the X questions that you could not answer.

Step 3: Every day or two, keep reviewing using a ✓ or X. Each time you review, your speed in answering will increase. When you accumulate three checkmarks, draw a circle around all the marks to indicate that you have mastered that question. Skip it in your next review.

Example: Explain Teddy Roosevelt's four main accomplishments as president of the United States.

Step 4: Continue to review regularly until you accumulate three checkmarks for each question.

Step 5: Return occasionally to review the circled questions in order to retain the material. Pay special attention to questions you did not answer correctly three consecutive times.

Step 6: For troublesome questions, use Q/A flashcards when you have free time for reviewing. Put a question on the front of the card and the answer on the back. Use the checkmark review method on the flashcards by marking an X or ✓ under the question each time you quiz yourself. After a total of three checkmarks, put the cards aside; return to them for an occasional review.

Sample of Checkmark Review Method

Topic: Influences on America   Political Science 10/2

How has geo.
influenced Am.?

(x√√√)

— large → need to be decentralized
— US isolated from Europe, Africa, Asia, etc.
  — until 20th c. = policy of isolationism
  – few international commitments
  – no military alliances
  — no foreign invasion

How has demography
influenced Am.?

(x√x√√)

– demography = analysis of pop. charac.
  (race, sex, age, etc.)
— growth
    –1790 - 4 m.
    –1974 - 211 m.
  c/c = U.S. av. 58 inhab. per sq. mi.
    China " 216 " " " "
— urbanization
— diversity

Knowledge is of two kinds. We know a subject ourselves or we know where we can find information upon it.
—Samuel Johnson

Seeking Alternate Sources to Explain Difficult Material

Most books, even easy-to-read ones, contain confusing passages. Too often students tend to zip right past these sections, hoping that they are not important. Here is a simple technique for handling difficult or confusing parts of your texts or lectures.

■ As you read your text and write questions in the margins, use a pencil to make question marks when you do not understand something.

■ Later, check an alternate source, such as an encyclopedia or reference book, that will help explain it. Another textbook might provide a clearer explanation.

■ Once you understand the difficult passage, erase your question mark.

Alternately, you can seek help from your instructor, a classmate, or a tutor.

Exercise 1

Think about the courses you are taking now. Is there a topic that you are confused about?

Course:_____ Topic: _____

List sources you can consult within the next two days:

1. _____ 2. _____

> **Suggested Activity:** Compare with a group of students those topics that are troubling you and what sources you plan to consult. Do your classmates have any other alternative sources to suggest?

Forming a Study Group

At the University of California, Berkeley, Professor Philip Uri Treisman studied Chinese students who did well in calculus and found that the key to their high grades was their dedication to group work. They studied together each week, doing their homework, comparing answers, working through old examinations, and tutoring each other. In contrast, Treisman found that African Americans did not tend to study together and did rather poorly on tests. After this study, Treisman formed Mathematics Workshops to create a supportive group approach to supplement regular math courses. As a result of these workshops, African American students with good SAT math scores outperformed white and Asian students with better SAT math scores.[2]

---

[2]Robert E. Fullilove and Philip Uri Treisman. (1990). "Mathematics Achievement at the University of California, Berkeley: An Evaluation of the Mathematics Workshop Program," *Journal of Negro Education*, vol. 59; 3:463–478.

Reviewing alone is only one way to study. Most people benefit from studying with others, at least to some extent. Much depends on your personality, your ability to find responsible group partners, and your available study time. A **study group** should consist of no more than three or four dedicated members, each willing to

- accept a specific group task to accomplish before the next meeting (e.g., write ten potential test questions for a chapter)

- be on time for study group meetings and stay until they conclude

- stick to the topic

- put forth sincere effort

Exercise 2

Write down the names of at least six students you would want in your study group for a course you are taking. (Some of your choices might not be available. Take into consideration ability, trust, compatibility, and responsibility.)

Title of course: _____

Names:

1. _____   4. _____

2. _____   5. _____

3. _____   6. _____

> **Suggested Activity:** Find out whether any of your classmates are taking the same courses you are and if any are interested in forming a study group.

The Memorizing Process

Most of us forget much of what we read in a text or hear in a lecture within a few hours—unless we review it. After a week's time, typical retention declines to 20 percent (see chart), and after a month to only 2 percent.[3] If you doubt these statistics, think about a lecture that you attended several weeks ago and have not reviewed. How much can you remember about the topic discussed? Unless you were fascinated by the lecture, you probably remember very little. But how many times have you chosen not to take notes because you thought, "Oh, I'll remember that!"? Your brain takes in so much information every day that the details can easily escape you if you do nothing with them.

---

[3] Ian M. L. Hunter. (1957). *Memory: Facts and Fallacies,* p. 83. Baltimore, MD: Penguin.

Typical Rate of Memory Loss[4]

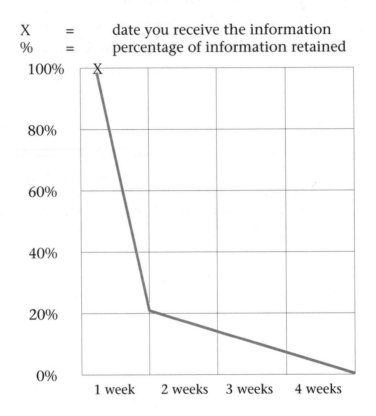

X   =   date you receive the information
%   =   percentage of information retained

One reason that people forget so quickly is the factor of *interference*. For example, assume that at 9 a.m. you attend an ecology class and are fascinated by a film about the destruction of tropical rain forests. At 10:30, you are in a German class but cannot concentrate because your mind is still on the rain forests. Or your concentration on German sentence structure causes you to forget much of the film.

New information constantly flows into your short-term memory, but you lose much of it in a matter of seconds if you do not "process" it into your long-term memory. A combination of memorization techniques will help you achieve this.

[4] Ian M. L. Hunter. (1957). *Memory: Facts and Fallacies,* p. 83. Baltimore: Penguin.

Short-Term and Long-Term Memory

Every waking moment, you're bombarded with data, much of which you ignore. While walking down a street, you cannot be aware of everything around you, each blade of grass or flower or tree; the sounds of horns honking, birds singing, and children playing; the aromas of cooking and car fumes. Consciously or unconsciously, you select what you want to notice.

Think of your memory as a series of systems for processing what you want to remember. Information that you receive via your sensory system (the senses of sight, hearing, touch, taste, and smell) stays with you for only a few seconds or minutes in the short-term memory system. For example, when you get a telephone number from Information, if you don't use it or write it down immediately, you'll probably forget it within seconds. The same thing may happen when you hear your biology instructor define *mitosis* as nuclear cell division in which the chromosome number remains unchanged. To remember such information, you must encode it into your long-term memory system so that it can be retrieved later on. Encoding involves putting information into your own words or into maps that you create.

Information is stored in the long-term memory system in an organized way, sorted into categories and subcategories just as though it were in a computer or file cabinet. This organizational system allows you to find prior knowledge and integrate new information with the old. For the definition of *mitosis,* for example, you would first go to your biology file and then to the reproduction subcategory, where you would create a folder labeled "mitosis."

Because of the organized way in which the long-term memory system works, you may have difficulty with subjects about which you have very little prior knowledge. For this reason alone, it's important to find out what the prerequisites are for the courses you plan to take so that you can acquire the necessary background.

Unless you review information that you have integrated into your long-term memory, it tends to slip into the storage bank, from which it may or may not be retrievable. For instance, a person who studies French for one year can retrieve memorized French vocabulary quite easily during that year, but if the vocabulary is not reviewed during the following year, a significant loss can occur. After five years without review, the person will probably remember very few words. If, however, that person should then visit France, he or she would recognize many French words while there because of the accumulation of French vocabulary in the storage bank from five years before. Also, if the person were to retake the same French class, the stored vocabulary would make learning much easier. In some cases, however, information that has gone into the storage bank cannot be recovered.

The diagram on the following page illustrates how the short- and long-term memory systems work together.

The Short- and Long-Term Memory Systems

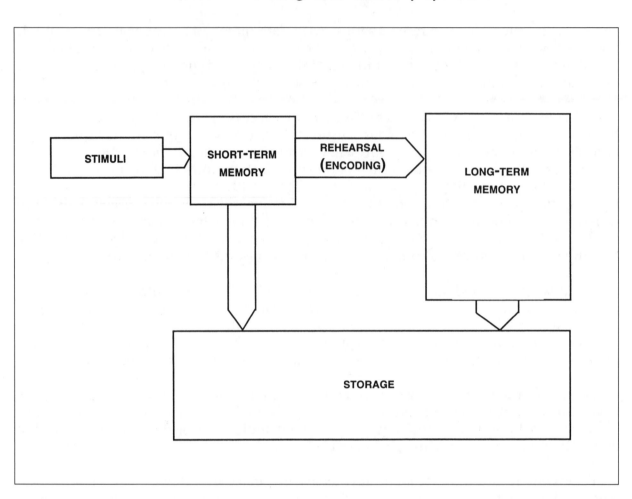

A combination of the following memorization techniques will help you process, encode, and retrieve information.

Memorizing Through Association

If you were asked to memorize the word *lugubrious,* how would you start? You probably have nothing to associate with the word, no way to link it with your own prior knowledge, experience, or feelings.

Learning something new is easier when you use **association**—when you can link the information to what you already know. For example, if you're studying the concept of repression in a psychology course, you might say, "This reminds me of some of the dynamics in my own family." You place the new word or idea into a category and then compare and contrast it with something you know in order to understand it better. If asked to compare censorship of the 1920s with today's, you can make your own connections. Making associations results in understanding and remembering new information more easily. In the following exercise you will be linking new information to what you know.

Exercise 3

Review "The Radio Revolution" and "Hollywood's Filmland Fantasies" on pages 320 and 321 and list the positive and negative effects of these media:

Negative effects of radio: _____

Positive effects of radio: _____

Negative effects of movies: _____

Positive effects of movies: _____ _____

Of these positive and negative effects, which are still being discussed today?

_____

_____

_____

_____

What would be the best improvements for today's "information age"?

_____

_____

_____

_____

Exercise 4

In a psychology class you will study about a defense mechanism called *projection,* the tendency to attribute one's own feelings, motives, and attitudes to another person—especially negative feelings that cause anxiety. For example, suppose that you feel insecure and anxious about yourself. At the same time, you are forever worrying that your supervisor at work is dissatisfied with your performance despite praise about the quality of your work. In effect, you are projecting your anxiety onto your supervisor.

List two examples of projection you have experienced or observed.

1. _____

2. _____

All knowledge has its origins in our perceptions.
—**Leonardo da Vinci**

Memorizing Through Visual, Auditory, and Kinesthetic Systems

If you are going to retain what you learn, it's helpful to bring into play as many of your five senses as possible. When you read, you use your **visual memory system.** When you read aloud, you use your **auditory memory system**—you are not only speaking but hearing yourself and thus using two memory systems at once to increase retention.

Reading specialists may warn against reading aloud because they are trying to build up your reading speed. However, if you find a passage difficult, the combination of seeing and hearing words may help you to understand and remember better.

The **kinesthetic memory system** involves using your body. Physical activities such as taking notes, drawing charts and pictures, working on a lab experiment, acting out a literary or historical event, or demonstrating vocabulary words can reinforce memory for many courses.

Memorizing Through Grouping

Research by psychologist George A. Miller indicates that the brain can only handle about seven words or facts at a time.[5] To take in and retain more than that, you must group information. As a case in point, complete the following exercise.

Exercise 5

Grouping Exercise A

Take 30 seconds to memorize the list in Column A. When you are finished, cover up the list and write the list from memory in Column B. (The items do not have to be in the same order.)

Column A	Column B

eggs
celery
tissue
hamburger
dish detergent
cheese
dog food
diet soda
apples
milk
birdseed
steak

---

[5]George A. Miller. (March 1956). "The Magical Number Seven, Plus or Minus Two: Some Limits on Our Capacity for Processing Information," *Psychological Review,* 63:81–97.

Grouping Exercise B

Now take 30 seconds to memorize the list in Column A below. Then cover it up and rewrite the list from memory in Column B. (The items do not have to be in the same order.)

Column A		Column B
forks	bed	
plates	pillow	
cups	sheets	
spoons	dresser	
couch		
chair		
television		
stereo		

What were the results of this memory exercise? Most people remember the words in Exercise B better because the items are grouped into meaningful units. In the next two exercises it will be up to you to determine the grouping.

Grouping Exercise C

Group the following items into two categories. Give each category a name, then write each item under the appropriate category.

Category A:	Category B:

heart
addition
veins
subtraction
total
liver
kidneys
division
multiplication

Grouping Exercise D

Group the following headings in the chapter on the "Roaring Twenties" into three categories. Fill in A, B, or C, to indicate the proper category. Before you begin, define your three categories, one of which should be social.

Category A: _____   Category B: _____   Category C: _____social_____

_____ The Prohibition "Experiment"

_____ The Golden Age of Gangsterism

_____ Monkey Business in Tennessee

_____ The Mass-Consumption Economy

_____ Putting America on Rubber Tires

_____ The Advent of the Gasoline Age

_____ Humans Develop Wings

_____ The Radio Revolution

_____ Hollywood's Filmland Fantasies

_____ The Dynamic Decade

Grouping will help you review main concepts in preparation for any examination. Textbook chapters are usually divided into approximately eight major concepts supported by a series of minor concepts. If you group information about each major concept and make Q/A flashcards, you can review quickly. For example, if you are studying the rising crime rate in New York City for a sociology class, rather than memorizing isolated information, you might group the material into several major concepts: past crime types and rates, current crime types and rates, causes of change, effects of change, comparisons with crime in other cities, proposed solutions, and predictions.

> *Suggested Activity:* Work with classmates to examine how many main concepts are included in this chapter (Step 7). How did you determine the main concepts or ideas?

Memorizing Through Repetition

The term **repetition** is not meant to imply that you should mimic your instructor, repeating information in the same words over and over. In this book, repetition means "interacting" with the same information in as many ways as possible: reading, reflecting, writing, speaking, listening, visualizing, and discussing it. Two methods can lead to meaningful repetition: pocket learning and distributed learning. Both are based on the theory that memorization works best if you absorb only a small amount of material at a time. The brain can handle only so much data before it becomes overloaded.

Pocket learning means that you review only a "pocketful" of information at a time. We all have many pockets of time: waiting for a class to start, taking a coffee break, waiting for a bus, sitting in a doctor's office.

> *The unfortunate thing about this world is that good habits are so much easier to give up than bad ones.*
> **—Somerset Maugham**

Exercise 6

List four pockets of time in your schedule that you can use (anywhere from three to ten minutes).

1._____   3._____

2._____   4._____

Distributed learning means spacing out your memorization and review so that you are repeatedly exposed to information over a period of time. Many students cram for a test in a single marathon study session. However, research indicates that when you distribute your learning into short, separate sessions, you reduce fatigue and boredom while allowing time for information to "jell" in the mind. Therefore, when reviewing a chapter, you would probably learn more if you put in 15 minutes at four different times than if you spent an hour on it.

There is no such thing as overlearning. Review as much as possible so that you can walk into a test feeling confident. Pocket and distributed learning can give you that confidence.

> *One of my favorite study techniques now is using flashcards. Learning how to use them was time-consuming at first, but in the long run they are worth it. They're small enough that they can go anywhere that you go. They've really made my grades shoot up.*
>
> —Bob Ingles

Memorizing Through Mnemonic Techniques

Mnemonic techniques involve creating words, sentences, or stories that are easy to remember and that aid you in retaining important information. Let's review several kinds of mnemonic techniques.

The Mnemonic Word Technique. Form a word (even if you have to invent it) from the initials of the words you want to remember. For example, in the history section you learned that "The Dynamic Decade" could be summarized using five characteristics:

The Dynamic Decade	
How did our changing lifestyles and values parallel the upsurge in our economy?	- Urban areas had the most population - Churches used modernist techniques to retain members - Advertisers exploited sexual allure to sell products - Jazz created racial pride from the growing centers of New Orleans and Harlem - New African American culture nourished Langston Hughes and others

By taking one letter from each of these situations, you can create a "word" to aid you in remembering the five factors:

U = Urban areas   C = Churches turn modern   N = New African American culture
A = Advertisers   J = Jazz a unifying factor

Mnemonic aid: CAJUN

The word CAJUN works as a mnemonic device; it is easy to remember because it reminds us of an identifying term of Louisiana, especially New Orleans. The term you choose need not be an actual word or even make sense to others—as long as it is pronounceable and you can remember what the word stands for.

Exercise 7

Assume you are taking a health class in which you have to learn the names of the four lobes of the brain. Create a mnemonic word as a memory aid. (The lobes can be arranged in any order.)

Four lobes of the brain: frontal, temporal, parietal, occipital

Your reordering of the lobes:

_____

Possible mnemonic words:_____

Which one works best for you? _____

How will you associate this word with the lobes of the brain so that you remember it?

_____

_____

Exercise 8

Before you can devise a mnemonic word, the information must be reduced to a few key words. For instance, assume you need a mnemonic word to help you remember what drove the mass-consumption economy in the 1920s. Key words include *energy, cars, advertising, sports,* and *debt.* Below, fill in your choice for a mnemonic word:

_____

How will you associate this word with the consumer economy of the 1920s?

_____

_____

_____

_____

> *Suggested Activity:* Share your answers for Exercises 7 and 8 with fellow students. Make note of words that you like better than the ones you chose.

The Mnemonic Sentence Technique.

In some situations you will need to remember items in a certain order but the mnemonic word technique won't work because you cannot create a pronounceable word. In this case, make a sentence by using the first letter of each item.

If you have ever taken music lessons, you probably learned this sentence to help you remember the notes on the musical staff: **E**very **G**ood **B**oy **D**oes **F**ine.

In a science class you can use the following sentence to remember the layers of the atmosphere in their order, starting with the troposphere, closest to earth: troposphere ___ stratosphere ___ mesosphere ___ thermosphere ___ exosphere.

Now create a mnemonic sentence using the letters TSMTE, in that order.

_____

_____

_____

> *Suggested Activity:* Work in a group to share your answers from above. Then discuss the advantages and disadvantages of both the mnemonic word and sentence techniques.

The "Linking Story" Mnemonic Techniques. This approach involves selecting key words and creating a story that includes them. The story should be short and humorous, even silly or ridiculous, but as distinctive as possible so that you'll remember it.

A famous mnemonic linking technique is the old ditty to help children memorize how many days are in each month of the year: *Thirty days have September, April, June, and November. All the rest have 31 (except February, which has 28).*

In another example, let us assume that in an American literature class you need to memorize that John Updike wrote the short story "A & P," John Steinbeck wrote the short story "Chrysanthemums," and John Gardner wrote the book *October Light.* You could make up the following scene to help you remember this list:

Up on the dike was an A & P store where a man named Steinbeck sold chrysanthemums raised by a gardener in the October light.

Exercise 9

Invent a similar story to link the following poets with their poetry. (You may change the order of the poets and their poems.)

Robert Frost, "The Wood-Pile;" Walt Whitman, "A Noiseless Patient Spider;" T. S. Elliot, "The Hollow Men"

Mnemonic aid:

_____

_____

_____

_____

Suggested Activity: An effective way to remember this story is to repeat it.

- Turn to a classmate and repeat your story.

- Listen to your classmate repeat his or her story.

- Close your textbook and jot down your story on a piece of paper.

- Now you have used auditory, visual, and kinesthetic memory systems.

At first you will find that using memory techniques requires time and mental exertion; working with a partner or a group will help. Mnemonics will become fun as you use your imagination and become faster at using them. Better grades will be your reward.

Every man's memory is his private literature.
　　　　　　　　　　　—Aldous Huxley

Application Assignments: History Text

Application 1

Turn to the heading "The Advent of the Gasoline Age" on page 318. Write key questions in the margins or make review notes with a question column. (If you saved your Q/A notes from Step 4, Application 1, you will be able to use them here.) In this section, the author pointed out important agents of change in the 1920s. Once you have found these "changes," list them below:

What were four significant changes brought about by the automobile?

1._____ 3._____

2._____ 4._____

Select one of the mnemonic techniques you have studied to help you memorize these four changes. Pick a key word to represent each problem. What are the key words?

1._____ 3._____

2._____ 4._____

Choice of mnemonic technique: _____

Mnemonic aid:

_____

_____

_____

The section titled "Monkey Business in Tennessee" includes key information to remember: John Dewey, Advancement in Science, Resurgence of Fundamentalism, and the Scopes Trial. Now select a different mnemonic technique to memorize them. (You may wish to review each key point in the "Roaring Twenties," starting on page 312.

Choice of mnemonic technique: _____

Mnemonic aid:

_____

_____

_____

> **Suggested Activity:** Discuss the importance of the other memory techniques suggested earlier in this chapter (grouping, association, repetition, and sensory/kinesthetic memory systems). Discuss the advantages and disadvantages of these techniques.

Application 2

In preparing for a test in another class, select information you are trying to memorize and choose a mnemonic technique.

Class: _____ Topic: _____

Choice of mnemonic technique: _____

Mnemonic aid:

_____

_____

_____

Using a different mnemonic technique, practice another topic, either for the same test or for a test in another class.

Class: _____ Topic: _____

Choice of mnemonic technique: _____

Mnemonic aid:

_____

_____

_____

> **Personal Response Check:** As a result of practicing memory techniques,
> I realize that   (1) _____
>   (2) _____

Self-Contract

As a result of learning about the reviewing and memorizing techniques in Step 7, I would like to adopt the following study strategies:

_____

_____

_____

_____

_____

_____

I will practice these new techniques for at least_____weeks to determine if I want to adopt them as a part of my permanent study strategies. Then I will complete the Progress Report below.

Signed:_____   Date:_____

Self-Contract Progress Report

Progress I have made toward these changes:_____

_____

_____

_____

_____

_____

_____Date:_____

Stage Three, Step Seven Journal Entry

Everybody is ignorant, only in different subjects
—Will Rogers

Date: _____

Discuss a plan of how you expect to use distributed learning (pocket learning) and the checkmark review method in your other classes. Evaluate how any new study strategies you have used so far are working for you. Include the positive and negative results of these new strategies.

_____

_____

_____

_____

_____

_____

_____

_____

_____

_____

_____

_____

_____

_____

_____

_____

A successful test-taker is a sucessful test-maker
                                            —Anonymous

Step Eight
Improving Your Test-Taking Skills

Objectives

❑ To think like a test maker by designing your own tests

❑ To plan strategies for before, during, and after the test

❑ To gain confidence in taking tests

Contents

❑ Strategies Before a Test

❑ Strategies During a Test

❑ Strategies After a Test
      Yellow and Blue Highlighter Technique
      Test Analysis Sheet
      Test Results Chart

❑ Types of Tests
      Understanding the True/False Test
      Understanding the Multiple-Choice Test
      Understanding the Matching Test
      Understanding the Completion Test
      Understanding the Short-Answer Test
      Understanding the Essay Test

❑ Application Assignments: History Text

❑ Application Assignments: Psychology Text

Key Terms

objective and subjective tests
positive and negative statements
double negatives
absolutes and qualifiers
stem and options
distractors
essay exam organizational patterns
test analysis

Self-Awareness Check:

Check the appropriate blanks:	Often	Sometimes	Rarely
1. I know in advance whether a test will be objective or subjective or both.	____	____	____
2. I regularly get high grades on tests and exams.	____	____	____
3. I recognize absolutes and qualifiers.	____	____	____
4. I have a successful formula for taking essay exams.	____	____	____
5. After each test, I analyze why I missed each question.	____	____	____

"A successful test-taker is a successful test-maker." Write down what you think this quotation means:

_____

_____

_____

_____

_____

_____

_____

The most obvious reason for poor grades is insufficient preparation. No strategy in this book can replace putting in the necessary study time. Students who do not allow enough time for systematic review tend to cram the night before a test and later wonder why they did not perform well. Some may zip through test questions that require only simple recognition, such as true/false, multiple choice, and matching items. However, when they are asked to answer essay questions, or otherwise demonstrate their understanding of the material, their grades plummet. Here we will look at strategies you can use before, during, and after a test to improve your test-taking abilities.

Strategies Before a Test

The First Week of Class

Begin preparing for tests as soon as your course begins. In this book, you have learned a variety of strategies to help you study efficiently and intelligently. These strategies include

- The overview
- TIPS (in linear and spatial maps)
- Question columns for text and notes
- Flashcards for difficult material
- Checkmark review method
- Memory techniques

As you study a subject, your instructor is also thinking about what topics (T), main ideas (I), and points (P) to include in test questions. It is up to you to anticipate what the instructor will ask.

Just Before a Test

The night before an exam, go over your review notes and flashcards. Get to class a few minutes early. Choose a seat away from any distractions. If you feel nervous or tense, practice a few relaxation techniques: concentrate on your breathing and take slow, deep breaths. Tell yourself that with each breath your anxious feelings will slowly unwind. Imagine a spring slowly uncoiling as you breathe. If you still can't relax, try tightening up a specific muscle group that feels tense. Hold the tension, then relax. Experience a sense of release, then let the rest of your body relax.

Strategies During a Test

Before you look at the test, jot down on the back any memorized information you do not want to risk forgetting.

Glance over the test to determine how much weight each section is given. For example, if there are 100 multiple-choice questions to answer in 50 minutes, with each question worth one point, you know you have about 30 seconds for each question. If you have 20 multiple-choice questions for 20 points and one essay question for 80 points, you need to put most of your time into the essay question. If you have 50 minutes for two essay questions at 50 points each, you will have to watch the time carefully so that you do not spend too much time on one question. (Wear a watch, or sit where you can see a clock.)

Read the directions *carefully;* not every student does. For example, one student ignored the directions on a true/false test and used T and F to answer the questions. The instructor marked every answer incorrect because the directions stipulated a plus sign (+) for true and a minus sign (–) for false. Essay exams commonly call for students to select two out of four topics, but some students struggle furiously to answer all four—because they didn't read the instructions. Do not assume anything on a test.

Begin with the easiest part of the test first. Then address the more difficult questions.

Do not be distressed by students who finish early. They usually realize they are going to fail the test and give up. "A" students tend to be the last ones to leave.

Proofread before you turn in your test. Are your T's and F's readable? Is your handwriting legible? Is your name on the paper? Have you made any grammatical errors? Have you answered every question and followed directions?

Suggested Activity: Brainstorm a list of other "Before a Test" and "During a Test" suggestions to share with the class.

Strategies After a Test

A crucial learning point is after the test, especially the first test for a class. Insights about the first class test provide clues for preparing for the next test, and probably all subsequent tests for that class. Following are two strategies you can use to follow up after a test.

Yellow and Blue Highlighter Technique

- Before a test, create a question column in your text and notes. Use a yellow highlighter to mark which questions in your question column you anticipate your instructor might ask on an exam.

- After the test, use a blue highlighter to mark what the instructor actually asked. The blue ink will turn the questions green. The more green you have, the more you and the instructor think alike.

Test Analysis Sheet

Use the form on the next page to analyze why you missed certain questions. You will need the test in front of you. If your instructor does not allow students to keep graded tests, show him or her your analysis sheet and request permission to fill out your form. Most instructors will be so impressed with your determination to improve that they will grant permission. The instructor may even offer to help you.

For each exam question missed, analyze why you missed the question and record the number of the question(s) beside the reason. Look for any pattern of errors to help you prepare better for the next test.

Below is an example of how to analyze your test results.

Form for Analyzing Your Returned Tests

(Sample Answers)

Class: _____ Test# _____ Date of Test: _____

Errors Related to Test Questions

1. Failed to understand the question: _____ *2,18* _____

2. Read question incompletely: _____ *11, 39* _____

3. Read question incorrectly: _____ *55, 61,70* _____

4. Did not understand vocabulary: _____ *21, 33, 49, 63* _____

   Other: _____

Analyzing Your Returned Tests

(Make a photocopy before using this page)

For each exam question missed, analyze why you missed the question and record the number of the question beside the reason. Look for a pattern of errors so that you can prepare more efficiently for the next test.

Class: _____ Test# _____ Date of Test: _____

Errors Related to Test Questions

1. Failed to understand the question:_____

2. Read question incompletely: _____

3. Read question incorrectly: _____

4. Did not understand vocabulary: _____

Other: _____

Errors Related to Answers

5. Incompletely answered the question: _____

6. Vaguely answered the question: _____

7. Provided incorrect information: _____

Other: _____

Errors Related to Subject

8. Did not understand material: _____

9. Did not study sufficiently: _____

10. Lacked basic background knowledge: _____

Other: _____

Errors Related to Test-Taking Procedures

11. Did not manage time well in test: _____

12. Blocked self due to anxiety: _____

13. Did not follow directions: _____

Other: _____

Test Results Chart

Just like a businessperson who needs profit and loss data to make decisions, you should keep track of how you are faring as a student. Maintain an up-to-date chart of your test grades along the lines of the sample below. (Photocopy the master form appearing on the next page.)

Results of Tests
(Sample Answers)

Semester: _____

Class: _____

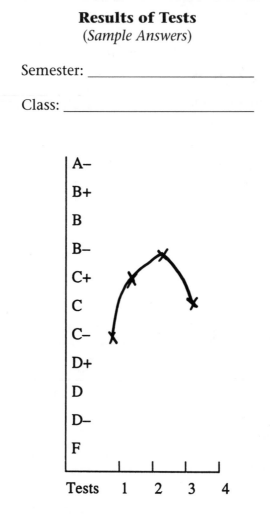

The great question is not whether you have failed, but whether you are content with failure.

—Laurence J. Peter

RESULTS OF TESTS
(Make photocopies before using)

Semester: _____ Year: _____ Dates: _____

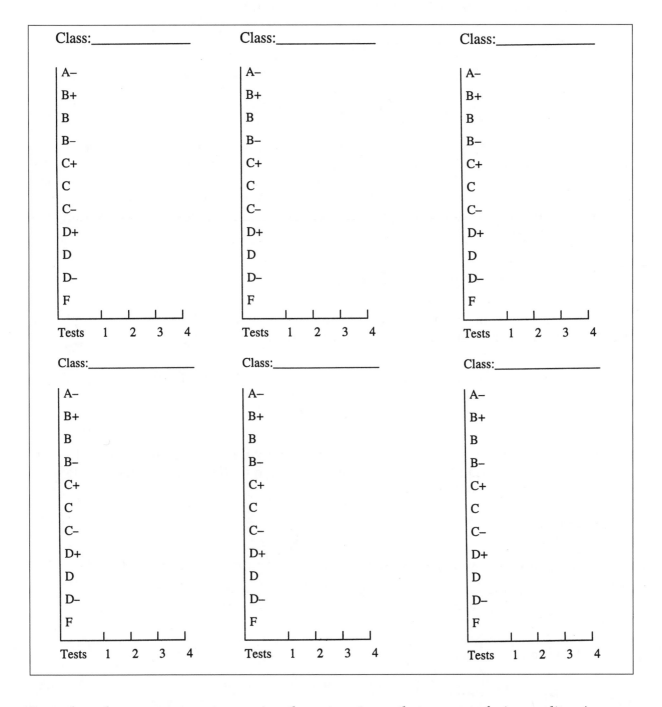

Record grades as soon as you receive them to ensure that you are facing reality. Are you neglecting some courses because others are easier or more enjoyable?

Types of Tests

As discussed earlier in this book, most tests fall into one of two categories: objective or subjective. **Objective tests** include

- true/false questions
- matching questions
- multiple-choice questions
- completion questions

Subjective tests, on the other hand, include

- short-answer questions
- essay questions

Subjective test scores can vary, depending on individual responses to the answers.

To score well on tests, you must learn to think like an instructor. If you already get A's and B's, you probably already know how to anticipate test questions as you study. If not, this chapter will give you new insights into the process of how instructors write test questions, because you will be writing some yourself. You will discover how difficult it is to create a fair, clear, challenging exam. More important, you will understand the testing process from your instructors' perspective.

Understanding the True/False Test

A true/false test is one of the most basic and widely used tests, consisting of *positive* and *negative statements* that are either true or false. For example:

1. The Mississippi River is the longest river in the United States. (True)

2. The Mississippi River is not the longest river in the United States. (False)

To understand this type of test, you will first play the role of the instructor. As the instructor, you must make certain decisions. Because tests begin with directions, first decide what directions you would provide for a true/false test.

Exercise 1

Check below how you want your students to respond in the answer blanks for a true/false test:

_____ 1. Write out True and False.

_____ 2. Write the symbols T and F.

_____ 3. Write + for True and – for False.

_____ 4. Other:_____

Decide whether you want to include other directions such as:

_____ 1. There is a penalty for guessing.

_____ 2. Correct any false sentences to make them true.

_____ 3. Other: _____

How many statements should have true answers? Most instructors choose to make half or more of the statements true.

Consider three types of key words to include in your true/false test: negatives, absolutes, and qualifiers.

Adding words like *not* can make statements more challenging but not necessarily false:

California is not a state in Canada. (True)

It is not true that Canada is north of the United States. (False)

Exercise 2

Underline the negative words in each statement. Mark each statement as true (T) or false (F).

_____ 1. Research papers are often assigned in composition classes.

_____ 2. Research papers are not often assigned in composition classes.

_____ 3. It is not true that mnemonics is a memorization technique.

_____ 4. Mnemonics is a memorization technique.

_____ 5. The abbreviation *e.g.* does not mean "for example."

_____ 6. The abbreviation *e.g.* means "for example."

Some questions contain **double negatives,** causing further confusion. Remember that two negatives make a positive:

*Aspirin is **not** an illegal drug* means that *aspirin is a legal drug.*

Cross out both negatives in the following sentences and rewrite them. Once the two negatives are removed, you simply need to identify whether the positive statement is true or false.

It is not true that organically grown apples are unhealthy.

_____

(true or false?)_____

It is unprovable that there is no life in outer space.

_____

(true or false?)_____

Exercise 3

Underline the two negative words or prefixes in each sentence. Rewrite the sentence without them and answer each as true (+) or false (-).

1. Lost textbooks are usually not irreplaceable.

    _____

    (true or false?)_____

2. "Facts are truth" is not an illogical statement.

    _____

    (true or false?)_____

3. Lies are not untruths.

    _____

    (true or false?) _____

Absolutes are words that imply that there are no exceptions, such as *all, always, never, everyone*—anything that implies *without exception*. Example: *Nobody* skis in July. The use of an absolute does not determine whether a statement is true or false; it is simply a signal to look closely.

Exercise 4

_____ 1. People always react to horror movies.

_____ 2. Students never allow enough time to study.

_____ 3. All types of cars have some kind of engine.

_____ 4. Everyone should exercise daily.

Qualifiers are words that imply that there are exceptions, such as *some, sometimes, usually, many, most, a few, often, tend to*. Example: *Some* people react negatively to horror movies.

Exercise 5

Underline the qualifiers and indicate true or false for the following statements:

_____ 1. Some students use drugs.

_____ 2. Many registered voters do not vote.

_____ 3. People tend to become defensive when they are angry.

_____ 4. Students often fail to read test directions.

Exercise 6

Write three true/false statements on the topic of college students.
- one with a negative
- one with a qualifier
- one with an absolute

1. _____

2. _____

3. _____

Suggested Activity: Trade your statements with those of a classmate. Answer each other's tests.

Personal Response Check: As a result of creating a true/false test,

I realize that   (1) _____

                   (2) _____

Understanding the Multiple-Choice Test

Another type of test asks you to choose one answer from multiple choices. Example:

A person who subconsciously buries feelings is using the defense mechanism of

a. projection b. introjection c. rationalization d. repression

The multiple-choice test is popular with instructors for three reasons:

1. Whereas a true/false test gives students a 50 percent chance of guessing correctly, a multiple-choice test lowers the odds to 25 percent (assuming there are four possible answers).

2. Multiple-choice questions demand more critical thinking skills than true/false tests because students must compare and contrast options.

3. These items are easier to grade than completion, short-answer, or essay questions. However, this kind of test is more difficult for the instructor to write; devising wrong answers that sound plausible is not an easy task, as you will soon find out.

The multiple-choice test contains two parts: the **stem** (the first part of the sentence) and the answer **options**. As a test maker, try to bury the correct answer among four or five options. The idea is to create distractions to draw students away from the correct answer. Therefore, all your options must appear logical.

Students tend to dislike options such as *all of the above, none of the above,* or *both a and c above.* When an instructor includes the option *all of the above,* this tends to be the correct choice because it is easier to use correct options than to think of **distractors;** similarly, the option *none of the above* is often a wrong answer. (Many instructors do not want to spend the time to devise four or five incorrect options.)

Another way to distract students is to include two similar answers. Consider this example:

The phrase "Your love is like a red, red, rose" is an example of a

a. *simulacrum*   b. *haiku*   c. *metonymy*   d. *simile*

Simulacrum and *simile* appear close, and many students would take a chance and pick one of these. (The correct answer is *simile*.)

Exercise 7

From the section "Dynamic Decade," on page 322, create a multiple-choice question. Here's an example:

> *The city of Los Angeles*
> *a. has a population of two million*
> *b. is the largest American city in terms of population*
> *c. was made an American city by the treaty of Guadalupe Hidalgo*
> *d. is the second largest city in California*

Now write your own question.

Stem: _____

a. _____   b. _____

c. _____   d. _____

Suggested Activity: Exchange questions with a classmate to test each other. Share your reactions as to how effective the questions were.

Personal Response Check: As a result of writing a multiple choice test item,
I realize that   (1) _____
                 (2) _____

When taking multiple-choice tests:

- Read all directions carefully. Sometimes you may need to choose more than one answer, or you may be asked to choose the best answer.

- When you read the stem, try to complete it in your own mind before glancing at options. This will help you avoid becoming confused by the choices.

- Answer easy questions first. Leave difficult questions for last.

- If the stem is long and complicated, find the subject and verb. Then restate sections of the stem in your own words.

- Consider every answer, mentally labeling each one as true, false, or maybe. A hasty decision can lead to the wrong answer.

- If both a general and a specific statement appear true, select the general one. Example: *The Fundamentalists at best won only a hollow victory when John T. Scopes was found guilty of teaching evolution because (a) the fine was only $100 (b) Clarence Darrow proved that the Bible was in error (c) church membership began a slow decline (d) the trial itself looked absurd and ridiculed the cause of Fundamentalism.* (While *c* might be proven true, *d* is the correct choice.)

- If two options are similar, determine how they differ. One is probably the correct answer. If two options are direct opposites, one may be correct.

- Sometimes longer options are correct because more words are needed to make them true. Options with qualifiers often signal a correct answer, just as absolutes often signal false options.

- The correct option is not likely to be a humorous, an emotional, or an illogical choice.

- *All of the above* tends to be the correct answer, but *none of the above* tends not to be.

Suggested Activity: Brainstorm to make a list of additional multiple-choice strategies to share with the class.

Understanding the Matching Test

The matching test asks students to match items from two columns, with the second column longer to add to distractors and allow for multiple answers. Study the example below.

Directions: Match the two columns by placing letters from Column B in the blanks. An item in Column A may have more than one answer from Column B. No item in Column B may be used more than once.

Column A	Column B
____ 1. *New York City*	a. *location of Golden Gate Bridge*
____ 2. *Chicago*	b. *site of Disney World*
____ 3. *San Francisco*	c. *location of O'Hare Airport*
	d. *home of Yankees baseball team*
	e. *home of Bears football team*

Exercise 8

Select three performers or politicians for Column A below, and write five identifications for Column B. Make Column B longer to include distractors. Indicate in the directions whether an item in Column B may be used more than once and whether items in Column A can have more than one answer.

Test directions: _____

_____

_____

Column A	Column B
1. _____	a. _____
2. _____	b. _____
3. _____	c. _____
	d. _____
	e. _____

> *Suggested Activity:* Exchange tests with a classmate and discuss them.

> *Personal Response Check:* As a result of creating a matching test,
> I realize that   (1) _____
>   (2) _____

When taking matching tests:

- Read the directions to find out whether an item can be used more than once.
- Decide which column you want to start with, the left or right.
- Read both columns before writing in answers.
- Do the easiest matches first.
- Mark the items used so that you do not have to keep rereading them.
- Check the logic of combining two items.

Understanding the Completion Test

The completion test is also called the *fill-in* test. Students complete a sentence by filling in a blank with the correct word or phrase. Example:

The _____ River, one of the longest rivers in the United States, flows from Minnesota to Louisiana and into the Gulf of Mexico.

When you compose a completion test for Exercise 9, decide carefully what word(s) to have students fill in so that there is only one correct answer. When asking for more than one word, you must also decide whether to use one blank or separate blanks. Example:

1. Rationalization is one example of _____.

   or

2. Rationalization is one example of _____ _____.

Exercise 9

Write three completion questions for the topic of food, a city or country, or a topic of your choice. Example:

The _____ was once considered a fruit but is now classified as a vegetable.

Directions: _____

_____

1. _____

_____

2. _____

_____

3. _____

_____

When taking a completion test:

- Check whether there are one or more separate blanks for multiple-word answers.

- Look for grammatical clues such as *a* and *an;* they will indicate whether the following word will begin with a vowel or a consonant (*a car, an apple*).

- When you cannot think of the precise word(s), write synonyms or an answer that is close. (Example: If you cannot remember the name of Charles Lindbergh, write "pilot of the *Spirit of St. Louis*.") The instructor may give you partial or full credit.

Understanding the Short-Answer Test

The short-answer test calls for a concise answer: a few sentences or a list of items. The amount of space provided is usually a clue to the length of the answer expected. Write your answer in regular sentences unless the question requests a list. Example: *List three African American jazz musicians whose popularity took them from New Orleans to Harlem.*

Exercise 10

1. Explain the TIPS method of taking textbook notes.

   _____

   _____

2. List three types of objective tests.

   _____

   _____

3. Define the term *absolutes*.

   _____

   _____

Understanding the Essay Test

An answer to an essay question is a brief composition. Many students dread essay exams, often because they do not feel confident about their writing.

What does your instructor want to see in your answers? In grading essay questions, instructors are faced with stacks of answers to read; therefore, the last thing they want is a long-winded, rambling, disorganized answer. They are reading for certain main ideas and want specific details as support. They do not need an elaborate introduction or ending. Too often, students spend more time on the introduction and conclusion than on the main body of their essays. Instructors want students to come to the point, prove it, and move on to the next question.

Following are examples of weak (Answer A) and stong (Answer B) answers to an essay question. Note that Answer B is organized in a way that directly reflects the question ("Discuss five ways. . . ") and gives specific examples for each of the five cultural aspects. Answer A, on the other hand, is not clearly organized and gives only vague examples to back up its claims.

Question:

Discuss five ways Spanish culture influenced the area that is now the Southwest of the United States.

Answer A:

Spain needed gold, so the king sent Cortez and his army to Mexico to find it. Cortez conquered the natives and destroyed their culture, but never did find gold.

Many people in the Southwest speak Spanish and their culture shows evidence of Spanish influence. Much of the architecture resembles what is found in Spain. Also, many Spanish-speaking people are Catholics, just like the Spaniards.

In some parts of Spain, cattle and sheep are raised, and in the Southwest cattle and sheep ranching are popular. The Southwest has rodeos too, an idea that came from Spain. Some of our laws have Spanish origins, as well as some of our words, such as patio.

We have much to be thankful for to Spain. We can see Spain's influence all around us.

Answer B:

The United States' Southwest is rich with the influence of Spanish culture.

One aspect is religion: the Catholic church has a strong foothold in the Southwest. When Spain wanted to control what is now the Southwest of the United States, Father Junipero Serra, a Franciscan missionary, established a network of missions that provided not only a religious influence, but protection and assistance to Spanish settlers as well.

Second is architecture, e.g., the ubiquitous plaza and red tile roofs. The plaza concept is very evident in Southwestern towns—a town square providing a center for religious, political, and social activity. Homes in the Southwest are often built with a patio. The red tile roof from southern Spain is also evident, especially in Southern California.

Third are the sheep and cattle brought from Spain. The Southwest raises both animals; with ranching came many ways of life, such as branding, the rodeo, and ranching vocabulary such as mustang *and* lasso.

Fourth is the Iberian agricultural economy. The Southwest has flourished from such imported crops as olives, limes, wheat, alfalfa, and peaches.

Fifth is the Spanish legal system. The Southwest has incorporated Spanish laws into its own, such as the separation of water and mineral rights as well as community property rights.

These five aspects reflect only a few of the Spanish influences on the Southwest, concrete examples which represent different aspects of daily life such as housing, food, and work—but only hint at the intellectual, religious, and cultural influences of Spain on the Southwestern way of life.

Exercise 11

Show how the two essay answers are similar and dissimilar. Sample answers are provided.

Compare Answers A & B	**Contrast Answers A & B**	
<u>Both</u>	<u>Answer A</u>	<u>Answer B</u>
mention architecture	*no example of architecture*	*3 examples of architecture*

In your role as test maker, after you select topics for essay exams, be specific in the types of organization patterns you want your students to follow as they structure their answers.

Understanding the differences between organizational patterns helps provide structure and direction for writing an exam essay. For example, the student who wrote Answer B on the influence of Spanish culture on the Southwest knew how to *discuss* five ways rather than to erroneously *trace* or *contrast* Spanish influence with some other influence.

Typical Essay Exam Organizational Patterns

Compare	Explain how two topics are alike. Examples: two experiments, two generals. (Note: Some instructors use the term *compare* when they really mean *compare and contrast.*)
Contrast	Explain how two subjects are not alike. Examples: an oak and a maple leaf; a dolphin and a porpoise.
Criticize (**Evaluate, Judge, Justify, Prove**)	Analyze a topic, discussing its positive and negative points with evidence. Choose a side. Examples: bilingual education; affirmative action.
Define	Provide the clear meaning of a term or topic. How is it similar to but different from a topic that is close in meaning? Examples: paranoia; schizophrenia.
Discuss (**Describe, Explain, Analyze, Examine**)	Examine a topic through examples and details. Examples: causes of the Civil War; toxic waste dumps.
Interpret	Describe your understanding of a topic. Examples: a poem; a current event; the meaning of truth.
Relate	Explain how one topic affects or connects to another. Examples: smoking and cancer; child abuse and co-dependency.
Trace	Show the steps or development from one point to another. Examples: procedure for an experiment; steps in child development.

Here is a sample essay exam for a literature class.

Directions: *Write about two of the following essay exam topics. 50 points each. Total time allotted: 60 minutes.*

1. *Compare and contrast the two sons in Arthur Miller's* Death of a Salesman: *their strengths, their weaknesses, and their relationship with their parents.*

2. *Trace the character development of Biff in* Death of a Salesman *from his childhood to the end of the play. What key events influence his development?*

3. *Evaluate whether* Death of a Salesman *is still relevant to today's society.*

Here is a sample essay exam for a marketing class:

Directions: Discuss one of the following topics. 100 points. Total time allotted: 30 minutes.

1. Consider an unknown actress being promoted as a new star. Trace her progress through the six stages of talent development.

2. Compare and contrast two computers manufactured by the same company, one sold under the company's well-known brand and the other as a discounted house brand. How are the two computers similar and dissimilar in components, quality, and function? How would the marketing of each compare and contrast?

3. Define the term *supply and demand* and discuss three examples in today's market.

Exercise 12

Write the directions for an essay exam consisting of three questions. Include how many questions to answer, how many points out of 100 each is worth, and how much time is allotted. Then write three essay questions, using the organizational patterns above and topics from another class you are taking.

Directions: _____

_____

Question 1: _____

_____

Question 2: _____

_____

Question 3: _____

_____

Personal Response Check: As a result of designing an essay exam,

I realize that   (1) _____

(2) _____

When taking an essay exam:

- Practice writing an essay answer at home, even if you have to guess at the topic. The practice will help you realize how much you can write in the time allotted and whether your answer is sufficiently organized and developed.

- Read the directions carefully: How many questions are there to answer? How many points is each worth? How much time do you have?

- If you must answer more than one question, decide which ones are the easiest. Start with them.

- After you decide which questions you plan to answer, take a few moments to jot down all the important details that you have memorized and will need to use in the essay. Don't worry about order or importance—get them out of your head and onto scratch paper before you forget them.

- Organize these notes by numbering them in the order in which you will use them, adding any new ones you may remember in the process.

- Begin your first sentence by making a clear, precise statement. Use key words from the question so that your reader knows immediately that you are on the right track. (See the first sentence of Answer B on the Southwest.)

- Use linking words such as *first, second, next, then, finally, last, in contrast, also, however,* and *therefore* as transitions to lead from one idea to the next.

- Provide sufficient examples and proof. Answer A on the Southwest is vague in support, while B offers specific Spanish crops, vocabulary, and examples of architecture.

- Keep your introduction and conclusion short.

- If you run out of time, quickly outline what you would have written. You might receive partial credit.

Now that you have practiced several study strategies for test taking, you will have an opportunity to practice what you have learned by taking tests on your reading from history and psychology.

Application Assignments: History Text

Application 1

The following test covers material you have studied in this book. It assumes that you have read all of "American Life in the 'Roaring Twenties,' 1919–1920" on pages 312–323.

Before you start, examine how the test is weighted. What sections contain most of the points? Skim the test quickly to mark the easiest questions. Decide where to start in order to get the most points. Then begin. (The answers are in the Instructor's Manual.)

"AMERICAN LIFE IN THE 'ROARING TWENTIES,' 1919–1929"

Part I: True and False   (10 points: 1 each)
Directions: Write *true* or *false* in each blank.

_____ 1. Opposition to the Eighteenth Amendment (Prohibition) was centered around the South and, to a lesser degree, the Midwest.

_____ 2. In spite of all his crimes, Al Capone was convicted of income tax evasion.

_____ 3. Fundamentalist Christians asserted that teaching Darwin's theory of evolution tended to destroy faith in God and the Bible.

_____ 4. Credit buying, "Possess today and pay tomorrow," was considered against the rules of economics and was severely regulated during the 1920s.

_____ 5. The development of the assembly line has customarily been attributed to Henry Ford, but the major share of the credit belongs to Frederick W. Taylor.

_____ 6. One of the great transformations in the 1920s was changing the auto from a luxury to a necessity.

_____ 7. Because Americans demanded more efficient transportation during the 1920s, railroads experienced an unprecedented growth throughout that period.

_____ 8. Surprisingly enough, the film industry became an astounding success as a result of the popularity of the anti-German propaganda films of World War I.

_____ 9. The airline industry grew slowly during the 1920s because people were afraid to fly.

_____ 10. At first, radio stations were government-owned so that people did not have to listen to "bothersome" commercials.

Part II: Multiple Choice   (20 points: 2 each)
Directions: Write the correct letter in the blank.

_____11. "The Atlantic Ocean was shriveling to about the size of the Aegean Sea in the days of Socrates, while isolation behind ocean moats was becoming a bygone dream." According to the above quote, the author was referring to what industrial marvel of the 1920s?

      a. the assembly line
      b. the advent of the automobile
      c. the development of the airplane
      d. the expected television revolution

_____12. The standardization of taste brought on by radio and motion pictures

      a. restored Old World cultures
      b. had a huge impact on immigrants trying to enter American main stream society
      c. stimulated the reading of serious literature
      d. nearly eliminated plays on the Broadway stage

_____13. The famous 1925 John T. Scopes or "Monkey Trial" took place in

      a. Hollywood
      b. Tennessee
      c. Detroit
      d. Chicago

_____14. The census of 1920 revealed that

      a. the so-called Modernists in religion lost ground to the "Fundamentalists"
      b. women found it more difficult to find employment
      c. women did not want to wear one-piece bathing suits
      d. most Americans lived in urban rather than rural areas

_____15. All the following factors accounted for the amazing prosperity of the 1920s <u>except</u>:

      a. business demands that purchases be paid for in cash
      b. cheap energy largely from new oil fields
      c. the influence of advertising
      d. the development of the assembly line

_____16. Organized crime during the 1920s became such a gigantic business that its annual income in 1930 was

      a. almost as large
      b. about the same
      c. twice as large
      d. several times as large as the income of the Washington government

_____17. Incredible as it might sound, the first single sporting event which the attendees paid more than a million dollars to see was

        a. the first professional football game
        b. the World Series with Babe Ruth
        c. Jack Dempsey knocking out Georges Carpentier
        d. there were no million-dollar gates until the 1930s

_____18. According to older generations, the recognized symbol of how our civilization was crumbling and leading to moral decay was the

        a. the flapper
        b. the gangster
        c. Sigmund Freud
        d. the darkened movie house

_____19. Side effects of the automobile revolution were evidenced by all the following except

        a. family life became far more closely knit
        b. thousands of miles of new roads were built using tax money from gasoline
        c. isolation among the different sections of the country was generally eliminated
        d. more families were moving to the suburbs

_____20. Harlem welcomed and nourished several African American poets during the 1920s, including

        a. Marcus Garvey
        b. W. C. Handy
        c. Langston Hughes
        d. Joseph King Oliver

Part III: Matching   (10 points: 2 each)
Directions: Fill in the blanks in Column A with the corresponding items from Column B.

Column A	Column B
_____ 21. Henry Ford	a. credited with the invention of wireless telegraphy
_____ 22. Clarence Darrow	b. attorney for John Scopes during the famous "Monkey Trial" of 1925
_____ 23. Charles Lindbergh	c. aviator who was the first to fly nonstop across the Atlantic Ocean
_____ 24. Guglielmo Marconi	d. a hypocritical legislator who toasted Prohibition from a hip flask
_____ 25. "Scarface" Al Capone	e. famous developer of the "Tin Lizzie"
	f. infamous gangster finally convicted of tax fraud

Part IV: Essay   (Total of 50 points: 25 for each answer)
Directions: Select two of the following topics for your essays. For each question, use the space provided for any notes.

1. Often portrayed as an era when "anything goes," how can it be said that the "Roaring Twenties" was also an era of intolerance?

2. Would you have liked to live in the 1920s? Supply three reasons and support each answer.

3. Select three far-reaching changes in the 1920s and compare them with the lifestyles and values of contemporary society.

4. Support the following with reasons and evidence: The 1920s was truly a "Dynamic Decade."

Notes for the first essay: _____

_____

_____

_____

_____

_____

_____

Notes for the second essay: _____

_____

_____

_____

_____

_____

_____

Begin your first essay here:

_____

_____

_____

_____

_____

_____

_____

_____

_____

Begin your second essay here:

_____

_____

_____

_____

_____

_____

_____

_____

_____

_____

_____

_____

_____

_____

_____

_____

_____

_____

_____

_____

_____

_____

_____

_____

_____

_____

_____

_____

_____

_____

_____

_____

_____

_____

_____

_____

_____

_____

_____

_____

_____

After your paper is graded, fill out the test analysis on the next page.

Analyzing Your Returned Test

For each exam question missed, analyze why you missed the question and record the number of the question beside the reason. Look for a pattern of errors so that you can prepare more efficiently for the next test.

Class: _____ Test# _____ Date of Test: _____

Errors Related to Test Questions

1. Failed to understand the question: _____

2. Read question incompletely: _____

3. Read question incorrectly: _____

4. Did not understand vocabulary: _____

   Other: _____

Errors Related to Answers

5. Incompletely answered the question: _____

6. Vaguely answered the question: _____

7. Provided incorrect information: _____

   Other: _____

Errors Related to Subject

8. Did not understand material: _____

9. Did not study sufficiently: _____

10. Lacked basic background knowledge: _____

    Other: _____

Errors Related to Test-Taking Procedures:

11. Did not manage time well in test: _____

12. Blocked self due to anxiety: _____

13. Did not follow directions: _____

    Other: _____

> **Personal Response Check:** As a result of taking a test using test strategies and analyzing the results,
>
> I realize that   (1) _____
>
> (2) _____

Application 2

For a test you are anticipating in one of your other classes, prepare a six-part exam. Put yourself in the role of your instructor. What are the directions? What will the test include? How will it be worded? How will the questions be weighted?

Your test should contain the following:

Part I:	5 true/false statements
Part II:	5 multiple choice
Part III:	matching (5 items in column A and 7 in column B)
Part IV:	3 completion
Part V:	3 short answer questions
Part VI:	3 essay questions

Answer sheet: Write answers for Parts I through V. For Part VI, write out the answer to one essay question (the one that will most help you to review for your test).

Turn your test in to your instructor. (If possible, type it.)

Application Assignments: Psychology Text

Application 3

Below is a test covering the material in the psychology chapter on stress and health on pages 330–335. Before you start, examine how the test is weighted. What sections contain most of the points? Skim the entire test to read all the questions quickly and mark the easiest ones. Decide where to start in order to get the most points. Then begin. (The answers are in the Instructor's Manual.)

Stress and Health Psychology

Part I: True and False   (10 points: 2 each)
Directions: Write the word *true* or *false*.

_____ 1. Stress can contribute to both pyschological and physical illness.

_____ 2. The time of greatest stress is not necessarily the moment when danger or something negative is occurring, but might be the time we are anticipating something we dread.

_____ 3. Positive things in our lives do not cause stress.

_____ 4. Most people find a sense of order and predictability boring.

_____ 5. Minor irritations can be as stressful as major events.

Part II: Multiple Choice   (20 points: 4 each)
Directions: Write the correct letter in the blank.

_____ 6. Health psychology is concerned with

        a. psychological factors in our lives
        b. the interaction of biological, psychological, and social factors
        c. the connection between stress and illness
        d. a and c
        e. all of the above

_____ 7. Stress is

        a. limited to life-and-death situations and other major events
        b. the result of both positive and negative situations
        c. the result of changes in our lives
        d. b and c
        e. all of the above

_____ 8. Defensive coping is identified as

     a. recognizing the source of stress
     b. understanding how to cope with stress
     c. deceiving ourselves about the cause of stress
     d. b and c
     e. all of the above

_____ 9. When drug users insist that they are merely experimenting with drugs, they are practicing

     a. repression
     b. denial
     c. reaction formation
     d. projection
     e. sublimation

_____10. An angry, aggressive child who excels at soccer has transformed negative feelings into a socially acceptable behavior called

     a. repression
     b. denial
     c. reaction formation
     d. projection
     e. sublimation

Part III: Matching   (10 points: 2 each)
Directions: Fill in the blanks in Column A with the corresponding items from Column B.

Column A	**Column B**
_____ 11. Person denied a job promotion may agree to a less desirable promotion.	a. confrontation
_____ 12. Person suspicious of being overcharged talks to the store manager.	b. compromise
_____ 13. Person afraid to walk past a house with a mean dog avoids that street.	c. withdrawal
_____ 14. Person who feels a best friend has lied drops the friendship without discussing this suspicion with the friend.	
_____ 15. Person attacks a problem head-on.	

Part IV: Completion   (10 points: 2 each)

Directions: Write the missing word in the blank by selecting from the list of defensive mechanisms listed below.

denial   repression   projection
identification   regression   intellectualization
reaction formation   displacement   sublimation

16. Blocking out painful feelings and memories is _____.

17. Parents who visit a child's teacher to discuss their child's misbehavior and choose to analyze their approach to educational theories rather than discuss their child's actions are in a subtle form of denial called _____.

18. An employee cries when the boss offers criticism; this behavior is known as _____.

19. A man accuses his girlfriend of being unfaithful without any proof because in the past he himself has been unfaithful; this transfer of guilt is known as _____.

20. A person who exaggerates praise for a rival to cover up jealousy may be acting out _____ _____.

Part V: Essay   (Total of 50 points: 25 for each answer)

Directions: Select *two* of the following topics for your essays. For each question, use the space provided for any notes or a simple outline to guide your writing.

1. Compare and contrast *direct coping* with *defensive coping;* include similarities and differences. Use specific examples to define each.

2. Discuss the effects of stress on the body, providing typical examples of sources of stress.

3. Argue whether defensive mechanisms are healthy or unhealthy. Provide examples of at least three different defensive mechanisms to prove your point.

Notes for the first essay:_____

_____

_____

_____

_____

_____

Notes for the second essay:_____

_____

_____

_____

_____

_____

Begin your first essay here:

_____

_____

_____

_____

_____

_____

_____

_____

_____

_____

_____

_____

_____

_____

_____

_____

_____

_____

_____

_____

_____

_____

_____

_____

_____

_____

_____

_____

_____

_____

Begin your second essay here:

_____

_____

_____

_____

_____

_____

_____

_____

_____

_____

_____

_____

_____

_____

_____

_____

_____

_____

_____

_____

_____

_____

_____

_____

After your paper is graded, fill out the **test analysis** on the next page.

Personal Response Check: As a result of designing a test for an upcoming exam,

I realize that　(1) _____

　　　　　　　　(2) _____

Analyzing Your Returned Test

For each exam question missed, analyze why you missed the question and record the number of the question beside the reason. Look for a pattern of errors so that you can prepare more efficiently for the next test.

Class: _____ Test # _____ Date of Test: _____

Errors Related to Test Questions

1. Failed to understand the question: _____

2. Read question incompletely: _____

3. Read question incorrectly: _____

4. Did not understand vocabulary: _____

   Other: _____

Errors Related to Answers

5. Incompletely answered the question: _____

6. Vaguely answered the question: _____

7. Provided incorrect information: _____

   Other: _____

Errors Related to Subject

8. Did not understand material: _____

9. Did not study sufficiently: _____

10. Lacked basic background knowledge: _____

    Other: _____

Errors Related to Test-Taking Procedures:

11. Did not manage time well in test: _____

12. Blocked self due to anxiety: _____

13. Did not follow directions: _____

    Other: _____

Self-Contract

As a result of my practice in being both a test maker and a test taker, I would like to adopt the following study strategies:

_____

_____

_____

_____

_____

_____

I will practice these new techniques for at least_____weeks to determine if I want to adopt them as a part of my permanent study strategies. Then I will complete the Progress Report below.

Signed:_____ Date:_____

Self-Contract Progress Report

Progress I have made toward these changes:_____

_____

_____

_____

_____

_____

_____Date:_____

Stage Three, Step Eight Journal Entry

A person needs at intervals to separate himself from family and companions and go to a new place. He must go without his familiar in order to be open to influences of change.
—Katherine Butler Hathaway

Date:_____

Freewrite about a test you have taken in your most difficult course. Are you satisfied with your grade? What is the relationship between how you prepared for the test and the grade? How has this test experience prepared you for the next test?

Respond to how the above quotation reflects your going to a "new place" by studying unfamiliar topics. What are examples of topics that have stimulated your thinking?

_____

_____

_____

_____

_____

_____

_____

_____

_____

_____

_____

_____

_____

_____

_____

_____

_____

_____

_____

_____

_____

_____

_____

_____

_____

_____

_____

_____

_____

_____

_____

_____

_____

_____

_____

_____

> *Research is formalized curiosity. It is poking and prying with a purpose.*
>
> **—Zora Neal Hurston**

Step Nine
Use Your Library

Key Terms

computerized card catalog
online catalog
key words
subject headings
periodicals
microfilm and microfiche

Finding Your Way Inside the Library

Walk into today's college library and you will find computers everywhere. Some check out books, keep track of circulation, and send out overdue notices. Others display the library's holdings, scan thousands of topics, and have extensive database search capabilities. Specialized subject-matter terminals sift through magazine articles, newspapers, abstracts, and journals. Reference tools have entered the information age, and the old-fashioned card catalog is fast disappearing.

You may have already used a **computerized card catalog.** If so, you have experienced its astonishing swiftness and efficiency. You have probably also noticed that the data on the screen do not include the number of subject listings and the cross-indexing commonly found on catalog cards. To seek out this information, the computer requires specialized instructions (known as Boolean commands) that help narrow the search. Take some time to master the program that will locate books for you, and don't be afraid to ask questions.

No matter how advanced electronic reference tools become, the problems you face when setting out to do research remain the same. What is my topic? How do I get started? Where can I find information? Where can I get help?

You might start by exploring the library to locate resources. At the minimum, you should know where reference books, periodicals (magazines), online databases, and card catalogs are located. Take a guided tour if one is offered. If there is no tour, ask the research librarian to direct you to the research tools and show you how to conduct online searches.

As useful as a tour can be, it will not answer your specific research questions. You want to find information on a specific topic and specific titles as quickly as possible. With that in mind, we recommend two valuable research tools, the online or card catalog and *The Reader's Guide to Periodical Literature.* Mastery of these tools will unlock the library's treasury of information.

Tool One: The Online or Card Catalog

Finding a Topic

Most school and public libraries are equipped with many up-to-date electronic research tools. Some include databases devoted to books, newspapers, journals, reviews, and documents. Many have made the Internet and the World Wide Web available. The tool that will best provide book sources remains the **online catalog** (also known as the card catalog in libraries that still use card drawers).

Among all the various commercial online catalog programs, you will find subtle but important differences for keyboarding. Therefore, start by reading the printed or on-screen instructions on how to use the program. You will find suggestions for using key word or subject heading searches. These two important "search engines" are invaluable for any researcher.

Key words are those terms you uncover when thinking about or asking questions of a topic. For instance, if you are interested in researching something about the film industry, the key words *film, movies, twentieth century, actors,* and *screenplays* may come to mind. The computer program will "nudge" you to enter specific key words. For example, *movies* will be best searched under *motion pictures.* Once you identify this term, try adding more terms, such as *1920–1930, United States,* or *history.* The program can combine these key words and automatically start narrowing your search to the history of motion pictures in the United States between 1920 and 1930.

You can also conduct a search using **subject headings.** Suppose you have been assigned to write a ten-page research paper in Economics 101. Your instructor has told you that you can write on any topic as long as it concerns the general subject of economics. Can you imagine how many topics can be found under this heading? Whether using cards or a monitor, look up *economics* and browse. The possible subtopics you'll find include domestic and international money systems, alternate systems, profit and loss, supply and demand, and macro- and microeconomics, just to name a few. Stop at a topic that sounds interesting or has been in the news.

Below is what one economics card or computer source might include as a subject heading:

HC110.D4.J3	**(Call Number)**
Janeway, Eliot (Author)	
1968	**(Date of Publication)**
Economics of Crisis: War, Politics, and the Dollar	**(Title)**
Subjects:	

      United States—Economic Policy
      United States—Politics and Government
      War—Economic Aspects—United States

The above entry may stimulate you to ask, "How does war affect our economy?" "Does war improve or weaken our economy?" These questions can lead to other questions, all providing key words that expand your search.

Before heading for the online or card catalog, think of questions that may guide you when you use key words and subject headings to conduct a search. Words in your questions may give you a head start with entering key words. The following exercise provides practice for such questioning.

Exercise 1

What questions do you have about the following topics?

Example: Olympic games. What is the history of the Olympics? How are sites for the games selected? How have the Olympics changed in the last 100 years? How are athletes chosen to participate?

Example: Music videos. Why are music videos so popular? Which groups and artists are having the greatest effect on videos? What kind of music dominates? What are three of the main messages in the lyrics?

Now fill in your questions for the topics below:

Educational system in Japan: _____

_____

_____

_____

Racial tension:_____

_____

_____

_____

Latest computer technology: _____

_____

_____

_____

Graffiti: _____

_____

_____

_____

Use one of your questions above to practice finding sources.

Finding Sources

Once you select a narrowed topic and are ready to find sources, you can start a subject heading search for books. Subject headings show how many different ways books are classified. For instance, if your general subject is the White House, then any specific book you find will list:

1. "Washington, D.C.—White House."

2. "Presidents—United States—Biography."

3. "Washington, D.C.—Social life and customs."

These three subject headings are crucial because you have uncovered the secret behind your library's main classification system. By using any of the three subject headings, you will be directed to many books from which you can choose. Depending on the terms you use, the same sources can be found by using key word and subject heading entries just in case one method leads you into a blind alley.

Finding sources that fit your subject always involves some detective work. If you are like most students, you would like to find the best and the latest information about your subject within a reasonable length of time. From the start, make sure you spend ample time at the online catalog. Don't be satisfied with listing a book or two and then running to the shelves. If not already checked out or misplaced, the books may be on subjects quite different than you expected. That's why you should search until you have at least a dozen sources, either books or periodicals, before you move away from the computer.

Tool Two: *The Reader's Guide to Periodical Literature*

The Reader's Guide to Periodical Literature is a reference index that steers you to other sources of information. Whereas the card catalog refers you to books, this index lists publications that are printed periodically: magazines, journals, and newspapers. *The Reader's Guide to Periodical Literature* is the most frequently used index for looking up topics to find out which magazines have published related articles.

Finding a Topic

If you do not have a narrowed topic, the *Reader's Guide* can help you. In each volume, broad topics are divided into narrower topics, one of which may be appropriate for your research. For example, let's assume you are doing a paper on the problems of immigrant workers in the United States. The broad topic of the United States has many subheadings, one of which is Immigration and Naturalization Service. Some topic entries also include a *See also* notation to refer you to other entries, similar to the following example:

United States - Immigration and Naturalization Service
    Immigration and Emigration

                See also
            Alien labor
            Asylum, Right of
            Deportation
            McCarran-Walter Act

These subheadings and the *See also* cross-references will help you pose questions that narrow or develop your theme. Why are immigrants deported? What rights do immigrants have to asylum? What rights do aliens have in our labor force? Look up the McCarran-Walter Act and find out what effects it had.

Finding Sources

To use the *Reader's Guide,* first determine what year or years you need. Each hardbound volume usually covers one year's magazine offerings. (Your library may have the *Reader's Guide* on computer, which is a tremendous time-saver. However, not all volumes may be available.) If you choose the topic of the Persian Gulf War, for instance, begin your search with the 1990 volume. For some topics, examine magazine articles from different years to follow your topic's development. Search for your topic in the alphabetical listings, which are listed by both subject and author.

If your topic is Mexican immigration in the United States, you might begin looking for the following topic and subtopic:

    Mexico

        Immigration to United States

If your topic is not listed, think of alternative wording. For example, look under *Immigration* and then seek your topic as a subtopic:

    Immigration
    Mexico

Or broaden your topic even more:

    United States
        Immigration
        Mexico

Suppose you are interested in Mexican immigrants who are deported as illegal aliens after many years of living and working in the United States. The *Reader's Guide* entries will offer specific information about articles, similar to the following example entry:

    Illegal aliens return home. C. Rodriguez. bibliog il *California Events*

        14:54-57 Je 1992

If you look at the magazine *California Events* for June 1992 (volume 14), on pages 54–57 is an article by C. Rodriguez titled "Illegal Aliens Return Home." *Bibliog* indicates that the article lists other sources, usually books and other periodicals; *il* means that illustrations are included.

Most libraries store recent periodical issues but preserve older issues on microform—that is, **microfilm** or **microfiche,** film that accommodates exact reproductions in reduced form.

Once you learn to use the *Reader's Guide,* you will have the skills to use other indexes, most of which are for specialized periodicals. For example, the *Essay and General Literature Index* leads you to essays and chapters about literature and authors that you would not find listed in either the card catalog or *The Reader's Guide to Periodical Literature.*

Exercise 2

Use *The Reader's Guide to Periodical Literature* to find three entries for your topic or question in Exercise 1, or for a topic you already have been assigned for a class paper. Copy the entry exactly as you find it or obtain a computer printout.

Topic: _____

Question: _____

_____

_____

Entry 1: _____

_____

_____

Entry 2: _____

_____

_____

Entry 3: _____

_____

_____

Other library resources to consider

1. *Librarians.* Your single most important resource in the library is the library staff. Ask a librarian to help you locate resources and learn how to use them.

2. *Indexes.* Consider using the many other indexes that list magazine, journal, and newspaper entries. Here are just a few:

Business Periodicals Index	*Humanities Index*
Editorials on File	*Music Index*
Education Index	*Public Affairs Information Index*
Bibliographic Index	*Environment Index*
Short Story Index	*Essay and General Literature Index*
Social Science Index	*General Science Index*
New York Times Index	*Los Angeles Times Index*

3. *Abstracts.* Abstracts not only refer you to specific entries in periodicals but also provide a brief summary of the article and sometimes a critique. After reading the abstract, you can determine whether you want to take the time to locate the article itself. Abstracts are published in many fields; here are just a few examples:

International Political Science Abstracts
Psychological Abstracts
Sociological Abstracts

4. *Encyclopedias and Dictionaries.* Every library includes general encyclopedias such as *Encyclopedia Britannica* and *World Book;* the same is true for general dictionaries. For college-level work, however, you will find specialized encyclopedias and dictionaries essential. A few examples include:

Catholic Encyclopedia	*Encyclopedia of Advertising*
Jewish Encyclopedia	*Dictionary of Film Makers*
Encyclopedia of Philosophy	*Dictionary of Mythology,*
Encyclopedia of Educational	*Folklore, and Symbols*
Research	

5. *Vertical File.* Certain publications are so small or odd-sized that they are stored in a specialized file cabinet: bulletins, charts, pamphlets, and newspaper clippings that are not on microfiche.

6. *Resources for Facts.* All libraries contain books that are compendiums of factual information: yearbooks, almanacs, atlases. For example:

Facts on File	*Who's Who in Finance*
Word Almanac	*Yearbook of Agriculture*
Archaeological Atlas of the World	

Remember, your best resource is always the librarian.

Finding Other Campus Resources

Too often students are not aware of the many resources almost every campus offers. Check off the following resources on your campus. Two blank spaces have been provided for you to fill in other resources available on your campus. Your college schedule and catalog indicate the location of these resources.

Check if available	Campus location	Resources: Add important information about each. (hours, names, services)
		Adult Reentry Center
		Audiovisual Center
		Benefits Office (Veterans and Social Security)
		Campus Police
		Career Center
		Counseling Services
		Disabled Students Center
		EOPS (Equal Opportunity Programs & Services)
		Financial Aid Office
		Health Center

Check if available	Campus location	Resources: Add important information about each. (hours, names, services)
		Psychological Counseling (ask in Health Center)
		Honors Program Office
		International Education Program
		Instructional Television Office
		Job Placement Office
		Learning Assistance Center
		Scholarship Office
		Transfer Center
		Tutoring Center
		Writing Center

Summary Map of Step Nine

Library Sources

Card/online Catalog	*Reader's Guide to Periodical Literature*	Other Sources

Finding a topic
Finding sources

Librarians
Indexes
Abstracts
Encyclopedias and dictionaries
Vertical file
Resources for facts

Other Campus Resources

Career Counseling
Counseling Services
Financial Aid Office
Health Center
Tutoring Center

> *Research is formalized curiosity. It is poking and prying with a purpose.*
>
> —**Zora Neale Hurston**

Step Ten
Write a Research Paper

Objectives

❏ To find and narrow a research topic

❏ To use questions to develop a simple outline

❏ To find and validate sources

❏ To practice taking notes from sources

❏ To develop a thesis statement

❏ To avoid plagiarism and a "cut and paste" paper

❏ To document a research paper

Contents

❏ Phase 1: How Do I Find and Narrow a Topic?

❏ Phase 2: What Do I Already Know About This Topic?

❏ Phase 3: Can I Find Sufficient Research Materials for My Topic? How valid are my Resources?

❏ Phase 4: How Do I Avoid Being Overwhelmed?

❏ Phase 5: How Do I Take Notes Once I Find Information?

❏ Phase 6: How Do I Avoid Plagiarism and a Dull "Cut and Paste" Paper?

❏ Phase 7: How Do I Document My Paper?

❏ Summary Map of Step Ten

Key Terms

topic
informative research paper
argumentative research paper
thesis statement
primary and secondary sources

> validity of sources
> bibliography cards
> summary and paraphrase
> plagiarism
> question sheet notes
> direct and indirect quotations
> documentation
> Works Cited

You have a research paper due in four weeks. Among other requirements, the paper should be approximately ten double-spaced typewritten pages with a minimum of eight resources. You must prove that you have done original research by providing documentation to cite your sources, including a Works Cited list.

This chapter will guide you through a stage-by-stage research procedure and explain skills that will apply to any assigned research paper, even for such diverse academic courses as English, psychology, chemistry, history, and astronomy.

Be assured that a research paper assignment challenges most students, mainly because it requires not only a systematic procedure for researching and writing a lengthy paper, but also such skills as locating research sources, taking notes, and documenting sources. Even the very length of a research paper may seem daunting.

Here are some questions that can bring about panic if students don't have the answers:

> How do I find and narrow a topic?
> What do I already know about this topic?
> What more do I need to know?
> Can I find sufficient research materials?
> How valid are my resources?
> How can I avoid being overwhelmed by researching and writing a lengthy paper?
> How do I take notes once I find information?
> How do I avoid plagiarism and a dull "cut and paste" paper?
> How do I document my paper?

Imagine answers to these questions as phases of research that lead to a paper. Most important, focus on one phase at a time rather than on all the phases at once, beginning with the question of a topic.

Phase 1: How Do I Find and Narrow a Topic?

Finding a **topic** depends on your instructor's assignment. Some instructors will let you select any topic that is course-related because they know that if you are not interested in your topic, the paper may be a dull reporting of information you have gathered and "pasted" together. The more excited you are about your topic, the easier your paper will be to write and the more interesting for your instructor to read.

One way to find your own topic is to think about what arouses your curiosity in your classes. You may be curious about a future election (political science), crime in your city (sociology), proper nutrition (health science), the latest developments in cloning (biology), or even a career you are considering (business).

Other instructors will offer broad topic categories, which you must narrow down to fit the length of the paper. An astronomy instructor may offer such broad topics as black holes, recent space exploration, or possible life on other planets. You need to narrow the topic because any of these three topics would be far too broad for a research paper; each would probably require a book-length text to cover the topic adequately.

As described in Step 9, you can use the library's computer databases to enter subject headings and key words to get ideas for topics or to narrow a topic.

In this textbook, you have been studying the 1920s in American history. Broad topics a history instructor might assign on this subject would include Prohibition, inventions, immigration, musicians, and a change in women's roles.

Exercise 1

From your reading of the 1920s in this textbook, pick four broad topics that you find interesting and list them below in the first column; you may include any of the ones mentioned above. Later you will fill in the other two columns. If you are working on a research paper assignment for one of your other courses, include that topic.

Broad Topic	Narrowed Topic	Question
Example: *Inventions*	*Radio*	*How did the invention of the radio influence American life?*
1. _____	_____	_____
2. _____	_____	_____
3. _____	_____	_____
4. _____	_____	_____

Exercise 2

A. "Inventions in the 1920s" is too broad a topic for even a ten-page paper; choosing the subject of radio is one way to narrow down your topic. Narrow down each of the four broad topics and write your choices in the second column.

B. Even "radio" is too broad a topic, but a question about one aspect of the invention of the radio can narrow you topic further.

How did the invention of the radio influence American life?

Go back to Exercise 1 and in the third column create a question for each of your narrowed topics.

C. Read over the four questions you have written to select one that you'll use for another exercise. Put an asterisk in the right margin next to the question.

Your instructor will more than likely specify whether you should be writing an **informative** or an **argumentative** research paper. You have probably written both types by either explaining a topic with information without taking any stance or explaining a topic for which you are arguing a point.

The question "How did the invention of the radio influence American life?" suggests an informative paper. For an argumentative paper, the question would be changed to wording that calls for the writer to prove an opinion, such as "Did the invention of the radio significantly influence American life?" After gathering proof, a student would develop a thesis statement (the main point of the paper) to support one side or the other: "The invention of the radio did not greatly influence American life" or "The invention of the radio significantly influenced American life."

If assigned an argumentative paper for a specific topic, you may already know what you want to prove. If not, proceed with seeking information about the topic until you have sufficient facts to determine what you want to prove.

Phase 2: What Do I Already Know About This Topic?

Now that you have a tentative topic and question, you'll explore your topic question by finding out what you already know. You may be surprised at how much you do know to answer the question. If you don't know much, that's okay. Curiosity usually leads people to a topic because they would like to know more about it.

Exercise 3

Write below your topic question and then for five minutes write freely about what you *already* know or think you know about the topic—don't worry about accuracy at this point. Feel free to include personal or family stories about your chosen topic. Freewriting allows you to write without worrying about accuracy, sentence or paragraph structure, spelling, or punctuation: *you just let thoughts flow freely.*

Example:

How did the invention of the radio influence American life?

The newly invented radio could now get news to Americans faster than newspapers, and listeners could actually hear voice tones, emotions, and sound effects, all of which could influence how people thought. Politicians didn't have to be in front of a live audience but could address all Americans rather than just a limited number. Another influence was probably on family life by bringing parents and children together to listen to and discuss the news, and to enjoy favorite programs together. Just as cars and airplanes were speeding up life and shrinking the nation and the world, so was the radio.

Your topic question: _____

Your freewriting: _____

_____

_____

_____

_____

_____

_____

_____

_____

Exercise 4

Now that you've summarized what you *do* know about your topic, list questions for what you do *not* know about the topic, questions that may need to be answered to write an in-depth paper. List any question, major or minor, that comes to mind so that you have many from which to choose.

Example:

Influences of the radio on American life

Questions:

1. *How many people owned radios in the 1920s, and could the average family afford one?*

2. *What were favorite programs in the 1920s?*

3. *What were types and themes of favorite programs in the 1920s?*

4. *How have the types and themes changed for radio programs?*

5. *What family values were promoted by the radio in the 1920s?*

6. *Were there children's programs in the 1920s? If so, what values were stressed?*

7. *Were crime and violence included in 1920s radio programs?*

8. *Did early radio have commercials? If so, what products were advertised?*

Your list of questions:

Topic: _____

1. _____

2. _____

3. _____

4. _____

5. _____

6. _____

7. _____

Taking time to make this list of questions has benefits beyond focusing your research reading. You may, for example, find that one of the questions offers a better topic or may be a substitute if you cannot find sufficient information for the topic you selected. A student who cannot find material on the influences of the radio on the 1920s lifestyle might change to the topic of "types of radio programs and their themes."

> ***Suggested Activity:*** Share your topic question, freewriting, and questions with a group of classmates so that they can offer more questions about your topic. Add for consideration any of their questions that interest you.

Exercise 5

Now that you have a list of questions in Exercise 4, both yours and those your classmates contributed, underline or circle what you consider the most important three or four questions on which to focus. For a short research paper of four to six pages, probably two to three questions will suffice; a longer paper may require more questions, but not necessarily so. *A good rule is to limit your questions so that each one can be answered in depth.*

At this time, don't worry about the questions that you don't select. They may be irrelevant or may eventually fit under one of your major questions. Also, don't worry about your paper's controlling idea, the **thesis statement.** You may have some idea what message you want to convey to your reader, whether you are writing an informative or argumentative research paper, but that message may change by the time you have researched your sources. Your notes may take you in a direction you have not considered.

Exercise 6

The next step in organizing a simple outline of questions may appear to be a waste of paper, but be assured that you will be using each of these pages for note-taking. You will need as many sheets of paper as you have major questions.

In the top margin of each sheet, write one of your major questions.

Example: for a research paper on the Ku Klux Klan (KKK):

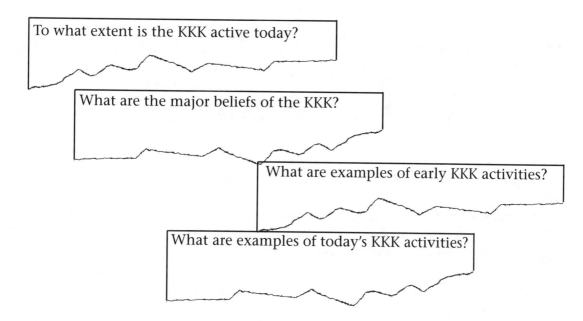

To what extent is the KKK active today?

What are the major beliefs of the KKK?

What are examples of early KKK activities?

What are examples of today's KKK activities?

Exercise 7

Now rearrange your question pages several times to determine the sequence of questions you prefer to use as the outline for your paper.

Exercise 8

Once you are satisfied with your sequence of questions, create a simple outline for your topic by listing the questions on one sheet of paper. This outline will guide your research so that when you begin your reading you know exactly what information you are seeking for each section of the paper. At this point your instructor may want to approve the outline and offer suggestions before you move forward. This approval can save you much time and effort.

Your simple outline:

Topic: _____

Outline: _____

_____

_____

_____

> **Suggested Activity:** Explain your sequence of question topics to your group for their responses.

Phase 3: Can I Find Sufficient Research Materials for My Topic? How Valid Are My Resources?

Before going further with any topic, you need to explore whether libraries that you have access to will offer sufficient primary and secondary sources. **Primary sources** are eyewitness reports that offer firsthand information about experiences and ideas: diaries, letters, editorials, autobiographies, some books and periodical writing, and speeches. Most books and periodicals (newspapers, magazines, and journals) are referred to as **secondary sources** because the information gathered is secondhand.

Too often students will delay taking inventory of sufficient primary and secondary sources by focusing on one source, often the first one they find, not realizing until too late that not much else is available. By then, changing topics can create a serious time problem. A typical situation is that the instructor requires ten sources but only five are available.

Before heading off to the library to check for sources, you may want to review Step 9 if you are not already a pro at using library offerings.

Your gathered information is only as reliable as your source. Find out who wrote the material you are reading, and check the background of a person you are interviewing. Is the person an authority on the topic? What credentials make this person a reliable source? For example, if your research topic is a new AIDS drug, a physician would be a reliable source to explain the drug chemistry as well as the probable benefits and side effects of the medicine. An AIDS patient taking this new drug could describe experiencing the results. Both doctor and patient are probably reliable sources in different aspects of the drug; however, facts gathered from only one patient may be weak proof. Other patients may have different reactions, and sometimes doctors may not agree about a new drug. Therefore compare and contrast what these "authorities" say.

Too often we readers assume we can count on respected, credentialed people for reliable, objective information, yet writers may let their personal opinion influence their writing. Some can influence readers with their word choices, or by omitting or distorting information. For example, in comparing and contrasting three historians whose writings describe the actions of John Brown, the controversial pre-Civil War abolitionist from Kansas, we find that each of the three historians views his subject with different eyes. One historian refers to John Brown as an "anti-slavery fanatic" whose "harebrained scheme" of capturing the Harpers Ferry arsenal in Virginia in 1859 increased the fear of slave uprisings (Angle 23). A second historian includes more information by describing John Brown as an "egomaniac" who, with his sons and followers before the Harpers Ferry incident, "hacked to death five innocent men [in Pottawatomie Creek, Kansas] who had actually come to Kansas to get away from slavery" (Leckie 387). A third historian not only omits the Pottawatomie massacre, saying only that Brown "had done his part to aid the anti-slavery forces in Kansas," but praises John Brown in comparison to others who "had died fighting for freedom, but none had done it so heroically or at such a propitious moment" (Franklin 268).

Ask yourself questions about your source: Does the writer or interviewee strive to remain objective? Does the person provide accurate facts rather than opinions that sound like facts? If the person provides opinions, does the author support opinions with proof? Does the writer cite where the facts came from, providing full documentation? Note in the preceeding paragraph the in-text parenthetical documentation (e.g., Angle 23) of authors and page numbers, for which full bibliographical information appears in a Works Cited list at the end of this section.

A book jacket usually offers the credentials of the writer, but if there is no book jacket or if you have read an article without sufficient details of the author's background, the Internet can often provide this information. If you enter the name of the third historian, "John Hope Franklin," a Web search engine will lead you to several sites that offer complete information about this respected American historian: his date and place of birth, education, teaching career, public offices, list of publications, honors and awards, and his research center focusing on African Americans.

In a few pages you will be reading about the Ku Klux Klan. By entering that key term on search engines, you can find many articles on this American hate group. One article that stands out as being detailed and factual is offered by the Southern Poverty Law Center, but you may wonder about its **validity** as a source. If you have not read much about civil rights, you may not recognize this center. By entering "Southern Poverty Law Center" as a key word, you will be led to its website (http://www.splcenter.org) and learn that it was founded in 1971, is located in Montgomery, Alabama, and is a nonprofit organization that combats hate, intolerance, and discrimination through education. Another method for checking validity is to ask your instructor about a source; in the case of the KKK, you would ask your history or government instructor.

Be especially wary of information you find on the Internet; anyone can create a website and produce writings about anything. You yourself could create a website to write your own version of John Brown's abolitionist actions without your being a valid source for readers.

Works Cited

Angle, Paul M. (1967). *A Pictorial History of the Civil War Years*. Garden City: Doubleday.

Franklin, John Hope. (1947). *From Slavery to Freedom: A History of Negro Americans*. New York: Alfred A. Knopf.

Leckie, Robert. (1968). *The Wars of America: Quebec to Appomattox*. Vol. 1. New York: Harper & Row.

Phase 4: How Do I Avoid Being Overwhelmed?

Often students leave the library overwhelmed by the thought of reading all the sources they have found. By creating a simple and temporary outline of questions to research, you have already taken a major step to give you confidence that you have the situation under control. You know what major questions you want to answer. You will limit your reading to skimming for answers to these questions. Also, you probably have been in classes, especially English classes, in which you have had to write short papers of two to three printed pages. *Consider your research paper as simply a series of short papers, each one a section of your outline.*

Now you need to estimate the length of each section of your paper. This step may alleviate your feeling overwhelmed by writing a long paper. Consider the KKK outline as an example:

The Ku Klux Klan

Introduction	1/2 page
When, where, and why did the KKK begin?	2 pages
What are the major beliefs of the KKK?	1 page
What are examples of KKK past activities?	4 pages
To what extent is the KKK active today?	2 pages
Conclusion	1/2 page
	10 pages

These estimates should reassure you that finding relevant information to answer each question is a manageable task. This outline places emphasis on examples of KKK activities because that section receives the largest number of pages. Another student may prefer to focus on today's KKK or emphasize how the KKK has influenced similar white supremacy groups today. This exercise may also reveal that too many questions are being asked to allow for sufficient in-depth discussion, leading to the omission of at least one question. The writer may have to decide between past and present KKK activities.

For your topic, you must determine the most important section or sections of your paper and estimate the number of pages accordingly. At this point of your research, you may not know what you want to emphasize until you finish your note-taking. That's understandable, so for now, just guess. You can always change this outline based on what you are—or are not—finding. Your outline is simply a temporary guide.

Exercise 9

Go back now to your simple outline on page 287 and assign an estimated number of pages for answering each of your section questions.

The task of writing a ten-page research paper will be far less daunting if you think in terms of writing two- to four-page sections. In summary, think small: *The research paper is a compilation of short papers on the same topic.*

Phase 5: How Do I Take Notes Once I Find Information?

Now that you know your school library, nearby libraries, and the Internet offer sufficient information and number of required sources for your topic, you can zoom in on your simple question outline to direct your readings.

By knowing in advance what information you are looking for, you can reduce your amount of reading; otherwise, you could feel you are drowning in a sea of information that sounds fascinating but may not be usable. There is no need to read an entire book if you check the Table of Contents and the Index for specific topics. In shorter sources, such as magazines, journals, and chapters, skim the text until you find answers to your questions.

Making Bibliography Cards Before Taking Notes

Once you find information that helps answer one of your questions, create **bibliography cards** to record full information for books and other sources from which you are working and taking notes. When you make your research paper's Works Cited list to document the sources you've actually mentioned (cited) in your text, all information will already be recorded and in the correct format. All you need to do is arrange the cards in alphabetical order to assemble your paper's Works Cited (see the end of Phase 3 above for a sample Works Cited). If you fail to make your bibliography cards before you take notes, you may forget to do so and end up having to go to the library to retrieve your sources, which may be checked out.

Sample Bibliography Card

Bailey, Thomas, and David Kennedy,
  The American Pageant, 10th Ed.
  Lexington, MA: DC Heath, 1994.

For purposes of this section, you'll follow the widely used Modern Language Association (MLA) research paper system. MLA uses citations in the text rather than footnotes or endnotes. Another style is the APA (American Psychological Association) style, often used in social science and science research papers (see page 296 for examples of MLA and APA styles).

You will need to use a style manual for the research paper style your instructor prefers. Regardless of which manual you use, formats vary for the bibliographic information that you need to include, such as the format for two authors as opposed to one, for more than one volume, for a new edition, for chapters written by different authors, or for information from websites, video, or television programs.

Types of Note-Taking

There are three types of note-taking. All three are often included in one set of notes, but you need to be aware of how you are recording information to avoid **plagiarism** (presenting another's words and ideas as your own):

- A **summary** of what you are reading (using your own words to capture main ideas; usually about one-fourth the length of the original)

- A **paraphrase** (using your own words, a restatement of the writer's thoughts that can be approximately the same length as, or shorter than the original)

- **Direct** and **indirect quotations**:
    - Direct quotation: "There was one shrill whistle."
    - Indirect quotation: The author stated that there was one shrill whistle.

One of the dangers in taking notes is a tendency to plagiarize without realizing that you are doing so. This unintended kind of plagiarism can occur if you fail to mark which words come directly from a source. This failure can cause you to blend your words and those of others without giving credit for their words and original ideas. In your **question sheet notes,** therefore, you must identify and document a writer's words, phrases, passages, as well as ideas that you have not found elsewhere.

Using Question Sheets to Record Information

Next, you should record information on each question sheet that will help answer the question. In the left margin record the author(s) and page number(s) in parentheses, the exact format that you will use for documentation in your paper. Indent on the second line so that you can quickly find the authors' names and new entries. The following is an example.

When, where, and why did the KKK begin?

(Bailey and Kennedy 50l–503)

KKK began in Tennessee in 1866 to prevent "the success, and ability of black legislators. . . . " The KKK, the "Invisible Empire of the South," wanted to discourage both Negroes and pro-Negro legislators from voting in black legislators.

[Note: example of summary that includes direct quotation]

Exercise 10

Below are bibliography cards that relate to notes for another question sheet on the KKK.

Kownslar, Allan O., and Donald B. Frizzle. *Discovering American History.* New York: Holt, Rinehart and Winston, 1970.

Boorstin, Daniel J., and Brooks Mather Kelley. *A History of the United States.* Lexington, MA: Ginn, 1981.

What are examples of KKK activities?

(Kownslar and Frizzle 225–228)

    Albion W. Tourgée was one of the Northerners who went to the South after the Civil War to participate in the reconstruction of the South, either to help or to take advantage of the freed, uneducated Negroes. Tourgée wrote the novel *A Fool's Errand* to record how Southern whites reacted to the new power of the freed Negroes. He includes a description of a secret group, the Ku Klux Klan, that terrorized and even killed Negroes to keep them in line. One passage includes an example of a KKK activity soon after the KKK organized: "It was a chill, dreary night. . . . There was one shrill whistle, some noise of quietly moving horses; and those who looked from their windows saw a black-gowned and grimly-masked horseman sitting upon a draped horse at every corner of the streets, and before each house,—grim, silent, threatening. Those who saw dared not move, or give any alarm. Instinctively they knew that the enemy they had feared had come, had them in his clutches, and would work his will of them, whether they resisted or not. . . . I should say there were from a hundred to a hundred and fifty still in line. They were all masked, and wore black robes. The horses were disguised, too, by draping. . . . I could not see precisely what they were at, but, from my back upper window, saw them down about the tree. After a while a signal was given, and just at that time a match was struck, and I saw a dark body slip down under the limb."
    [Note: example of paraphrase and direct quotation]

(Boorstin and Kelley 311–312)

    Some Southerners who wanted to maintain the Old South style of life formed a secret army. The Ku Klux Klan, coming from a Greek word *kyklos* meaning circle, could be violent in their attempt to prevent blacks from voting and presuming they were "the white man's equal."
    "Thousands of blacks were driven from their homes, maimed, or tortured. Whole communities were terrorized by masked thugs on parade, by burning crosses, by kidnapping and tar-and-feathering."

> *Suggested Activity:* In a small group, share the notes you just recorded. Discuss how each of you may have varied in what you considered main ideas to record. Offer examples of summary, paraphrase, and direct and indirect quotations.

Developing a Final Thesis Statement and Outline

Once you have completed your note-taking, you have sufficient information to determine your final thesis statement. Since you may have changed your mind about the focus of your paper or changed your point of view, make certain your simple outline matches your final thesis statement before you start your rough draft.

Phase 6: How Do I Avoid Plagiarism and a Dull "Cut and Paste" Paper?

Now you are ready to start your rough draft. After writing an introduction, turn to your Question/Answer sheets for the first part of your outline. Read the question and then all the notes that answer this question. Then reread the answers over and over until you think that you can write without referring to your notes. You want to freewrite this section with all the information synthesized in your head so that your thoughts and voice flow on the page. Freewriting means that you are free to write without worry about order of thoughts, spelling, sentence structure, or forgetting information. After you finish a freewriting draft of this section, you can go back and insert **direct** and **indirect quotations,** missing information, and in-text parenthetical documentation to avoid plagiarism. At this point, don't worry about spelling or effective sentence structure, just get the first draft down on paper.

Notice in the freewriting example below that the student has captured the bare essence of the detailed notes with her own voice, words, and style with full awareness that she can select and insert missing information later. What follows is her first partial draft with blanks left for insertions.

Rough draft for partial answer on "What are examples of KKK activities?"

Writers have recorded many examples of KKK discrimination and cruelty toward Negroes after the Civil War. Historians_____
and_____summarized the widespread terror by stating that thousands of blacks were victims of the KKK's burning crosses, tar-and-feathering, torturing blacks, and driving them from their homes.

One Northerner describes an eerie scene of masked horsemen moving silently through a town, with even their horses disguised. About 150 of these black-robed horsemen paralyzed the townspeople as they moved through the streets. Then a signal, followed by a match lit to reveal a dark body under a tree limb. . . .

After adding the missing information, the student will be ready to write the next draft to smoothly tie in the insertions.

Phase 7: How Do I Document My Paper?

There are two steps to acknowledging your sources: in-text parenthetical **documentation,** which provides either the author's name and page number (MLA), or the author's name and year (APA); and a **Works Cited** (or Bibliography), which offers full information about each source. Disciplines interested in the latest research usually require a research paper style, such as APA, that puts the date of the information in the forefront. Here is an example of MLA documentation:

> One Northerner describes an eerie scene of masked horsemen moving silently through a town, with even their horses disguised. About 150 of these black-robed horsemen paralyzed the townspeople as they moved through the streets. Then a signal, followed by a match lit to reveal a dark body under a tree limb (Kownslar and Frizzle 225–228).

The APA style would be:

(Kownslar and Frizzle, 1970, pp. 225–228).

Here are examples of how Kownslar and Frizzle would be listed in the Works Cited for the two different styles:

MLA:
Kownslar, Allan O., and Donald B. Frizzle. *Discovering American history.* New York: Holt, Rinehart and Winston.

APA:
Kownslar, A. O., & Frizzle, D. B. (1970). *Discovering American history.* New York: Holt, Rinehart and Winston.

Exercise 11

Work with a partner to summarize the differences in the MLA and APA styles for:

A. In-text documentation

   Example: MLA style does not use the year of publication, but APA does.

   _____

   _____

   _____

   _____

   _____

B. Works cited

Example: APA capitalizes only the first word and proper nouns in a book title, but MLA uses standard capitalization for titles (all main words).

   _____

   _____

   _____

   _____

   _____

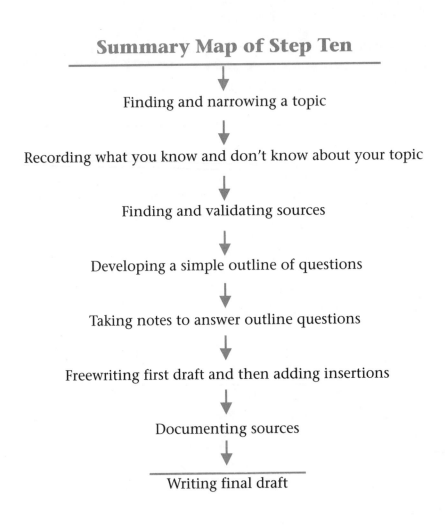

Summary Map of Step Ten

Finding and narrowing a topic

Recording what you know and don't know about your topic

Finding and validating sources

Developing a simple outline of questions

Taking notes to answer outline questions

Freewriting first draft and then adding insertions

Documenting sources

Writing final draft

Stage Four

Create a Personal Study Profile

Using the metacognitive process, you observe your own learning process, evaluate which study strategies fit the way you learn best, and fine-tune or adjust them as needed.

—A. L. Brown

Objectives

❏ To understand how you prefer to learn

❏ To match study strategies to the demands of the subject

Contents

❏ Personal Study Profile

Key Terms

auditory and visual stimuli
basic strategy
alternative strategy

From learning more about yourself as a student, you now have a more realistic understanding about how you prefer to learn. You also know how to tailor your learning style to your instructor's teaching style. For example, if you are a visual learner but your instructor provides only **auditory stimuli** through lectures, your lecture notes will, nevertheless, offer **visual stimuli.**

You now also know how to save time by choosing the right strategy for the appropriate situation; for example, writing summaries is worth the effort in preparing for essay exams while flashcards are efficient for memorizing answers to difficult questions or definitions.

You know how to manage your time, to make appointments with yourself to study, and to allot sufficient hours per week for studying.

With these and other new awarenesses, you are ready to make a list of what strategies in this book work best for you. Here is a sample of a Personal Study Profile entry:

10. Using Alternate Sources

Basic Strategies:

Example: *Read about a topic in periodicals.*

1. Get a Tutor.
2. Form a study group.
3. Check encyclopedia.
4. Call a classmate.

Alternative Strategies:

1. Read in a different textbook.
2. Talk to instructor.

Take your time filling in your Personal Study Profile. Refer back to your Personal Response Checks, Self-Contracts, Journal Entries, and each chapter's Contents to review strategies that have been useful. For example, if you found 'Beat the Clock' helpful, record it under "Concentrating" as a **basic strategy.** If it is not a technique that you plan to use regularly, record it as an **alternative strategy.** (You may find alternative strategies useful in the future even if you have not used them often or did not like them when you first tried them.)

When finished, remove these profile sheets and keep them in the front of your notebook as a quick reference when you study.

Personal Study Profile

1. Using an Overview to Get the Big Picture

Basic Strategies:

Example: *Read a textbook preface, foreword, or introduction.*

1. _____

2. _____

3. _____

4. _____

Alternative Strategies:

1. _____

2. _____

2. Studying a Textbook

Basic Strategies:

Example: *Make a TIPS for important or difficult material.*

1. _____

2. _____

3. _____

4. _____

Alternative Strategies:

1. _____

2. _____

3. Taking Lecture Notes

Basic Strategies:

Example: *Create abbreviations for a course's key terms.*

1. _____

2. _____

3. _____

4. _____

Alternative Strategies:

1. _____

2. _____

4. Learning Course Vocabulary

Basic Strategies:

Example: *Use a new word or term in a sentence.*

1. _____

2. _____

3. _____

4. _____

Alternative Strategies:

1. _____

2. _____

304 Part One / Study Strategies and Techniques

5. Anticipating Test Questions

Basic Strategies:

Example: *Concentrate on* what, why, *and* how *rather than* who, when, *and* where.

1. _____

2. _____

3. _____

4. _____

Alternative Strategies:

1. _____

2. _____

6. Managing Time

Basic Strategies:

Example: *Make a daily list of things to do.*

1. _____

2. _____

3. _____

4. _____

Alternative Strategies:

1. _____

2. _____

7. Concentrating

Basic Strategies:

Example: *Keep a tally list of distractions while I study.*

1. _____

2. _____

3. _____

4. _____

Alternative Strategies:

1. _____

2. _____

8. Memorizing for a Test

Basic Strategies:

Example: *Make flashcards.*

1. _____

2. _____

3. _____

4. _____

Alternative Strategies:

1. _____

2. _____

9. Working with a Study Group

Basic Strategies:

Example: *Limit a study group to three or four committed people.*

1. _____

2. _____

3. _____

4. _____

Alternative Strategies:

1. _____

2. _____

10. Using Alternate Sources

Basic Strategies:

Example: *Read about a topic in periodicals.*

1. _____

2. _____

3. _____

4. _____

Alternative Strategies:

1. _____

2. _____

11. Reviewing and Preparing for a Test

Basic Strategies:

Example: *Use the checkmark review method.*

1. _____

2. _____

3. _____

4. _____

Alternative Strategies:

1. _____

2. _____

12. Taking the Test

Basic Strategies:

Example: *After reading the directions, glance over the test and answer the easiest questions first.*

1. _____

2. _____

3. _____

4. _____

Alternative Strategies:

1. _____

2. _____

13. Analyzing the Test Results

Basic Strategies:

Example: *Fill out an analysis sheet to determine why specific questions were missed.*

1. _____

2. _____

3. _____

4. _____

Alternative Strategies:

1. _____

2. _____

Part Two

College Texts

History Excerpt

"American Life in the 'Roaring Twenties,' 1919–1929"*

Contents

---

*Thomas Bailey and David Kennedy. (1994). *The American Pageant,* 10th ed., copyright (c) by D.C. Heath & Company. Reprinted by permission of Houghton Mifflin, pp. 749–762.

> *America's present need is not heroics but healing; not nostrums but normalcy; not revolution but restoration;. . . not surgery but serenity.*
>
> **—Warren G. Harding, 1920**

President Harding's explanation for the "Roaring Twenties" was probably close to the mark. The previous two decades had seen Americans try to reform their own country and then the world. The first, known as The Progressive Movement (1900–1912), found Americans energetically improving city and state governments, creating a new banking system, and attempting cures for a variety of social problems. The second (1912–1920) extended from our experiences with World War I. Reluctantly, we joined that conflict because we were convinced that democracy was in jeopardy if Germany's war machine conquered all of Europe. Guided and persuaded by President Woodrow Wilson, we began a mission "to make the world safe for democracy." Coupled with this mission, we put great hope in our president's idea that permanent world peace was possible only if directed by a League of Nations. Unhappily, the harsh nature of the peace treaty, along with our unanticipated failure to join the League, led to a disillusionment unparalleled in our history. Almost overnight, reform and grand visions lost their luster. As President Harding noted, we had enough of "cure-alls" and wanted our familiar lives back. As a result we plunged into an era where gangsters, jazz, and sports replaced slum clearance, city improvements, and attempts at world peace. The 1920s became a time to catch our breath and enjoy a new-found prosperity.

The "Roaring Twenties" was also a time to turn inward. We passed laws restricting immigration and jailed people who stood for foreign ideas. Infected with this "nativist" mood, we endured a fearsome revival of the Ku Klux Klan, a terrorist organization pledged to keep former slaves from gaining civil or political rights. We witnessed the controversial trial of Nicola Sacco and Bartolomeo Vanzetti, who were convicted and executed, not so much by evidence, but because they were Italians, atheists, anarchists, and draft dodgers. Separated by language, religion, and customs, Jews, Russians, Poles, Hungarians appeared destined to live in divided communities. Yet, at the same time, there were changes that tended to bring these groups together. You will discover these social modifications as you read about Prohibition, mass consumption, skyrocketing stock prices, electrifying jazz, a radio craze, and sensational Hollywood. The meaning behind this transformation can be found in the following history of the "Roaring Twenties."

The Prohibition 'Experiment'

One of the last peculiar spasms of the progressive reform movement was Prohibition, loudly supported by crusading churches and by many women. The arid new order was authorized in 1919 by the Eighteenth Amendment, as implemented by the Volstead Act passed by Congress later that year. Together these laws made the world "safe for hypocrisy."

The legal abolition of alcohol was fairly popular in the Midwest, and especially so in the South. Southern whites were eager to keep stimulants out of the hands of blacks, lest they burst out of "their place." But despite the overwhelming ratification of the "dry" amendment, strong opposition persisted in the larger eastern cities. Concentrated colonies of "wet" foreign-born peoples hated to abandon their Old World drinking habits. Yet most Americans now assumed that Prohibition had come to stay. Everywhere there were last wild flings, as the nation prepared to enter upon a permanent "alcoholiday."

But Prohibitionists were naive in the extreme. They overlooked the tenacious American tradition of strong drink and of weak control by the central government, especially over private lives. They forgot that the federal authorities had never satisfactorily enforced a law where the majority of the people—or a strong minority—were hostile to it. They ignored the fact that one cannot make a crime overnight out of something that millions of people had never regarded as a crime. Lawmakers could not legislate away a thirst.

Peculiar conditions hampered the enforcement of Prohibition. Profound disillusionment over the aftermath of the war raised serious questions as to the wisdom of further self-denial. Slaking thirst became a cherished personal liberty, and many ardent wets believed that the way to bring about repeal was to violate the law on a large enough scale. Hypocritical, hip-flasked legislators spoke or voted dry while privately drinking wet. ("Let us strike a blow for liberty" was an ironic toast.) Frustrated soldiers, returning from France, complained that Prohibition had been "put over" on them while they were "over there." Grimy workers bemoaned the loss of their cheap beer, while pointing out that the idle rich could buy all the illicit alcohol they wanted. Flaming youth of the jazz age thought it "smart" to swill bootleg liquor—"liquid tonsillectomies." Millions of older citizens likewise found forbidden fruit fascinating, as they engaged in "bar hunts."

Prohibition might have started off on a better foot if there had been a larger army of enforcement officials. But the state and federal agencies were understaffed, and their snoopers, susceptible to bribery, were underpaid. The public was increasingly distressed as scores of people, including innocent bystanders, were killed by quick-triggered dry agents.

Prohibition simply did not prohibit. The old-time "men only" corner saloons were replaced by thousands of "speakeasies," each with its tiny grilled window through which the thirsty spoke softly before the barred door was opened. Hard liquor, especially the cocktail, was drunk in staggering volume by both men and women. Largely because of the difficulties of transporting and concealing bottles, beverages of high alcoholic content were popular. Foreign rumrunners, often from the West Indies, had their inning, and countless cases of liquor leaked down from Canada. The zeal of American Prohibition agents on occasion strained diplomatic relations with Uncle Sam's northern neighbor.

"Home brew" and "bathtub gin" became popular, as law-evading adults engaged in "alky cooking" with toy stills. The worst of the homemade "rotgut" produced blindness, even death. The affable bootlegger worked in silent partnership with the friendly undertaker.

Yet the "noble experiment" was not entirely a failure. Bank savings increased, and absenteeism in industry decreased, presumably because of the newly sober ways of formerly soused barflies. On the whole, probably less liquor was consumed than in the days before Prohibition. though strong drink continued to be available. As the legendary tippler remarked, Prohibition was "a darn sight better than no liquor at all."

The Golden Age of Gangsterism

Prohibition spawned shocking crimes. The lush profits of illegal alcohol led to bribery of the police, many of whom were induced to see and smell no evil. Violent gang wars broke out in the big cities between rivals seeking to corner the rich market in booze. Rival triggermen used their sawed-off shotguns and chattering "typewriters" (machine guns) to "erase" bootlegging competitors who were trying to "muscle in" on their "racket." In the gang wars of the 1920s in Chicago, about five hundred low characters were murdered. Arrests were few and convictions were even fewer, as the button-lipped gangsters covered for one another with the underworld's code of silence.

Chicago was by far the most spectacular example of lawlessness. In 1925 "Scarface" Al Capone, a grasping and murderous booze distributor, began six years of gang warfare that netted him millions of blood-spattered dollars. He zoomed through the streets in an armor-plated car with bulletproof windows. A Brooklyn newspaper quipped,

> And the pistols' red glare
> Bombs bursting in air
> Give proof through the night
> That Chicago's still there.

Capone, though branded "Public Enemy Number One," could not be convicted of the cold-blooded massacre, on St. Valentine's Day in 1929, of seven disarmed members of a rival gang. But after serving most of an eleven-year sentence in a federal penitentiary for income-tax evasion, he was released as a syphilitic wreck.

Gangsters rapidly moved into other profitable and illicit activities: prostitution, gambling, and narcotics. Honest merchants were forced to pay "protection money" to the organized thugs; otherwise their windows would be smashed, their trucks overturned, or their employees or themselves beaten up. Racketeers even invaded the ranks of local labor unions as organizers and promoters. Organized crime had come to be one of the nation's most gigantic businesses. By 1930 the annual "take" of the underworld was estimated to be from $12 billion to $18 billion—several times the income of the Washington government.

Criminal callousness sank to new depths in 1932 with the kidnapping for ransom, and eventual murder, of the infant son of aviator-hero Charles A. Lindbergh. The entire nation was inexpressibly shocked and saddened, causing Congress in 1932 to pass the so-called Lindbergh Law, making interstate abduction in certain circumstances a death-penalty offense.

Monkey Business in Tennessee

Education in the 1920s continued to make giant bootstrides. More and more states were requiring young people to remain in

William Jennings Bryan. This perennial presidential candidate and Christian Fundamentalist was destroyed by biology and Clarence Darrow. (Library of Congress).

school until age sixteen or eighteen, or until graduation from high school. The proportion of 17-year-olds who finished high school almost doubled in the 1920s, to more than one in four.

The most revolutionary contribution to educational theory during these yeasty years was made by mild-mannered Professor John Dewey, who was on the faculty of Columbia University from 1904 to 1930. By common consent one of America's few front-rank philosophers, he set forth the principles of "learning by doing" that formed the foundation of so-called progressive education, with its greater "permissiveness." He believed that the workbench was as essential as the blackboard and that "education for life" should be a primary goal of the teacher.

This new emphasis on creating socially useful adults rendered many schools more attractive. No longer was the schoolhouse a kind of juvenile jail, from which the pupils burst at the end of the year chanting, as young Dewey had when a youngster in Vermont, "Good-bye school, good-bye teacher, damned old fool."

Science also scored wondrous advances in these years. A massive public-health program, launched by the Rockefeller Foundation in the South in 1909, had virtually wiped out the ancient affliction of hookworm by the 1920s. Better nutrition and health care helped to increase the life expectancy of a newborn infant from 50 years in 1901 to 59 years in 1929.

Yet both science and progressive education in the 1920s were subjected to unfriendly fire from the Fundamentalists. These old-time religionists charged that the teaching of Darwinian evolution was destroying faith in God and the Bible, while contributing to the moral breakdown of youth in the jazz age. Numerous attempts were made to secure laws prohibiting the teaching of evolution, "the bestial hypothesis," in the public schools, and three Southern states adopted such shackling measures. The trio of states included Tennessee, in the heart of the so-called Bible Belt South, where

the spirit of evangelical religion was still robust.

The stage was set for the memorable "Monkey Trial" at the hamlet of Dayton, eastern Tennessee, in 1925. A likable high-school biology teacher, John T. Scopes, was indicted for teaching evolution. Batteries of newspaper reporters, armed with notebooks and cameras, descended upon the quiet town to witness the spectacle. Scopes was defended by nationally known attorneys, while William Jennings Bryan, an ardent Presbyterian Fundamentalist, joined the prosecution. Taking the stand as an expert on the Bible, Bryan was made to appear foolish by the famed criminal lawyer Clarence Darrow. Five days after the trial was over, Bryan died of a stroke, no doubt brought on by the heat and strain.

This historic clash between theology and biology proved inconclusive. Scopes, the forgotten man of the drama, was found guilty and fined $100. But the Supreme Court of Tennessee, while upholding the law, set aside the fine on a technicality. The Fundamentalists at best won only a hollow victory, for the absurdities of the trial cast ridicule on their cause. Yet even though increasing numbers of Christians were coming to reconcile the revelations of religion with the findings of modern science, Fundamentalism, with its emphasis on literal reading of the Bible, remained a vibrant force in American spiritual life. It was especially strong in the Baptist church and in the rapidly growing Churches of Christ, organized in 1906.

The Mass-Consumption Economy

Prosperity—real, sustained, and widely shared—put much of the "roar" in the twenties. The economy kicked off its war harness in 1919, faltered a few steps in the recession of 1920–1921, and then sprinted forward for nearly seven years. Both the recent war and Treasury Secretary Andrew Mellon's tax policies favored the rapid expansion of capital investment. Ingenious machines, powered by relatively cheap energy from newly tapped oil fields, dramatically increased the productivity of the laborer. Assembly-line production reached such perfection in Henry Ford's famed Rouge River plant near Detroit that a finished automobile emerged every ten seconds.

Great new industries suddenly sprouted forth. Supplying electrical power for the humming new machines became a giant business in the 1920s. Above all, the automobile, once the horseless chariot of the rich, now became the carriage of the common citizen. By 1930 Americans owned almost 30 million cars.

The nation's deepening "love affair" with the automobile headlined a momentous shift in the character of the economy. American manufacturers seemed to have mastered the problems of production; their worries now focused on consumption. Could they find the mass markets for the goods they had contrived to spew forth in such profusion?

Responding to this need, a new arm of American commerce came into being: advertising. By persuasion and ploy, allure and sexual suggestion, advertisers sought to make Americans chronically discontented with their paltry possessions and want more, more, more. A founder of this new "profession" was Bruce Barton, prominent New York partner in a Madison Avenue firm. In 1925 Barton published a best-seller, *The Man Nobody Knows,* setting forth the seductive thesis that Jesus Christ was the greatest adman of all time. "Every advertising man ought to study the parables of Jesus," Barton preached. "They are marvelously condensed, as all good advertising should be." Barton even had a good word to say for Christ's executive ability: "He picked up twelve men from the bottom ranks of business and forged them into an organization that conquered the world."

In this commercialized atmosphere, even sports were becoming a big business. Ballyhooed by the "image makers," home-run heroes like George H. "Babe" Ruth were far better known than most statesmen. The fans bought tickets in such numbers that "Babe's" hometown park, Yankee Stadium, became known as "the house that Ruth built." In 1921 the slugging heavyweight champion, Jack Dempsey, knocked out the dapper French light heavyweight, Georges Carpentier. The Jersey City crowd in attendance had paid more than a million dollars—the first in a series of million-dollar "gates" in the golden years.

Buying on credit was another innovative feature of the postwar economy. "Possess today and pay tomorrow" was the message directed at buyers. Once-frugal descendants of Puritans went ever deeper into debt to own all kinds of newfangled marvels—refrigerators, vacuum cleaners, and especially cars and radios—now. Prosperity thus accumulated an overhanging cloud of debt, and the economy became increasingly vulnerable to disruptions of the credit structure.

Putting America on Rubber Tires

A new industrial revolution slipped into high gear in America in the 1920s. Thrusting out steel tentacles, it changed the daily life of the people in unprecedented ways. Machinery was the new messiah—and the automobile was its principal prophet.

Of all the inventions of the era, the automobile cut the deepest mark. It heralded an amazing new industrial system, based on assembly-line methods and mass-production techniques.

Americans adapted rather than invented the gasoline engine; Europeans can claim the original honor. By the 1890s a few daring American inventors and promoters, including Henry Ford and Ransom E. Olds (Oldsmobile), were developing the infant automotive industry. By 1910 there were 69 companies, with a total annual production of 181,000 units. The early contraptions were neither speedy nor reliable. Many a stalled motorist, profanely cranking a balky automobile, had to endure the jeer "Get a horse" from the occupants of a passing dobbin-drawn carriage.

An enormous industry sprang into being, as Detroit became the motorcar capital of America. The mechanized colossus owed much to the stopwatch efficiency techniques of Frederick W. Taylor, a prominent inventor, engineer, and tennis player, who sought to eliminate wasted motion. His epitaph reads "Father of Scientific Management."

Best known of the new crop of industrial wizards was Henry Ford, who more than any other individual put America on rubber tires. His high and hideous Model T ("Tin Lizzie") was cheap, rugged, and reasonably reliable, though rough and clattering. The parts of Ford's "flivver" were highly standardized, but the behavior of this "rattling good car" was so individualized that it became the butt of numberless jokes.

Lean and silent Henry Ford, who was said to have wheels in his head, erected an immense personal empire on the cornerstone of his mechanical genius, though his associates provided much of the organizational talent. Ill educated, this multimillionaire mechanic was socially and culturally narrow; "History is bunk," he once testified. But he dedicated himself with one-track devotion to the gospel of standardization. After two early failures, he grasped and applied fully the techniques of assembly-line production—"Fordism." He is supposed to have remarked that the purchaser could have his automobile any color he desired—just as long as it was black. So economical were his methods that in the mid-1920s he was selling the Ford roadster for $260—well within the purse of a thrifty worker.

The flood of Fords was phenomenal. In 1914 the "Automobile Wizard" turned out his 500,000th Model T. By 1930 his total had risen to 20 million, or, on a bumper-to-bumper basis, more than enough to encircle the globe. A national newspaper and magazine poll conducted in 1923 revealed Ford to be the people's choice for

Ford Sedan. Automobiles, along with cheap gas, provided quick escape from the confines of home. (Library of Congress)

the presidential nomination in 1924. By 1929, when the great bull market collapsed, 26 million motor vehicles were registered in the United States. This figure, averaging 1 for every 4.9 Americans, represented far more automobiles than existed in all the rest of the world.

The Advent of the Gasoline Age

The impact of the self-propelled carriage on various aspects of American life was tremendous. A gigantic new industry emerged, dependent on steel but displacing steel from its kingpin role. Employing directly or indirectly about 6 million people by 1930, it was a major prop of the nation's prosperity. Thousands of new jobs, moreover, were created by supporting industries. The lengthening list would include rubber, glass, and fabrics, to say nothing of highway construction and thousands of service stations and garages. America's standard of living, responding to this infectious prosperity, rose to an enviable level.

New industries boomed lustily; older ones grew sickly. The petroleum business experienced an explosive development. Hundreds of oil derricks shot up in California, Texas, and Oklahoma, as these states expanded wondrously and the wilderness frontier became an industrial frontier. The once-feared railroad octopus, on the other hand, was hard hit by the competition of passenger cars, buses, and trucks. An age-old story was repeated: one industry's gains were another industry's pains.

Other effects were widely felt. Speedy marketing of perishable foodstuffs, such as fresh fruits, was accelerated. A new prosperity enriched outlying farms, as city dwellers were provided with produce at attractive prices. Countless new roads ribboned out to meet the demand of the American motorist for smoother and faster highways, often paid for by taxes on gasoline. The era of mud ended as the nation made haste to construct the finest network of hard-surfaced roadways in the world. Lured by new seductiveness in advertising, and encouraged by the perfecting of installment-plan buying, countless Americans with shallow purses acquired the habit of riding as they paid.

Zooming motor cars were agents of social change. At first a luxury, they rapidly became a necessity. Essentially devices for needed transportation, they soon developed into a badge of freedom and equality—a necessary prop for self-respect. To some, ostentation seemed more important than transportation. Leisure hours could now be spent more pleasurably, as tens of thousands of cooped-up souls responded to the call of the open road on joyriding vacations. Women were further freed from clinging-vine dependence on men. Isolation among the sections was broken down, and the less attractive states lost population at an alarming rate. By the late 1920s, Americans owned more automobiles than bathtubs. "I can't go to town in a bathtub," one homemaker explained.

Other social by-products of the automobile were visible. Autobuses made possible the consolidation of schools and to some extent of churches. The sprawling suburbs spread out still farther from the urban core, as America became a nation of commuters.

The demon machine, on the other hand, exacted a terrible toll by catering to the American mania for speed. Citizens were becoming statistics. Not counting the hundreds of thousands of injured and crippled, the one millionth American had died in a motor vehicle accident by 1951—more than all those killed on all the battlefields of all the nation's wars to that date. "The public be rammed" seemed to be the motto of the new age.

Virtuous home life partially broke down as joyriders of all ages forsook the ancestral hearth for the wide-open spaces. The morals of flaming youth sagged correspondingly—at least in the judgment of their elders. Even the disgraceful crime waves of the 1920s and 1930s were partly stimulated by the motorcar, for gangsters could now make quick getaways.

Yet no sane American would plead for a return of the old horse and buggy, complete with fly-breeding manure. The automobile contributed notably to improved air and environmental quality, despite its later notoriety as a polluter. Life might be cut short on the highways, and smog might poison the air, but the automobile brought more convenience, pleasure, and excitement into people's lives than almost any other single invention.

Humans Develop Wings

Gasoline engines also provided the power that enabled humans to fulfill the age-old dream of sprouting wings. After near-successful experiments by others with heavier-than-air craft, the Wright brothers, Orville and Wilbur, performed "the miracle at Kitty Hawk," North Carolina. On a historic day—

December 17, 1903—Orville Wright took aloft a feebly engined plane that stayed airborne for 12 seconds and 120 feet (37 meters). Thus the air age was launched by two obscure bicycle repairmen.

As aviation gradually got off the ground, the world slowly shrank. The public was made increasingly air-minded by unsung heroes—often martyrs—who appeared as stunt fliers at fairs and other public gatherings. Airplanes—"flying coffins"—were used with marked success for various purposes during the Great War of 1914–1918. Shortly thereafter private companies began to operate passenger lines with airmail contracts, which were in effect a subsidy from Washington. The first transcontinental airmail route was established from New York to San Francisco in 1920.

In 1927 modest and skillful Charles A. Lindbergh, the so-called Flying Fool, electrified the world by the first solo west-to-

Charles Lindbergh. His solo flight across the Atlantic won him the notoriety of a "super star." (Library of Congress)

east conquest of the Atlantic. Seeking a prize of $25,000, the lanky stunt flier courageously piloted his single-engined plane, the *Spirit of St. Louis,* from New York to Paris in a grueling 33 hours and 39 minutes.

Lindbergh's exploit swept Americans off their feet. Fed up with the cynicism and debunking of the jazz age, they found in this wholesome and handsome youth a genuine hero. They clasped the fluttering "Lone Eagle" to their hearts much more warmly than the bashful young man desired. "Lucky Lindy" received an uproarious welcome in the "hero canyon" of lower Broadway, as eighteen hundred tons of ticker tape and other improvised confetti showered upon him. Lindbergh's achievement—it was more than a "stunt"—did much to dramatize and popularize flying, while giving a strong boost to the infant aviation industry.

The impact of the airship was tremendous. It provided the soaring American spirit with yet another dimension. At the same time, it gave birth to a giant new industry. Unfortunately, the accident rate in the pio-

neer stages of aviation was high, though hardly more so than on the early railroads. But by the 1930s and 1940s, travel by air on regularly scheduled airlines was markedly safer than on many overcrowded highways.

Humanity's new wings also increased the tempo of an already breathless civilization. The floundering railroad received another setback through the loss of passengers and mail. A lethal new weapon was given to the gods of war; and with the coming of city-busting aerial bombs, people could well debate whether the conquest of the air was a blessing or a curse. The Atlantic Ocean was shriveling to about the size of the Aegean Sea in the days of Socrates, while isolation behind ocean moats was becoming a bygone dream.

The Radio Revolution

The speed of the airplane was far eclipsed by the speed of radio waves. Guglielmo Marconi, an Italian, invented wireless

Rural Oregonians at the radio. Talking furniture gave new meaning to family life. (Library of Congress)

telegraphy in the 1890s, and his brainchild was used for long-range communication during World War I.

Next came the voice-carrying radio, a triumph of many minds. A red-letter day was posted in November 1920, when the Pittsburgh station KDKA broadcast the news of the Harding landslide. Later miracles were achieved in transatlantic wireless photographs, radiotelephones, and television. In harmony with American free enterprise, radio programs were generally sustained by bothersome "commercials," as contrasted with the drabber government-owned systems of Europe.

Like other marvels, the radio not only created a new industry but added richness to the fabric of American life. More joy was given to leisure hours, and many children who had been lured from the fireside by the automobile were brought back by the radio. The nation was better knit together. Various sections heard Americans with standardized accents, and countless millions "tuned in" on perennial comedy favorites like *Amos n' Andy.* Advertising was further perfected as an art. Educationally and culturally, the radio made a significant contribution. Sports were further stimulated. Politicians had to adjust their speaking techniques to the new medium, and millions rather than thousands of voters heard their pleas. A host of listeners swallowed the gospel of their favorite newscaster or were even ringside participants in world-shaking events. Finally, the music of famous artists and symphony orchestras was beamed into countless homes.

Hollywood's Filmland Fantasies

The flickering movie was the fruit of numerous geniuses, including Thomas A. Edison. As early as the 1890s this novel contraption, though still in crude form, had attained some popularity in the naughty peek-show penny arcades. The real birth of the movie came in 1903, when the first story sequence reached the screen. This breathless melodrama—*The Great Train Robbery*—was featured in the five-cent theaters, popularly called "nickelodeons." Spectacular among the first full-length classics was D. W. Griffith's *The Birth of a Nation* (1915), which glorified the Ku Klux Klan of Reconstruction days and defamed the blacks. White southerners would fire guns at the screen during the attempted "rape" scene.

A fascinating industry was thus launched. Hollywood, in southern California, quickly became the movie capital of the world, for it enjoyed a maximum of sunshine and other advantages. Early producers featured nudity and heavy-lidded female vampires "vamps," and an outraged public forced the screen magnates to set up their own rigorous code of censorship. The motion picture really arrived during the World War of 1914–1918, when it was used as an engine of anti-German propaganda. Specially prepared "hang the kaiser" films aided powerfully in selling war bonds and in boosting morale.

A new era began in 1927 with the success of the first "talkie"—*The Jazz Singer,* starring the white performer Al Jolson in blackface. The age of the "silents" was ushered out as theaters everywhere were "wired for sound." At about the same time, reasonably satisfactory color films were being produced.

Movies eclipsed all other new forms of amusement in the phenomenal growth of their popularity. Movie "stars" of the first pulchritude commanded much larger salaries than the president of the United States, in some cases as much as $100,000 for a single picture. Many actors and actresses were far more widely known than the nation's political leaders.

Critics bemoaned the vulgarization of popular tastes wrought by the new technologies of radio and motion pictures. But the effects of the new mass media were not all negative. The parochialism of insular ethnic communities eroded as the immigrants' children, especially, forsook the neighborhood vaudeville theater for the downtown movie palace or turned away from Grandma's Yiddish storytelling to tune in *Amos n' Andy.* Much of the rich diversity of the immigrants' Old Country cultures was lost, but the standardization of tastes and of language hastened entry into the American mainstream—and set the stage for the emergence of a working-class political coalition that, for a time, would overcome the divisive ethnic differences of the past.

The Dynamic Decade

Far-reaching changes in lifestyles and values paralleled the dramatic upsurge of the economy. The census of 1920 revealed that for the first time most Americans no longer lived in the countryside but in urban areas. Women continued to find opportunities for employ-ment in the cities, though they tended to cluster in a few low-paying jobs (such as retail clerking and office typing) that became classified as "women's work." An organized birth-control movement, led by fiery feminist Margaret Sanger, openly championed the use of contraceptives. A National Women's Party began in 1923 to campaign for an Equal Rights Amendment to the Constitution. (The campaign was still stalled short of success seven decades later.) To some defenders of traditional ways, it seemed that the world had suddenly gone mad.

Even the churches were affected. The Fundamentalist champions of the old-time religion lost ground to the Modernists, who liked to think that God was a "good

Measuring a bathing suit. The Charleston, birth control, jazz and even the length of a bathing suit challenged taboos and shocked the older generation. (Library of Congress)

guy" and the universe a pretty chummy place.

Some churches tried to fight the Devil with worldly weapons. Competing with joy-riding automobiles and golf links, they turned to quality entertainment of their own, including wholesome moving pictures for young people. One uptown house of the Lord in New York advertised on a billboard, "Come to Church: Christian Worship Increases Your Efficiency."

Even before the war, one observer thought the chimes had "struck sex o'clock in America," and the 1920s witnessed what many old-timers regarded as a veritable erotic eruption. Advertisers exploited sexual allure to sell everything from soap to car tires. Once-modest maidens now proclaimed their new freedom as "flappers" in bobbed tresses and dresses. Young women appeared with hemlines elevated, stockings rolled, breasts taped flat, cheeks rouged, and lips a "crimson gash" that held a dangling cigarette. Thus did the "flapper" symbolize a yearned-for and devil-may-care independence (some said wild abandon) in some American women. Still more adventuresome females shocked their elders when they sported the new one-piece bathing suits.

Justification for this new sexual frankness could be found in the recently translated writings of Dr. Sigmund Freud. This Viennese physician appeared to argue that sexual repression was responsible for a variety of nervous and emotional ills. Thus not pleasure alone, but health, demanded sexual gratification and liberation.

Many taboos flew out the window as sex-conscious Americans let themselves go. As unknowing Freudians, teenagers pioneered the sexual frontiers. Glued together in syncopated embrace, they danced to jazz music squeaking from phonographs. In an earlier day a kiss had been the equivalent of a proposal of marriage. But in the new era, exploratory young folk sat in darkened movie houses or took to the highways and byways in automobiles—branded "houses of prosti-

tution on wheels" by straitlaced elders. There, the youthful "neckers" and "petters" poached upon the forbidden territory of each other's bodies.

If the flapper was the goddess of the "era of wonderful nonsense," jazz was its sacred music. With its virtuoso wanderings and tricky syncopation, jazz moved up from New Orleans along with the migrating blacks during World War I. Tunes like W. C. Handy's "St. Louis Blues" became instant classics, as the wailing saxophone became the trumpet of the new era. Blacks such as Handy, "Jelly Roll" Morton, and Joseph "Joe" King Oliver gave birth to jazz, but the entertainment industry soon spawned all-white bands—notably Paul Whiteman's. Caucasian impresarios cornered the profits, though not the creative soul, of America's most native music.

A new racial pride also blossomed in the northern black communities that grew so rapidly during and after the war. Harlem in New York City, counting some 100,000 African-American residents in the 1920s, was one of the largest black communities in the world. Harlem sustained a vibrant, creative culture that nourished poets like Langston Hughes, whose first volume of verses, *Weary Blues,* appeared in 1926. Harlem in the 1920s also spawned at least one messianic leader, Marcus Garvy. A colorful West Indian who affected plume-hatted uniforms and an imperial lifestyle, Garvey founded the United Negro Improvement Association (UNIA) to promote the resettlement of American blacks in Africa. His Black Star Line Steamship Company, intended to transport his numerous followers to the new African Eden, went bankrupt in 1923, and Garvey was eventually convicted of fraud and imprisoned. But his vigor and visibility did much to cultivate feelings of self-confidence and self-reliance among blacks, and his example proved important to the later founding of the Nation of Islam (Black Muslim) movement.

Glossary

The Prohibition 'Experiment'

Affable   Friendly and courteous; easy to talk to.

Ardent   A feeling of enthusiasm, especially passionate for a cause.

Arid   Without moisture; extremely dry.

Bemoan   To express pity or to moan for.

Hypocrisy   A pretense that one believes in certain principles but acts otherwise. (Commonly, saying one thing and doing another.)

Illicit   Unlawful; strictly forbidden.

Ironic   A statement that is in contradiction with what is meant or believed. Example—"Isn't it ironic that some lawmakers drank alcoholic toasts in the name of liberty after voting for Prohibition?"

Progressive Reform Movement   A period of city, state, and national reform from the 1890s to 1920.

Ratify   To confirm or sanction a bill or a law.

Slaking   To lessen or allay thirst through drinking.

The Golden Age of Gangsterism

Abduction   Stealing away another, usually by force; kidnapping.

Callousness   Unbending or unyielding feelings for others.

Monkey Business in Tennessee

Affliction   Something that causes pain or grief.

Ardent   Having a strong or passionate belief.

Bestial Hypothesis   Scornful nickname given to the teaching of evolution in schools. *Bestial* refers to those brutal qualities associated with the behaviors of beasts.

Bible Belt   Section of the country generally located in the Midwest and parts of the South populated by those who hold Fundamentalist beliefs.

Evangelical   Pertaining to one who has experienced personal guilt for sins and acclaims the ideas of the New Testament.

Fundamentalist	Person or group who believes in the literal truth of the Bible, the virgin birth, and the authenticity of miracles. Especially important in the 1920s while opposing Darwin's theories of evolution.
Permissiveness	A tendency toward permitting or allowing behaviors considered natural and normal. Acting without restraint or refusal.

The Mass-Consumption Economy

Allure	Attractive through fascination or temptation.
Capital Investment	Purchasing part ownership in a business in expectation of increasing its wealth. Expanding property assets through investment.
Dapper	Appearing elegant, well-dressed, smart.
Innovative	To make changes in or create something new.
Paltry	A petty, trifling, or meager amount.
Parable	Generally, a short story that explains a spiritual idea or moral truth.
Ploy	A trick or strategy to gain advantage, especially in conversation.

Putting America on Rubber Tires

Dobbin-drawn	Referring to a carriage or buggy drawn by a horse.
Epitaph	A tribute to a deceased, usually found written on a tomb or tombstone; a memorial.
Great Bull Market	Heavy investment in the stock market in expectation that stock prices will continue to rise.
Hideous	Extremely ugly.
Messiah	Originally the savior of the Jewish people. Any person expected to save or deliver people from earthly harm.

The Advent of the Gasoline Age

Advent	At the start of.
Ancestral Hearth	Place of birth.
Consolidation	Bringing together; uniting, or combining.
Forsook	To have rejected or given up entirely.
Lustily	Full of vigor and strength.
Ostentation	A front or showy display meant to impress others.

Humans Develop Wings

Cynicism   Doubting the goodness of another's motives; pertaining to people who immediately find fault in attempts to reform society.

Debunking   To prove the opposite of beliefs or sentiments.

Exploit   A feat of such consequence that it might qualify as a heroic deed.

"Hero Canyon"   Name given to that street in New York where honors are bestowed on national heroes as they are paraded down Broadway.

Martyrs   Persons who undergo great suffering or death for an idea or a cause.

Notoriety   Widely known although not necessarily favorably.

Uproarious   Depicting a disorderly or near-riotous assembly or unruly crowd.

The Radio Revolution

Drabber   Comparative form of *drab* meaning dull, colorless, or cheerless.

Gospel   A doctrine or set of firmly held beliefs upheld as truth.

Medium   An instrument used to accomplish a purpose. *Example:* Television is a medium for advertising.

Perennial   Seemingly endless or seasonal. Familiar event that seems to repeat continuously.

Sustain   To provide financial backing to support a program or institution.

Hollywood's Filmland Fantasies

Coalition   An alliance among persons, groups, or nations for a specific purpose.

Divisive   Referring to words or actions intended to create disunity.

Ethnic   Referring to a group of people identified by their language, history, or nationality.

Insular   A feeling of being detached or alone, much like living on an island.

Magnates   Dominant persons in business, such as a shipping magnate.

Parochialism   Given to an exclusive interest into one's own country, region, or activities. A narrowness of view.

Pulchritude   Having exquisite beauty or loveliness.

Vulgarization   Taking something lovely and changing it into something base, crude, tasteless, or common.

Yiddish   The special language, an admixture of Hebrew and Slavic, generally spoken by Jewish immigrants from Eastern Europe.

The Dynamic Decade

Exploited	To find and use the resources of others (including nations) for personal gain.
Impresario	Usually a personal manager or trainer of an artist, especially a musician.
Messianic	Pertaining to a deliverer, especially of those who are chosen.
Poach	To take from another.
Syncopation	Placing accents on rhythmic beats that are normally unaccented.
Bobbed Tresses	Formerly long hair that has been cut short to affect a more "mannish" style.
Veritable	A genuine or real statement; being truly such.
Virtuoso	One who excels in a field, especially music.
Repression	The ability of the mind to remove painful memories of feelings or ideas from consciousness.

Psychology Excerpt:
Stress and Health Psychology*

Contents

* From Charles G. Morris, with Albert A. Maisto. (1999). *Psychology: An Introduction,* 10th ed. Upper Saddle River, NJ: Prentice Hall. Reprinted with permission, pp. 476–489.

Stress and Health Psychology

Most people must adjust to a life that is less than perfect, a life in which bad events happen and even pleasures come with built-in complications. We need to adapt to stress, not just the stress of crises or unexpected strokes of good fortune, but also the stress of everyday minor demands.

Every **adjustment** is an attempt—successful or not—to balance our desires against the demands of the environment, to weigh our needs against realistic possibilities, and to cope as well as we can within the limits of our situation. The student who fails to get the lead in the school play may quit the production in a huff, accept a smaller role, serve as theater critic for the school paper, or join the debating team. Each response is an adjustment to failure, although some of these responses will probably be less constructive in the long run than others.

How we adjust to the stresses—both major and minor—that we encounter is crucial to our health and the quality of our lives. As we shall see in this section and the following one on psychological disorders, stress can contribute to both psychological and physical illness. In fact some medical experts believe that all physical ailments, from colds to ulcers to cancer, have a psychological as well as a physical component. For this reason, stress and its effects on people's lives is a key focus of **health psychology,** a subfield of psychology concerned with the relationship between psychological factors and physical health and illness. Health psychologists seek to understand the relationship between stress and illness: Why do some people manage stress well enough to remain healthy? Why do others become ill? Can personality traits influence recovery from serious illness? How can we promote healthy behaviors? To answer these questions, they study the interaction of biological, psychological, and social factors, an approach we follow in this section.

Sources of Stress

Stress refers to any environmental demand that creates a state of tension or threat and requires change or adaptation. Many situations prompt us to change our behavior in some way: We stop our car when a traffic light turns red; we switch television channels to avoid a boring program and find an interesting one to watch; we go inside when it starts to rain. Normally, these situations are not stressful because they are not accompanied by tension or threat. Now imagine that when the light turned red you were rushing to make an important appointment, or that the person watching TV with you definitely does not want to switch the channel, or that you are about to host a large outdoor party when it starts to rain. Now these situations can be quite stressful.

Some events, such as wars and natural disasters, are inherently stressful, because the danger is real. But even in inherently stressful situations, the time of greatest stress is not necessarily the time when danger is most imminent. We feel the most stress when we're anticipating the danger. Parachutists, for example, report feeling most afraid as the time for the jump approaches. Once they are in line and cannot turn back, they calm down. By the time they reach the most dangerous part of the jump—in free fall and waiting for their chutes to open—their fears have subsided (Epstein 1962).

Of course, stress is not limited to life-and-death situations, nor even to unpleasant or tension-filled experiences. Even good things can cause stress, because they require us to change or adapt in order to meet our needs (Morris 1990). A wedding is stressful as well as exciting: Most weddings are very complicated affairs to arrange, and marriage marks a profound change in many relationships. Being promoted is gratifying—but it demands that we relate to new people in new ways, learn new skills, perhaps dress differently or work longer hours. We'll look more closely now at some factors that cause stress.

Change

All of the stressful events we have considered so far involve change. Most people have a strong preference for order, continuity, and predictability in their lives. Therefore, they experience any event, good or bad, that brings about change as stressful. . . .

Hassles

. . . psychologists have pointed out that much stress is generated by "hassles," life's petty annoyances, irritations, and frustrations. Such seemingly minor matters as being stuck in traffic, misplacing car keys, and getting into a trivial argument may be as stressful as major life events. . . .Whether minor or major, these events are stressful because they lead to feelings of pressure, frustration, conflict, and anxiety.

Pressure

Pressure occurs when we feel forced to speed up, intensify, or shift direction in our behavior, or when we feel compelled to meet a higher standard of performance.

Frustration

Frustration also contributes to stress. Frustration occurs when a person is prevented from reaching a goal because something or someone stands in the way. A high school student who does poorly on his college boards does not get into his father's alma mater; a woman looking forward to a well-deserved promotion is denied it for sexist reasons. These people must either give up their goals as unattainable, modify their goals, or find some way to overcome the obstacles blocking their way.

Conflict

Of all life's troubles, conflict is probably the most common. A student finds that both the required courses she wanted to take this semester are given at the same hours on the same days. We find ourselves in agreement with one political candidate's views on policy, but prefer the personality of the opponent. A boy does not want to go to his aunt's for dinner, but neither does he want to listen to his parents complain about his decision if he stays home.

Conflict arises when we face two or more incompatible demands, opportunities, needs, or goals. We can never resolve conflict completely. We must either give up some of our goals, modify some of them, delay our pursuit of some of them, or resign ourselves to not attaining all of our goals. Whatever we do, we are bound to experience some frustration, which adds to the stressfulness of conflicts.

Self-Imposed Stress

People sometimes create problems for themselves quite apart from stressful events in their environment. Albert Ellis has proposed that many people carry around a set of irrational, self-defeating beliefs that add unnecessarily to the normal stresses of living (Ellis and Harper 1975). For example, some people believe "It is essential to be loved or approved by almost everyone for everything I do"; for people who share this belief, any sign of disapproval will be a source of considerable stress. Other people believe "I must be competent, adequate, and successful at everything I do"; such people take the slightest sign of failure or inadequacy as evidence that they are worthless human beings. Still others believe "It is disastrous if everything doesn't go the way I would like"; when things don't go perfectly, such people feel upset, miserable, and unhappy.

Coping With Stress

Whatever its source, stress calls for adjustment. Psychologists distinguish between two general types of adjustment: direct coping and defensive coping. *Direct coping* refers to any action we take to change an uncomfortable situation. When our needs or desires are frustrated, for example, we attempt to remove the obstacles between ourselves and our goal or we give up. Similarly, when we are threatened, we try to eliminate the source of the threat, either by attacking it or by escaping from it.

Defensive coping refers to the ways people convince themselves that they are not really threatened or that they do not really want something they cannot get. A form of self-deception, defensive coping is characteristic of internal, often unconscious conflicts. When we are emotionally unable to bring a problem to the surface of consciousness and deal with it directly because it is too threatening, our only option may be to cope with it defensively.

Direct Coping

When we are threatened, frustrated, or in conflict, we have three basic choices for coping directly: *confrontation, compromise,* or *withdrawal.* We can meet a situation head-on and intensify our efforts to get what we want (confrontation). We can give up some of what we want and perhaps persuade others to give up part of what they want (compromise). Or we can admit defeat and stop fighting (withdrawal).

Confrontation. Facing a stressful situation forthrightly, acknowledging to oneself that there is a problem for which a solution must be found, attacking the problem head-on, and pushing resolutely toward one's goals is called **confrontation.** The hallmark of the "confrontational style" (Morris 1990) is making intense efforts to cope with stress and to accomplish one's aims. This may involve learning skills, enlisting other people's help, or just trying harder. Or it may require steps to change either oneself or the situation. The woman whom we have been describing might decide that if she wants very much to move up in the company, she will have to agree to relocate. Or she might try to change the situation itself in one of several ways. She could challenge the assumption that working at the branch office would give her the kind of experience

her supervisor thinks she needs. She could try to persuade her boss that she is ready to handle a better job in the main office. Or she could remind her supervisor of the company's stated goal of promoting more women to top-level positions.

Confrontation may also include expressions of anger. Anger may be effective, especially if we really have been treated unfairly and if we express our anger with restraint instead of exploding in rage. A national magazine once reported an amusing, and effective, example of controlled anger in response to an annoying little hassle. As a motorist came to an intersection, he had to stop for a frail old lady crossing the street. The driver of the car behind him honked his horn impatiently, whereupon the first driver shut off his ignition, removed the key, walked back to the other car, and handed the key to the second driver. "Here," he said, "you run over her, I can't do it. She reminds me of my grandmother."

Compromise. One of the most common, and effective, ways of coping directly with conflict or frustration is **compromise.** We often recognize that we cannot have everything we want and that we cannot expect others to do just what we would like them to do. In such cases, we may decide to settle for less than we originally sought. The woman denied a job promotion may agree to take a less desirable position that doesn't require branch office experience, or she may strike a bargain to go to the branch office for a shorter period of time.

Withdrawal. In some circumstances, the most effective way of coping with stress is withdrawal from the situation. A person at an amusement park who is overcome by anxiety just looking at a roller coaster may simply move on to a less threatening ride or even leave the park entirely. The woman whose promotion depends on temporarily relocating might just quit her job and join another company.

We often disparage withdrawal as a refusal to face problems. But sometimes withdrawal is a positive and realistic response, such as when we realize that our adversary is more powerful than we are, or reach a compromise and that any form of aggression would be self-destructive. In seemingly hopeless situations, such as submarine and mining disasters, few people panic. Believing there is nothing they can do to save themselves, they give up. If a situation, in fact, is hopeless, resignation may be the most effective way of coping with it.

Perhaps the greatest danger of coping by withdrawal is that we will come to avoid all similar situations. Someone who grew extremely anxious looking at the roller coaster may refuse to go to an amusement park again. The woman who did not want to relocate to her company's branch office may quit her job without even looking for a new one. In such cases, coping by withdrawal becomes maladaptive avoidance. Moreover, people who have given up on a situation can miss out on an effective solution.

Withdrawal, in whatever form, is a mixed blessing. Although it can be an effective method of coping, it has built-in danger. The same tends to be true of defensive coping.

Defensive Coping

So far, we have focused on stress that arises from recognizable sources, but at times, we either cannot identify or cannot deal directly with the source of our stress. For example, you return to a parking lot to discover that someone has damaged your new car and then left the scene. Or a trip you have planned for months is delayed by an airline strike. Some problems are too emotionally threatening to be faced directly. Perhaps you find out that someone close to you is seriously ill. Or you learn that after four years of hard work you have not been admitted to medical school and may have to abandon your plan to become a doctor.

In such situations, many people automatically adopt defense mechanism as a way of coping. Defense mechanisms are techniques for deceiving oneself about the causes of a stressful situation in order to reduce pressure, frustrations, conflict, and anxiety. The self-deceptive nature of such adjustments led Freud to conclude that they are entirely unconscious. He was particularly interested in distortions of memory and in irrational feelings and behavior, all of which he considered symptoms of a struggle against unconscious impulses. Not all psychologists accept Freud's interpretation of defensive coping as always springing from unconscious conflicts. Often we are aware that we are pushing something out of our memory or otherwise deceiving ourselves. For example, all of us have blown up at one person when we knew we were really angry at someone else. Whether defense mechanisms operate consciously or unconsciously, they do provide a means of coping with stress that might otherwise be unbearable. We review the defense mechanisms below.

Denial. Denial is the refusal to acknowledge a painful or threatening reality. Although denial is a positive response in some situations, in other situations it clearly is not. Students who deny their need to study and instead spend several nights a week at the movies may fail their exams. Similarly, frequent drug users who insist that they are merely experimenting with drugs are also deluding themselves.

Repression. The most common mechanism for blocking out painful feelings and memories is repression, a form of forgetting that excludes painful thoughts from consciousness. Soldiers who break down in the field often block out the memory of the experiences that led to their collapse (Grinker and Spiegel 1945). Repression may indicate that the person is struggling against impulses (such as aggression) that conflict with conscious values. For example, most of us were taught in childhood that violence and aggression are wrong. This conflict between our feelings and our values can create stress, and one way of coping defensively with that stress is to repress our feelings, to block out completely any awareness of our underlying anger and hostility.

Denial and repression are the most basic defense mechanisms. In denial, we block out situations we can't cope with; in repression, we block out unacceptable impulses or thoughts. These psychic strategies form the bases for several other defensive ways of coping, discussed below.

Projection. If a problem cannot be denied or completely repressed, we may distort its nature so that we can handle it more easily. One example of this is projection, the attribution of one's own repressed motives, ideas, or feelings to others. We ascribe feelings to someone else that we do not want to acknowledge as our own, locating the source of our conflict outside ourselves. A corporate executive who feels guilty about the way he rose to power may project his own ruthless ambition onto his colleagues. He is simply doing his job, he believes, while his associates are all crassly ambitious and consumed with power.

Identification. The reverse of projection is identification. Through projection, we rid ourselves of undesirable characteristics that we have repressed by attributing them to someone else. Through identification, we take on the characteristics of someone else so that we can vicariously share in that person's triumphs and overcome feeling inadequate. The admired person's actions, that is, become a substitute for our own. A parent with unfulfilled career ambitions may share emotionally in a son's or daughter's professional success. When the child is promoted, the parent may feel personally triumphant. Identification is often used as a form of self-defense in situations where a person feels utterly helpless, including being taken as a hostage or being a prisoner. Some prisoners gradually come to identify with their guards as a way of defensively coping with unbearable and inescapable stress.

Regression. People under severe stress may revert to childlike behavior through a process called regression. Why do people regress? Some psychologists say that it is because an adult cannot stand feeling helpless. Children, on the other hand, feel helpless and dependent every day, so becoming more childlike can make total dependency or helplessness more bearable.

Regression is sometimes used as a manipulative strategy, too, albeit an immature and inappropriate one. Adults who cry or throw temper tantrums when their arguments fail may expect those around them to react sympathetically, as their parents did when they were children.

Intellectualization. Intellectualization is a subtle form of denial in which we detach ourselves from our feelings about problems by analyzing them intellectually and thinking of them almost as if they concerned other people. Parents who start out intending to discuss their child's difficulties with a teacher, but instead talk to her about educational philosophy, may be intellectualizing a very upsetting situation. They appear to be dealing with their problems, but in fact they are not because they have cut themselves off from their emotions.

Reaction Formation. Reaction formation is a form of denial in which people express with exaggerated intensity ideas and emotions that are the opposite of their own. Exaggeration is the clue to this behavior: Someone who extravagantly praises a rival may be covering up jealousy over the opponent's success. Reaction formation may also be a way of convincing oneself that one's motives are pure. The man who feels ambivalent about being a father may devote a disproportionate amount of time to his children in an attempt to prove to himself that he is a good father.

Displacement. Displacement involves the redirection of repressed motives and emotions from their original objects to substitute objects. The woman who has always wanted to be a mother may feel inadequate when she learns that she cannot have children. As a result, she may become extremely attached to a pet or a niece or nephew. In another example of displacement, the person who must smile and agree with a difficult boss may yell at family members for no reason.

Sublimation. Sublimation refers to transforming repressed motives or feelings into more socially acceptable forms. Aggressiveness, for instance, might be channeled into competitiveness in business or sports. A strong and persistent desire for attention might be transformed into an interest in acting or politics. Freud believed that sublimation is not only necessary but desirable. People who can transform their sexual and aggressive drives into more socially acceptable forms are clearly better off, for they are able to at least partially gratify instinctual drives with relatively little anxiety and guilt. Moreover, society benefits from the energy and effort such people channel into the arts, literature, science, and other socially useful activities.

Does defensive coping mean that a person is immature, unstable, or on the edge of a "breakdown"? Not at all. In some cases of prolonged and severe stress, defensive coping not only contributes to our overall ability to adapt and adjust, but even becomes essential to survival. And even in less extreme situations, people may rely on defense mechanisms to get through everyday problems and stress. As Coleman et al. (1987) point out, defenses are "essential for softening failure, alleviating tension and anxiety, repairing emotional hurt, and maintaining our feelings of adequacy and worth" (190). Only when a defense mechanism interferes with a person's ability to function or creates more problems than it solves is it considered maladaptive.

References

Ellis, A., and Harper, R. A. (1975). *A new guide to rational living.* North Hollywood, CA: Wilshire Book Co.

Epstein, S. (1962). The measurement of drive and conflict in humans: Theory and experiment. in M. R. Jones (ed.), *Nebraska Symposium on Motivation.* Lincoln: University of Nebraska Press.

Grinker, R. R., and Spiegel, J. P. (1945). *War neurosis.* Philadelphia: Blakiston.

Morris, C. (1990). *Contemporary psychology and effective behavior* (7th ed.). Glenview, IL: Scott, Foresman.

Index